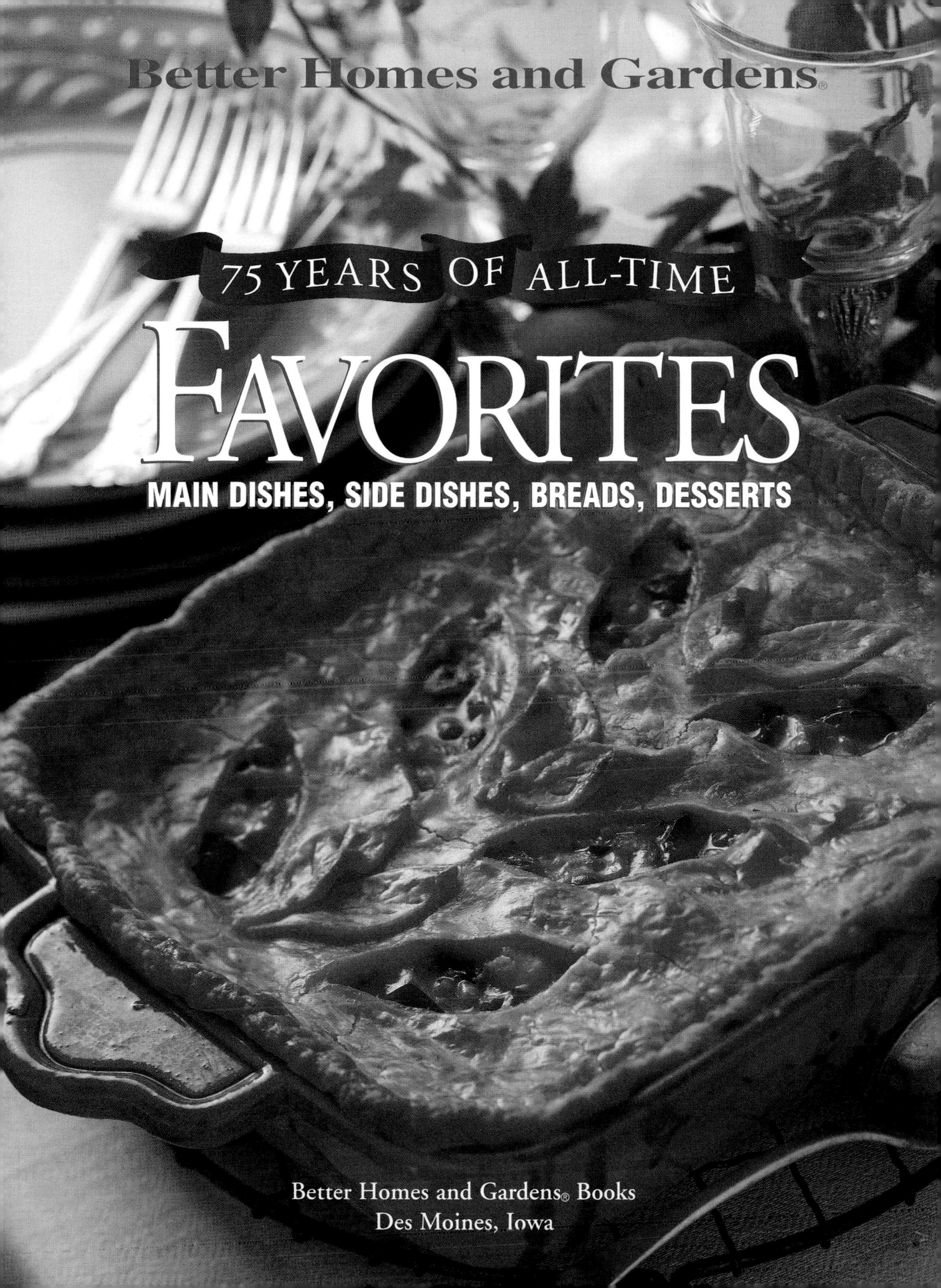

Better Homes and Gardens®

75 YEARS OF ALL-TIME

FAVORITES

MAIN DISHES, SIDE DISHES, BREADS, DESSERTS

Better Homes and Gardens® Books
Des Moines, Iowa

Better Homes and Gardens® Books
An imprint of Meredith® Books

Better Homes and Gardens®
75 Years of All-Time Favorites
Project Editor: *Kristi M. Fuller*
Contributing Editors: *Shelli McConnell, Mary Major Williams,*
Joyce Trollope, Spectrum Communication Services
Associate Art Director: *Lynda Haupert*
Copy Chief: *Angela K. Renkoski*
Editorial and Design Assistants: *Judy Bailey,*
Jennifer Norris, Karen Schirm
Test Kitchen Director: *Sharon Stilwell*
Test Kitchen Project Supervisor: *Marilyn Cornelius*
Food Stylist: *Dora Jonassen*
Photographers: *Mark Thomas, King Au*
Cover photo: *Scott Little*
Electronic Production Coordinator: *Paula Forest*
Production Manager: *Douglas M. Johnston*
Prepress Coordinator: *Margie J. Schenkelberg*

Meredith® Books
Editor in Chief: *James D. Blume*
Managing Editor: *Christopher Cavanaugh*
Director, New Product Development: *Ray Wolf*

Vice President, General Manager: *Jamie L. Martin*

Better Homes and Gardens® Magazine
Editor in Chief: *Jean LemMon*
Executive Food Editor: *Nancy Byal*
Senior Editor: *Joy Taylor*
Senior Associate Editors: *Jeanne Ambrose, David Feder, R.D.*

Meredith® Publishing Group
President, Publishing Group: *Christopher M. Little*
Vice President and Publishing Director: *John P. Loughlin*

Meredith® Corporation
Chairman of the Board and Chief Executive Officer: *Jack D. Rehm*
President and Chief Operating Officer: *William T. Kerr*

Chairman of the Executive Committee: *E. T. Meredith III*

Our seal assures you that every recipe in
75 Years of All-Time Favorites has been
tested in the Better Homes and Gardens® Test Kitchen.
This means that each recipe is practical and
reliable, and meets our high standards of taste appeal.
We guarantee your satisfaction with this book for
as long as you own it.

Cover photograph: *Sweet Potato Shortcakes with Berries (page 292)*
Photograph on page 1: *Deep-Dish Chicken Pie (page 171)*

All of us at Better Homes and Gardens Books are dedicated
to providing you with the information and ideas you
need to create tasty foods. We welcome your comments
and suggestions. Write to us at: Better Homes and
Gardens Books, Cookbook Editorial Department,
1716 Locust Street RW–240,
Des Moines, IA 50309–3023.

*S*ome things are enduring. Who can forget the smell of lilacs on a spring morning, the exuberance of the last day of school each year, or your mom's Sunday dinners? Food—like flowers and freedom—makes lasting impressions in our memories to be recalled and enjoyed years later.

If ever there was an opportunity to recall and enjoy favorite foods, it's here on the pages of this very special cookbook created to celebrate the 75th anniversary of *Better Homes and Gardens*® magazine. *75 Years of All-Time Favorites* is a heaping measureful of all the ingredients you need to relive the best of times and tastes from Grandmother's, Mom's, and even your very own kitchen. Carefully selected from all the past years of *Better Homes and Gardens* magazine, the recipes in this new cookbook include picks from our editors, our Test Kitchen experts, and—thanks to you—our readers.

One of the nicest things about all these longtime, good-time recipes is that each has been modified in our Test Kitchen to fit the way we live and cook today—with concern for health and nutrition.

Being the editor in chief of *Better Homes and Gardens* magazine as it celebrates its 75th birthday is a privilege I'd never imagined when I first started cooking. I remember browsing each month's issue for recipes that sounded good—as I'm sure we all did. But, at that time, I never thought I would be involved in any way with what I considered (and still do) the gold standard of food and recipes.

That's why I'm thrilled to write the welcome for this unique cookbook that gathers all of our favorite recipes into one intergenerational collection.

I wish you happy memories and happy moments in your kitchen! And remember, what you cook today will be tomorrow's fond memories when your children look back and pick their all-time favorites.

Jean LemMon
Editor in Chief
Better Homes and Gardens magazine

Contents

Introduction 6

Morning Glories 11

For Starters & Snacks 47

Super Salads 79

The Bakery 109

75 years of Cooking in America

Lovingly handed down from generation to generation, recipes often remain in a family for years. Tattered and stained from use, handwritten notes of ingredients and measurements are carefully tucked into cherished recipe boxes. This cookbook represents our own recipe box. In celebration of the 75th anniversary of *Better Homes and Gardens* magazine, we're sharing our favorite collection of recipes gathered from the pages of the magazine.

When our magazine arrived in readers' homes for the first time in 1922, it was called *Fruit, Garden and Home,* a publication devoted to home and family. The name was changed in 1924 to more accurately reflect its mission: *Better Homes and Gardens.* No matter the name, throughout three-quarters of a century, the magazine has dedicated itself to providing clear direction and encouragement that inspire its readers to *do* something—to build it, grow it, or cook it. The magazine's founder, E. T. Meredith, had a vision: to help Americans make better homes and home lives for their families. As we celebrate our diamond anniversary, that vision is preserved with the same passion today as it was 75 years ago—especially in the realm of cooking. From the simplest roasted chicken presented in the '30s to the elaborate pastries of the '90s, preparing recipes in novel ways for sharing with friends and family always has been the hallmark of *Better Homes and Gardens.*

Shaping the Way America Cooks

The back issues of *Better Homes and Gardens* chronicle a rich historical perspective of America's love of food—how we cooked and what we've cooked since 1922. Browse through back issues and you'll find the threads that make up the fabric of American lives. Discover how home canning became a necessity in the '40s as a way to preserve produce grown in Victory Gardens during World War II. See how the magazine taught readers to use fondue pots when these new gizmos swept the country in the '60s. Or, experience the miracle of frozen foods as consumers did in the '30s when this long-awaited technology was first made available. (Look for our "Vintage Views" throughout the book containing these tidbits of historical information.)

Since its beginning, *Better Homes and Gardens* has not only responded to the times, but helped mold them, too. On one trip to the West Coast prior to World War II, food editor Myrna Johnston (a real pioneer in the area of step-by-step cooking) discovered built-in backyard barbecues. She had one built in her own backyard and introduced the concept to readers in June 1941. The war years intervened, but Myrna, undaunted, helped her readers rediscover barbecuing in the early '50s. The backyard barbecue has since become a major theme in both the magazine and American cooking.

Myrna also helped popularize the tossed salad by introducing the first "Toss a Salad" feature. Her salad campaign continued through the '50s and '60s, dubbed "the lettuce years" by our editors.

Myrna recognized, too, that men often were interested in cooking. "Show the men how enjoyable cooking can be," she counseled her primarily female audience in the '30s. To that end, she used the magazine as a vehicle to feature men in a variety of cooking situations, from outdoor cooking to saladmaking in the "His Turn to Cook" column.

Better Homes and Gardens also was there to herald the appliance innovations that revolutionized cooking. Issues published in the '30s and '40s included a feature article each month on appliances that were new to the market—dishwashers, mixers, refrigerators, gas stoves—and brought the Industrial Age into the kitchen. Today's magazine continues this tradition by teaching our microchip-age readers about food processors, microwave ovens, and bread machines.

Testing and Tasting: The Introduction of the Test Kitchen

For a recipe to be published in *Better Homes and Gardens* magazine, it first must be tested and approved. This tradition began in 1923, when household editor Genevieve Callahan tested recipes in her own home. In 1928, we introduced our first in-house facility called The Testing-Tasting Kitchen. This innovation, located just across the hall from the *Better Homes and Gardens* editorial offices, took years of planning. The editors told readers in 1929, "It was remodeled and rearranged dozens of times on paper before it took form in wood and plaster." Step-saving devices included cupboards built around the refrigerator and a work table that also served as a dining surface. There was an enormous sink and gas stove along with colored enamelware displayed on counters and ledges that matched the woodwork and curtains.

In 1929, the editors stated with pride that their new facility for testing and tasting recipes was "a modern workshop as near as possible in size and equipment to what you might find in a home."

Today, our Test Kitchen actually houses 10 separate kitchens, where our team of home economists test as many as 50 recipes each day. But our purpose remains the same—to make sure every recipe is both delicious and easy to duplicate in your kitchen at home.

The Evolution of a Recipe

Possibly the most dramatic change we have made to the food pages of *Better Homes and Gardens* is in the way the recipes are written. In the infant years of the magazine, our editors thought it sufficient to provide this recipe—printed in its entirety—for Currant Raspberry Pie:

Add one cup of raspberries to three cups of ripe currants and bake in two crusts. Serve plain or with whipped cream.

That's it. No directions on preparing the fruit for the pie, no instructions on making or rolling piecrusts, and no mention of time or oven temperature for baking. It was a complete recipe for the cooks of that era. Today's version, though, would provide a color photograph of the pie, a precise list of ingredients, exact measurements, and nutritional information regarding the number of fat grams and calories in every slice.

Since the establishment of the Better Homes and Gardens Test Kitchen in 1928, our home economists have been part of a campaign to nudge the American public into a new, more scientific era of cooking. They use exact measurements and detailed cooking descriptions; there are no more Currant Raspberry Pie assumptions and generalizations. Instead, each recipe is measured, mixed, and baked just as readers would do it at home, ensuring complete success every time.

"There's a reason the word 'better' is in the title of our magazine. We feel a strong sense of responsibility to better the lives of American families. And that includes the food that people buy and eat."

—Nancy Byal, executive food editor, *Better Homes and Gardens*® magazine

*The magazine's founder,
E. T. Meredith*

About This Book

This diamond anniversary cookbook is a tribute to E. T. Meredith's commitment to bettering the lives of Americans. Here you'll find an extraordinary collection of more than 230 recipes we've handpicked from the thousands published since 1922. We also asked you, our readers, to send us your favorite recipes from the magazine—the ones you've loved enough to clip out and paste on 3×5 cards for your personal recipe files (the recipes sent in by readers are marked with a star throughout the book).

The selections also include choices from the "Cook's Round Table," a past feature where readers shared their favorite recipes for publication, and from today's ever-popular Prize Tested Recipe Contest (quite possibly the magazine world's longest-running food contest). Every month since 1937, our *Better Homes and Gardens* readers have competed for prizes by sending us the best of their best recipes.

To make the book as handy to use as possible, we organized the recipes by types of dishes, from breakfast Morning Glories to Memorable Main Dishes. We also marked all low-fat recipes with a heart symbol.

But we didn't stop there. Many of the recipes are supplemented with historical information—stories that set the food in the context of its time or give you insight to the changes in American cooking and tastes over the decades. Each recipe retains the personality and flavor of its time, but they all have been updated for today's cooking techniques and tastes.

We hope you'll enjoy the best of our best by creating new memories for yourselves and your families with these treasures from our past.

THE COOK'S ROUND TABLE

Conducted by Better Homes and Gardens readers

NOVEMBER 1933

10 CENTS

BETTER HOMES & GARDENS

Meredith Publishing Company· Des Moines, Iowa
More Than 1,400,000 Circulation

*The magazine's first
food cover, 1933*

Better Homes and Gardens

JANUARY 1997
$1.99

75
Helping
families live
better lives
for 75
years

Best ever
Readers' all-time favorite recipes

Decorating
The blues are back

New style
Top trends for 1997

*Our 75th anniversary
cover, 1997*

Morning Glories

Zucchini Frittata

1977

Brunches became popular in the '70s because they fit in perfectly with the relaxed entertaining style of the era. Brunches often featured international-inspired dishes such as this Italian-style frittata made with the ever-popular zucchini, also an Italian native.

1 cup thinly sliced zucchini (1 small)
½ cup thinly sliced leek (1 medium)
1 tablespoon margarine or butter
6 eggs
2 tablespoons snipped parsley
2 tablespoons water

½ teaspoon snipped fresh rosemary or ⅛ teaspoon dried rosemary, crushed
½ teaspoon salt
⅛ teaspoon pepper
½ of a 4½-ounce package Camembert cheese or 2 tablespoons freshly shredded Parmesan cheese

1 In an omelet pan or 10-inch oven-going skillet cook zucchini and leek in hot margarine or butter just until tender.

2 Meanwhile, beat together eggs, parsley, water, rosemary, salt, and pepper. Pour egg mixture over vegetables. Cook over medium-low heat. As mixture sets, run a spatula around edge of skillet, lifting egg mixture to allow uncooked portion to flow underneath. Continue cooking and lifting until egg mixture is almost set (surface will be moist).

3 Place pan in a 400° oven. Bake, uncovered, about 4 minutes or until top is set. Cut the half circle of Camembert horizontally (if using); cut each half into 2 or 3 wedges and place on the frittata or, sprinkle frittata with Parmesan cheese. Allow cheese to melt slightly before serving. Makes 4 to 6 servings.

Nutrition facts per serving: 201 calories, 14 g total fat (5 g saturated fat), 331 mg cholesterol, 534 mg sodium, 5 g carbohydrate, 1 g fiber, 13 g protein.

Farmer's Breakfast

1970

2 tablespoons cooking oil
2 cups frozen diced hash brown potatoes with onions and peppers, thawed (about ⅓ of a 24-ounce package)
1 cup diced cooked ham
6 beaten eggs
⅓ cup water
¼ cup shredded cheddar cheese (1 ounce)

1 Coat a large skillet with the oil. Add potatoes in a single layer. Cook, covered, over medium heat 5 to 7 minutes or until the potatoes are tender, stirring once. Stir in ham.

2 Combine eggs and water; pour over ham-potato mixture. Cook, uncovered, over medium heat until eggs are just set, turning mixture occasionally with a wide spatula. Sprinkle with cheese and serve immediately. Makes 4 servings.

Nutrition facts per serving: 338 calories, 19 g total fat (6 g saturated fat), 346 mg cholesterol, 583 mg sodium, 20 g carbohydrate, 2 g fiber, 21 g protein.

Farmers, who tend to eat breakfast early in the morning, often have a second breakfast at mid morning. One of the traditional dishes served is a "hash" of eggs, potatoes, and sausage or ham. Over the years, dishes that contained all or some of these ingredients were called a farmer's breakfast. This delicious version, adapted from a 1970 recipe, uses frozen hash-brown potatoes with onions and peppers.

Turkey-Asparagus Brunch Bake

1989

1 pound fresh asparagus or
    one 10-ounce package
    frozen cut asparagus or
    cut broccoli
1 pound ground turkey
1 cup chopped onion
½ cup chopped red sweet
    pepper
3 eggs

2 cups milk
1 cup all-purpose flour
¼ cup grated Parmesan cheese
1 teaspoon lemon-pepper
    seasoning
½ teaspoon dried tarragon,
    basil, or thyme, crushed
1 cup shredded Swiss cheese
    (4 ounces)

Plan a memorable brunch with the menu below, which was featured in May 1989.

---

*Turkey-Asparagus
Brunch Bake*

---

*Super-Colossal Cinnamon-
Pecan Ring (page 40)*

Fresh mixed fruit

---

*Assorted fruit juices or
wine coolers*

1 To cook fresh asparagus, wash and scrape off scales. Break off and discard woody bases of asparagus. Cut asparagus into 1½-inch pieces. In a covered saucepan cook asparagus in a small amount of boiling water for 4 to 8 minutes or until crisp-tender. (For frozen asparagus or broccoli, cook according to package directions; drain and set aside.)

2 In a large skillet cook turkey, onion, and sweet pepper until vegetables are just tender and no pink remains in turkey. Remove from heat; drain. Set aside. Grease a 3-quart rectangular baking dish. Arrange meat mixture in dish; top with cooked asparagus.

3 In a large mixing bowl combine eggs, milk, flour, Parmesan cheese, lemon-pepper seasoning, and tarragon; beat until smooth with a wire whisk or rotary beater. (Or, combine these ingredients in a blender container; cover and blend for 20 seconds.)* Pour egg mixture evenly over layers in baking dish.

4 Bake in a 425° oven about 20 minutes or until a knife inserted near the center comes out clean. Sprinkle with the Swiss cheese; bake 3 to 5 minutes more or until the cheese is melted. Makes 6 servings.

To make ahead: Prepare as directed to the asterisk (*). Pour egg mixture into a bowl or pitcher; cover and refrigerate. Cover and refrigerate turkey and asparagus in the baking dish. To bake, stir egg mixture well and pour over turkey mixture. Bake, uncovered, in 425° oven about 30 minutes or until a knife inserted near the center comes out clean. Continue as directed.

Nutrition facts per serving: 355 calories, 17 g total fat (8 g saturated fat), 161 mg cholesterol, 417 mg sodium, 24 g carbohydrate, 2 g fiber, 26 g protein.

Cheese & Mushroom Brunch Eggs

1990

Need an easy entrée for brunch for six? In the May 1990 issue, Mary Kay Phillips, a featured cook, shared part of her strategy of serving scrambled eggs casserole-style. She said this recipe was her favorite because the eggs stay warm while all the guests are being served.

2 tablespoons margarine or butter
2 tablespoons all-purpose flour
1 cup milk
⅓ cup shredded process Swiss cheese (1½ ounces)
3 tablespoons grated Parmesan cheese
2 tablespoons dry white wine or milk*
   Nonstick spray coating
1½ cups sliced fresh mushrooms
¼ cup thinly sliced green onions
1 tablespoon margarine or butter
12 beaten eggs
1 medium tomato, chopped

1 For sauce, in a medium saucepan melt the 2 tablespoons margarine or butter. Stir in flour. Cook for 1 minute. Add the 1 cup milk all at once. Cook and stir over medium heat until thickened and bubbly. Stir in cheeses. Cook and stir over medium heat until cheeses melt. Remove from heat; stir in 2 tablespoons wine or milk. Set aside.

2 For eggs, spray an unheated large skillet with nonstick coating. Preheat skillet over medium heat. Add mushrooms and green onions to the hot skillet; cook 2 to 3 minutes or until tender. Transfer vegetables to a small bowl; set aside.

3 In the same skillet melt the 1 tablespoon margarine or butter. Add eggs. Cook over medium heat without stirring until eggs begin to set around the edge. Using a large spatula, lift and fold the partially cooked egg mixture so the uncooked portion flows underneath. Continue cooking until eggs are set, but still glossy and moist. Transfer half of the scrambled eggs to a 2-quart square baking dish or an au gratin dish.

4 Spread half of the mushroom mixture over the eggs in the baking dish. Drizzle about half the sauce over. Top with the remaining scrambled eggs, remaining mushroom mixture, and remaining sauce.

5 Bake, uncovered, in a 350° oven about 20 minutes or until heated through. Top with tomato. Let stand 10 minutes. Makes 6 servings.

For a lower-fat version: Use skim milk and reduced-fat Swiss cheese and use 2½ cups refrigerated or frozen egg product, thawed, instead of the whole eggs.

*Note: If using milk instead of wine, stir ½ teaspoon dry mustard in with the 2 tablespoons milk.

Nutrition facts per serving: 284 calories, 20 g total fat (7 g saturated fat), 438 mg cholesterol, 293 mg sodium, 7 g carbohydrate, 1 g fiber, 18 g protein.
Lower-fat version: 207 calories, 11 g total fat (3 g saturated fat), 8 mg cholesterol, 421 mg sodium, 7 g carbohydrate, 1 g fiber, 18 g protein.

Florentine Eggs Benedict

1991

1 cup water
4 eggs
⅓ cup plain fat-free yogurt
3 tablespoons light
    mayonnaise dressing or
    salad dressing
2 teaspoons cornstarch
1 teaspoon prepared mustard
    Dash ground red pepper
¼ cup skim milk

Salt
Pepper
4 toasted French bread slices
    or English muffin halves
1 large tomato, sliced
12 large spinach leaves, stems
    removed
2 ounces very thinly sliced
    cooked smoked turkey or
    chicken

The exact origin of Eggs Benedict is hazy. Some experts say it was first prepared for a regular customer at Delmonico's Restaurant in New York City. Others say it was named after Wall Street wizard Lemuel Benedict. The recipe has become so popular that most restaurants that serve breakfast serve Eggs Benedict. In 1990, we made over the classic to make it more healthful. While we were at it, we adapted the recipe for the microwave oven.

1 For eggs, place water in a 1-quart microwave-safe casserole. Microwave, uncovered, on high for 2 to 3 minutes or until boiling. Gently break eggs into water. Prick each yolk and white. Cover with waxed paper; cook on high for 2 minutes. Let eggs stand, covered, while preparing sauce.

2 For sauce, in a 1-quart microwave-safe bowl stir together yogurt, mayonnaise dressing, cornstarch, mustard, and red pepper; stir in milk. Cook, uncovered, on high for 2 to 3 minutes or until slightly thickened and bubbly, stirring after every minute. Season to taste with salt and pepper. Cover; set aside.

3 Arrange bread slices or muffin halves on a large microwave-safe plate. Top each with *one* slice of tomato, *3* spinach leaves, and *one-fourth* of the turkey. With a slotted spoon, remove eggs from water; place on top of the turkey slices. Spoon some sauce over each serving. Cook, uncovered, on high for 1 to 2 minutes or just until heated through. Makes 4 servings.

♥ *Nutrition facts per serving: 233 calories, 10 g total fat (3 g saturated fat), 221 mg cholesterol, 535 mg sodium, 21 g carbohydrate, 1 g fiber, 14 g protein.*

Creole Olive Omelet

1938

This is not your average omelet. It's light like a soufflé and filled with a zippy Creole sauce. Although Cajun-style stewed tomatoes weren't available in 1938, we punched up the flavor by using them here. You can use regular stewed tomatoes if you prefer. The original sauce did not use any added spices, which is in keeping with Creole cooking. Cajun-style cooking relies on more spices than Creole cooking, but both use plenty of onion, green sweet pepper, and celery.

2 **tablespoons margarine or butter**
¼ **cup all-purpose flour**
¼ **teaspoon salt**
   Dash pepper
1 **cup milk**

4 **well-beaten egg yolks**
4 **egg whites**
2 **tablespoons margarine or butter**
1 **recipe Creole Sauce**

1 In a medium saucepan melt 2 tablespoons margarine or butter; stir in flour, salt, and pepper. Stir in milk all at once. Cook and stir over medium heat until thickened and bubbly. Gradually stir hot mixture into egg yolks; set aside. In a large mixing bowl beat egg whites with an electric mixer on high speed until stiff peaks form (tips stand straight). Fold into yolk mixture.

2 In a 10-inch oven-going skillet heat the remaining 2 tablespoons margarine or butter until a drop of water sizzles. Spoon in egg mixture, mounding it slightly higher at the side. Cook over low heat for 8 to 10 minutes or until puffed, set, and golden brown on the bottom. Bake, uncovered, in a 325° oven for 8 to 10 minutes or until a knife inserted near the center comes out clean.

3 Meanwhile, prepare Creole Sauce. Loosen side of the omelet with a metal spatula. Make a shallow cut slightly off-center across the omelet. Fold smaller side over the larger side. Transfer to a warm platter. Lift edge of omelet and fill center with Creole Sauce. To serve, cut into four portions. Pass extra sauce. Makes 4 servings.

Creole Sauce: In a medium saucepan melt 2 tablespoons *margarine* or *butter;* add ¼ cup chopped *green sweet pepper* and 3 tablespoons chopped *onion.* Cook and stir until vegetables are tender. Add one 14½-ounce can *Cajun-style stewed tomatoes,* 1 teaspoon *sugar,* and dash *black pepper.* Bring mixture to boiling. Reduce heat; simmer, uncovered, about 10 minutes or until mixture is slightly thickened and reduced to 1¾ cups. Stir in ¼ cup sliced *pimiento-stuffed green olives;* heat through.

Nutrition facts per serving: 331 calories, 25 g total fat (6 g saturated fat), 218 mg cholesterol, 948 mg sodium, 18 g carbohydrate, 1 g fiber, 11 g protein.

Brunch Egg Casserole

1970

This easy brunch recipe boasts all-American eggs, bacon, and toast—all in one dish. The "toast" is actually timesaving purchased plain croutons. Today, a health-conscious cook may want to use turkey bacon.

2 **cups plain croutons**
1 **cup shredded cheddar cheese (4 ounces)**
4 **eggs**
2 **cups milk**
1 **teaspoon prepared mustard**

Dash pepper
4 **slices bacon, crisp-cooked and crumbled**
Crisp-cooked bacon curls (optional)

1 In a greased 2-quart square baking dish combine croutons and cheese. Set aside. In a medium mixing bowl combine eggs, milk, mustard, and pepper; beat until combined. Pour egg mixture over croutons. Sprinkle with the crumbled bacon.

2 Bake, uncovered, in a 325° oven about 45 minutes or until knife inserted off-center comes out clean. Let stand 10 minutes before serving. If desired, garnish with bacon curls. Makes 6 servings.

For a lower-fat version: Use reduced-fat cheddar cheese and skim milk and use 1 cup refrigerated or frozen egg product, thawed, instead of the whole eggs.

Nutrition facts per serving: 242 calories, 14 g total fat (7 g saturated fat), 172 mg cholesterol, 372 mg sodium, 14 g carbohydrate, 0 g fiber, 14 g protein.
♥ *Lower-fat version: 199 calories, 8 g total fat (3 g saturated fat), 19 mg cholesterol, 422 mg sodium, 14 g carbohydrate, 0 g fiber, 16 g protein.*

Egg & Sausage Quiche

1976

Pastry for a single crust
   9-inch pie
8 ounces ground turkey
   sausage or bulk pork
   sausage
1 tablespoon margarine or
   butter
1 cup chopped vegetables
   (such as asparagus,
   onion, green sweet
   pepper, and/or broccoli)

¾ cup shredded Swiss cheese
   (3 ounces)
¾ cup shredded cheddar
   cheese (3 ounces)
1 tablespoon flour
3 beaten eggs
1½ cups milk, half-and-half, or
   light cream
⅛ teaspoon ground black
   pepper

During the late '60s and early '70s, quiche was definitely "in," and real women and men everywhere were eating it for brunch, lunch, and as an appetizer. Our magazine published numerous recipes based on the French classic, including this one for brunch.

1 Line a 9-inch pie plate with the pastry; flute edges. *Do not prick.* Line pastry shell with a double thickness of foil. Bake pastry in a 450° oven for 8 minutes. Remove foil. Bake 5 minutes more. Reduce oven temperature to 325°.

2 Meanwhile, in a medium skillet cook sausage until browned; drain well. In a small saucepan melt margarine or butter over medium heat; add vegetables and cook for 3 to 5 minutes or until tender. In a medium mixing bowl toss together cheeses and flour.

3 Sprinkle cooked vegetables in bottom of prebaked pastry shell; top with cooked sausage and cheese mixture. In a mixing bowl combine beaten eggs, milk or cream, and black pepper. Pour over mixture in pastry shell. Bake in a 325° oven for 35 to 40 minutes or until a knife inserted in center comes out clean. Let stand 10 minutes before serving. Makes 8 servings.

For a lower-fat version: Omit the margarine and cook the vegetables in a small amount of water until crisp-tender. Use reduced-fat Swiss and cheddar cheeses and skim milk instead of regular cheeses and milk. Substitute refrigerated or frozen egg product, thawed, for the whole eggs.

Nutrition facts per serving: 352 calories, 23 g total fat (9 g saturated fat), 115 mg cholesterol, 442 mg sodium, 18 g carbohydrate, 1 g fiber, 18 g protein.
Lower-fat version: 310 calories, 17 g total fat (6 g saturated fat), 104 mg cholesterol, 539 mg sodium, 19 g carbohydrate, 1 g fiber, 18 g protein.

Eggs Sonoma

This Mexican-inspired breakfast dish did its cast-iron skillet proud in a 1974 story about the benefits of the nonstick, even-cooking cookware. "Consider yourself lucky if you inherited a well-seasoned cast-iron skillet," we wrote. "Today many young homemakers are searching antique shops for this prized cookware." The article helped readers season their own skillets: "Coat the inside with unsalted shortening, then place it in a 350° oven for two hours. Wipe off the excess grease with a dry cloth. Before using the skillet again, you may need to wipe it out. After cooking, wash it in hot soapy water, then rinse and wipe dry. Never scour or scrub the skillet with cleanser or put it in the dishwasher."

⅓ cup seeded, chopped tomato
1 4½-ounce can chopped green chili peppers, drained
2 tablespoons finely chopped celery
1 tablespoon finely chopped onion
1 teaspoon white wine vinegar
½ teaspoon sugar
⅛ teaspoon dried rosemary, crushed
6 eggs
¼ teaspoon salt
Dash pepper
1 tablespoon margarine or butter
4 6- to 7-inch corn or flour tortillas

1 In a small bowl combine the tomato, chili peppers, celery, onion, vinegar, sugar, and rosemary; set aside. Beat together the eggs, salt, and pepper; add tomato mixture.

2 In a large skillet melt margarine or butter over medium heat; pour in egg mixture. Cook, without stirring, until mixture begins to set on the bottom and around the edge. Using a large spoon or spatula, lift and fold partially cooked egg mixture so uncooked portion flows underneath. Continue cooking over medium heat for 2 to 3 minutes or until eggs are set throughout but are still glossy and moist. Remove from the heat.

3 Meanwhile, heat tortillas according to package directions. To serve, top each tortilla with some of the egg mixture. Makes 4 servings.

Nutrition facts per serving: 207 calories, 12 g total fat (3 g saturated fat), 320 mg cholesterol, 385 mg sodium, 15 g carbohydrate, 0 g fiber, 12 g protein.

Jiffy Orange Pancakes

1959

To please today's lower-fat tastes and in the interest of convenience, our Test Kitchen home economists tried using milk in this pancake. The result was one tough flapjack. For a lighter, fluffier pancake, their recommendation is to stick with the half-and-half or light cream.

1 beaten egg
1 cup half-and-half or light cream
1 6-ounce can frozen orange juice concentrate, thawed (¾ cup)

1 cup packaged regular pancake mix (not complete mix)
½ cup sugar
¼ cup margarine or butter, cut up

1 Combine beaten egg, cream, and *¼ cup* of the orange juice concentrate. Add pancake mix. Stir just until combined but still slightly lumpy. Heat a lightly greased griddle or heavy skillet over medium heat until a few drops of water dance across the surface. Pour about 2 tablespoons of batter onto the hot griddle for each pancake. Cook over medium heat 1 to 2 minutes on each side or until pancakes are golden brown, turning to cook second sides when pancakes have bubbly surfaces and slightly dry edges. Serve immediately, or place in a lightly covered ovenproof dish and keep warm in a 300° oven.

2 For sauce, in a small saucepan combine sugar, margarine or butter, and the remaining orange juice concentrate. Bring mixture to boiling, stirring occasionally. Serve the warm sauce over pancakes. Makes about 16 pancakes (4 servings).

♥ *Nutrition facts per pancake with 1 tablespoon sauce: 118 calories, 5 g total fat (2 g saturated fat), 19 mg cholesterol, 152 mg sodium, 17 g carbohydrate, 0 g fiber, 2 g protein.*

Hot Mince Pancakes

1955

1¼ cups all-purpose flour
2 teaspoons baking powder
1 slightly beaten egg
½ cup half-and-half or light cream

¼ cup milk
3 tablespoons cooking oil
1 cup prepared mincemeat
1 recipe Orange Hard Sauce

1 In a mixing bowl stir together flour and baking powder. In another mixing bowl combine egg, half-and-half, milk, and oil; stir into flour mixture just until combined. Gently fold in mincemeat.

2 Heat a lightly greased griddle or heavy skillet over medium heat until a few drops of water dance across the surface. For each pancake, pour about ¼ cup of the batter onto the hot griddle. Cook over medium heat 1 to 2 minutes on each side or until pancakes are golden brown, turning to cook second sides when pancakes have bubbly surfaces and slightly dry edges. Serve immediately, or place in a lightly covered ovenproof dish and keep warm in a 300° oven. Serve with Orange Hard Sauce. Makes about 12 pancakes (6 servings).

Orange Hard Sauce: In medium mixing bowl beat ¼ cup *butter* with an electric mixer on medium speed for 30 seconds or until softened; gradually add 1 cup sifted *powdered sugar,* beating until light and fluffy. Beat in ¼ teaspoon grated *orange peel* and 1 tablespoon *orange juice.*

♥ *Nutrition facts per pancake with 1 tablespoon sauce: 212 calories, 10 g total fat (4 g saturated fat), 32 mg cholesterol, 182 mg sodium, 30 g carbohydrate, 0 g fiber, 3 g protein.*

The most famous pancake story comes from Olney, England, where the women hold a pancake race every Shrove Tuesday in anticipation of Lent, honoring a folklore tale from the 1400s. Many churches across the United States sponsor pancake breakfasts on Shrove Tuesday in honor of this pancake-flipping tradition. Although the magazine has never held such a race, you may want to start your own tradition with these Hot Mince Pancakes.

Peanut Waffles
With Butterscotch Sauce

1938

In the '30s, waffles were an all-time favorite dessert. Today most people serve them for breakfast. Although our original recipe contained cake flour (2 cups), we've substituted the more widely available all-purpose flour without sacrificing a bit of flavor or lightness.

1¾ cups all-purpose flour
2 tablespoons granulated sugar
1 tablespoon baking powder
¼ teaspoon salt
2 slightly beaten egg yolks
1¾ cups milk

½ cup cooking oil
½ cup chopped peanuts
2 egg whites
  Margarine or butter (optional)
1 recipe Butterscotch Sauce
  Fresh or frozen berries (optional)

1 In a mixing bowl stir together the flour, sugar, baking powder, and salt. In another bowl combine the egg yolks, milk, and oil; stir into dry ingredients all at once, stirring just until combined but still slightly lumpy. Stir chopped peanuts into batter. Set aside. In a small bowl beat egg whites until stiff peaks form (tips stand straight). Gently fold egg whites into batter, leaving a few fluffs of egg white. *Do not overmix.*

2 Pour about 1 cup of batter onto grids of a preheated, lightly greased waffle baker. Close lid quickly; do not open during baking. Bake according to manufacturer's directions. When done, use a fork to lift waffle off grid. Repeat with remaining batter.

3 Serve hot with margarine or butter, if desired, and Butterscotch Sauce. If desired, top with berries. Makes 12 (4-inch) waffles.

Butterscotch Sauce: In a medium saucepan combine 1¼ cups packed *brown sugar,* ⅔ cup *light-colored corn syrup,* ¼ cup *milk,* and ¼ cup *margarine* or *butter.* Bring just to boiling; reduce heat. Simmer, stirring occasionally, for 20 minutes. Serve warm. (Refrigerate any remaining sauce; reheat in saucepan over low heat.) Makes about 1⅔ cups.

Nutrition facts per waffle with 2 tablespoons sauce: 375 calories, 18 g total fat (3 g saturated fat), 39 mg cholesterol, 279 mg sodium, 50 g carbohydrate, 1 g fiber, 6 g protein.

Ginger Waffles

1972

3 cups finely crushed
   gingersnaps (about
   42 cookies)
2 teaspoons baking powder
½ teaspoon salt
3 beaten egg yolks

1 cup milk
¼ cup margarine or butter,
   melted
3 egg whites
1 recipe Citrus Sauce

The recipe for these ginger-flavored waffles was included in a 1972 story titled "Food for People Who Love to Cook." What better way to add ginger flavor than with gingersnaps? If you have any leftover sauce, serve it with vanilla ice cream.

1 In a mixing bowl combine the crushed gingersnaps, baking powder, and salt. Combine beaten egg yolks, milk, and margarine or butter; stir into gingersnap mixture.

2 In a small bowl beat egg whites until stiff peaks form (tips stand straight). Gently fold beaten egg whites into the gingersnap mixture, leaving a few fluffs of egg white. *Do not overmix.* Pour 1 to 1¼ cups batter onto the grids of a preheated, lightly greased waffle baker. Close the lid quickly; do not open during baking. Bake according to the manufacturer's directions. When done, use a fork to lift waffle off the grid. Repeat with remaining batter. Serve warm with Citrus Sauce. Makes 16 (4-inch) waffles.

Citrus Sauce: In a small saucepan combine ½ cup *sugar,* 2 tablespoons *cornstarch,* and dash *salt.* Stir in ¾ cup *water;* bring to boiling. Cook and stir until thickened and bubbly. Stir in ½ teaspoon grated *orange peel,* ½ cup *orange juice,* ½ teaspoon grated *lemon peel,* 1 tablespoon *lemon juice,* and 1 tablespoon *margarine* or *butter;* heat through. Serve warm. Makes 1½ cups.

♥ *Nutrition facts per waffle with 2 tablespoons sauce: 164 calories, 6 g total fat (2 g saturated fat), 41 mg cholesterol, 287 mg sodium, 24 g carbohydrate, 0 g fiber, 2 g protein.*

1982

Stuffed French Toast

1 **8-ounce package cream cheese, softened**
1 **12-ounce jar apricot preserves (about 1 cup)**
1 **teaspoon vanilla**
½ **cup chopped walnuts**
1 **16-ounce loaf French bread**

4 **eggs**
1 **cup whipping cream**
½ **teaspoon ground nutmeg**
½ **teaspoon vanilla**
½ **cup orange juice**
  Fresh or frozen raspberries (optional)

1 In a small mixing bowl beat together cream cheese, *2 tablespoons* of the apricot preserves, and the 1 teaspoon vanilla until fluffy. Stir in nuts; set aside. Cut bread into ten to twelve 1½-inch-thick slices; cut a pocket in the top of each. Fill each pocket with about 1½ tablespoons of the cheese mixture.

2 Beat together eggs, whipping cream, nutmeg, and the ½ teaspoon vanilla. Using tongs, dip the filled bread slices in the egg mixture, being careful not to squeeze out the filling. Cook on a lightly greased griddle over medium heat about 2 minutes on each side or until golden brown. Keep warm in 300° oven while cooking remaining slices.

3 Meanwhile, in a small saucepan heat together the remaining apricot preserves and the orange juice. To serve, drizzle the apricot preserves mixture over hot French toast. If desired, top with raspberries. Makes 10 to 12 slices.

For a lower-fat version: Use reduced-fat cream cheese (Neufchâtel); substitute 1 cup refrigerated or frozen egg product, thawed, for the whole eggs; and use skim milk instead of the whipping cream.

Nutrition facts per slice: 456 calories, 24 g total fat (12 g saturated fat), 143 mg cholesterol, 383 mg sodium, 52 g carbohydrate, 1 g fiber, 10 g protein.
♥*Lower-fat version: 353 calories, 11 g total fat (4 g saturated fat), 18 mg cholesterol, 428 mg sodium, 52 g carbohydrate, 1 g fiber, 11 g protein.*

Sugar-Crusted French Toast

1953

Testing this recipe was a challenge because the directions for broiling in a 1953 oven weren't suitable for today's ovens. (The recipe could have been more appropriately named Blackened French Toast!) A few minor adjustments—and a few more helpful details in the directions—produced this caramelized-sugar-topped French toast.

2 eggs
⅔ cup milk
2 tablespoons sugar
1 teaspoon vanilla
6 1-inch-thick slices French bread

2 tablespoons margarine or butter
1 tablespoon margarine or butter, melted
2 tablespoons sugar
½ teaspoon ground cinnamon

1 In a small bowl beat together eggs, milk, the 2 tablespoons sugar, and vanilla. Place bread in a 2-quart baking dish. Pour egg mixture over bread; turn bread to coat. Refrigerate 20 to 30 minutes or until egg mixture is absorbed.

2 In a large skillet or on a griddle melt the 2 tablespoons margarine or butter over medium heat. Cook bread on both sides in hot margarine for 2 to 3 minutes on each side or until golden brown. Transfer to a baking sheet. Brush tops of bread slices with the 1 tablespoon melted margarine or butter. Combine the 2 tablespoons sugar and the cinnamon; sprinkle on bread slices. Broil 4 inches from heat for 1½ to 2 minutes or just until sugar is caramelized. Makes 6 slices.

♥ *Nutrition facts per slice: 228 calories, 9 g total fat (2 g saturated fat), 73 mg cholesterol, 330 mg sodium, 30 g carbohydrate, 0 g fiber, 6 g protein.*

Cowboy Coffee Cake

1943

1½ cups all-purpose flour	¼ teaspoon ground cinnamon
1 cup packed brown sugar	¼ teaspoon ground nutmeg
⅓ cup butter	½ cup buttermilk
1 teaspoon baking powder	1 beaten egg
¼ teaspoon baking soda	

1 In a mixing bowl stir together flour and brown sugar. Cut in butter until mixture resembles fine crumbs; set aside ½ cup of the crumb mixture to sprinkle over batter. To remaining crumb mixture, add baking powder, baking soda, cinnamon, and nutmeg; mix well. Add buttermilk and egg; mix well.

2 Pour into a greased 8×8×2-inch baking pan and spread evenly; sprinkle with the reserved crumb mixture. Bake in a 375° oven about 25 minutes or until a wooden toothpick inserted near center comes out clean. Serve warm. Makes 1 coffee cake (9 servings).

♥ *Nutrition facts per serving: 218 calories, 8 g total fat (4 g saturated fat), 42 mg cholesterol, 172 mg sodium, 35 g carbohydrate, 1 g fiber, 3 g protein.*

This delectable quick bread is a Better Homes and Gardens classic and has appeared in our cookbooks since the '30s. Although we've updated it over the years to fit changing tastes and ingredients, the recipe has kept its original buttery flavor. What we haven't kept, unfortunately, is the explanation for how the recipe got its name.

Vintage Views
1923

Meal-Planning Blues

Planning meals is an age-old chore, as a September 1923 *Fruit, Garden and Home* (the magazine's original name) article relates: "The regularity of three meals a day, year in and year out, is sufficiently appalling to give one a case of good, old-fashioned nerves. Meal planning becomes such a great, big, mountain high task that it is no small wonder our average housewife gets sick and tired of it." What to do? "The keynote of all successful meal planning is something new." That suggestion is as relevant today as it was in 1923. Surprise your family with this "new" coffee cake.

Cram-Jam Braid

1 **package active dry yeast**	½ **cup apricot preserves or**
½ **cup warm water**	**seedless raspberry jam**
(110° to 115°)	½ **cup snipped pitted dates**
2½ **cups packaged biscuit mix**	½ **cup chopped walnuts**
1 **tablespoon sugar**	**Margarine or butter,**
1 **beaten egg**	**melted (optional)**
	Sugar (optional)

1 Dissolve yeast in warm water; set aside. In a large mixing bowl stir together the biscuit mix and the 1 tablespoon sugar; add egg and yeast mixture, stirring until smooth. Turn out onto a lightly floured surface; knead 10 to 15 strokes. Roll dough to a 9-inch square. Place on greased baking sheet.

2 In a small mixing bowl combine preserves or jam, dates, and nuts. Spread mixture down center one-third of dough. Make 3-inch-long cuts from the edges of opposite sides toward the center at 1½-inch intervals. Starting at an end, alternately fold opposite strips of dough, at an angle, across the filling. Slightly press ends together in the center to seal. Cover and let rise in a warm place until nearly double (about 30 minutes).

3 Bake in a 350° oven about 20 minutes or until golden brown. If desired, brush with melted margarine or butter and sprinkle with additional sugar. Serve warm or cool. Makes 10 servings.

♥ *Nutrition facts per serving: 241 calories, 8 g total fat (0 g saturated fat), 21 mg cholesterol, 360 mg sodium, 39 g carbohydrate, 2 g fiber, 4 g protein.*

Our September 1965 call for "Homemade Breads in Half the Time" garnered several contest-winning kaffeeklatsch breads, all of which started with a timesaving base such as hot roll or muffin mix. This recipe, submitted by a reader from Maine, rose to the occasion using a biscuit mix, a convenience product that appeared on the market in 1931. We can only assume this recipe got its name because it's crammed with jam or preserves.

Raspberry-Cream Cheese Coffee Cake

1970

Packaged biscuit mix has changed since the 1970s, so the original recipe for this coffee cake flopped in recent Test Kitchen trials. Today's mix caused the coffee cake to spread too much when baked. Our home economists determined that we needed to cut back on the fat. We cut the ¼ cup margarine or butter out of the dough, and we had a winner.

1 **3-ounce package cream cheese**
2 **cups packaged biscuit mix**
⅓ **cup milk**
⅓ **cup raspberry preserves**

¾ **cup sifted powdered sugar**
½ **teaspoon vanilla**
1 **to 3 teaspoons milk**
1 **tablespoon sliced almonds, toasted (optional)**

1 In a medium mixing bowl cut cream cheese into biscuit mix until crumbly. Stir in the ⅓ cup milk. Turn out onto a lightly floured surface; knead gently 8 to 10 strokes.

2 On waxed paper roll dough to a 12×8-inch rectangle. Turn onto a greased baking sheet; remove paper. Spread preserves down center of dough. Make 2½-inch-long cuts, at 1-inch intervals, from edges of long sides toward the center. Starting at an end, alternately fold opposite strips of dough, at an angle, across the filling. Slightly press ends together in the center to seal. Bake in a 425° oven for 15 to 17 minutes or until golden brown.

3 In a small mixing bowl combine powdered sugar, vanilla, and enough of the 1 to 3 teaspoons milk to make it of drizzling consistency. Drizzle over warm coffee cake. If desired, sprinkle with almonds. Makes 12 servings.

♥*Nutrition facts per serving: 158 calories, 5 g total fat (2 g saturated fat), 8 mg cholesterol, 259 mg sodium, 26 g carbohydrate, 1 g fiber, 2 g protein.*

Sourdough Coffee Cake

1¼ cups all-purpose flour
½ cup granulated sugar
1½ teaspoons baking powder
¼ teaspoon salt
¼ cup butter
⅔ cup Sourdough Starter*
1 beaten egg

1 teaspoon vanilla
1 21-ounce can cherry pie
   filling
½ cup all-purpose flour
¼ cup packed brown sugar
½ teaspoon ground cinnamon
¼ cup butter

Pioneers used sourdough starter to leaven their breads. But with the introduction of commercial yeast, these homey breads went out of fashion. By 1978, when this recipe appeared in our magazine, cooks had rediscovered the wonderful tang the starter gives to all types of baked goods. Sample this cherry-filled coffee cake and see for yourself how sensational sourdough breads can be.

1 In a large mixing bowl stir together the 1¼ cups flour, the granulated sugar, baking powder, and salt. Cut in ¼ cup butter until mixture resembles coarse crumbs. Combine Sourdough Starter, egg, and vanilla. Add to dry ingredients; stir well.

2 Spread in a greased 2-quart rectangular baking dish. Spoon pie filling over top. Combine the ½ cup flour, brown sugar, and cinnamon. Cut in the ¼ cup butter until mixture resembles coarse crumbs; sprinkle over fruit. Bake in a 350° oven for 45 minutes. Cool on wire rack for at least 45 minutes. Serve warm or cool. Makes 10 to 12 servings.

Sourdough Starter: Soften 1 package *active dry yeast* in ½ cup *warm water* (110°). Stir in 2 cups *warm water,* 2 cups *all-purpose flour,* and 1 tablespoon *granulated sugar.* Beat until smooth. Cover with cheesecloth; let stand at room temperature 5 to 10 days, stirring 2 or 3 times a day. Cover and refrigerate until ready to use.

To replenish starter after using part of it, add ¾ cup *water,* ¾ cup *all-purpose flour,* and 1 teaspoon *granulated sugar* to starter. Let stand at room temperature until bubbly, at least 1 day. Cover and refrigerate for later use. If not used within 10 days, add 1 teaspoon *granulated sugar.* Repeat adding sugar every 10 days.

*Note: Measure the starter, then let it stand until it's at room temperature before using.

♥*Nutrition facts per serving: 311 calories, 10 g total fat (6 g saturated fat), 46 mg cholesterol, 215 mg sodium, 53 g carbohydrate, 1 g fiber, 4 g protein.*

Graham-Streusel Coffee Cake

1992

Packaged cake mixes became available in the '40s. When novel convenience products such as this became staples, we looked for new ways to incorporate them into recipes. Martha Myers of Missouri takes credit for this coffee cake based around a cake mix. She won second place with this recipe in the Prize Tested Recipes contest in 1992.

1½ cups graham cracker crumbs (about 21 crackers)
¾ cup chopped pecans or walnuts
¾ cup packed brown sugar
1½ teaspoons ground cinnamon
⅔ cup butter or margarine, melted
1 package 2-layer-size yellow or white cake mix
1 cup water
¼ cup cooking oil
3 eggs
Powdered Sugar Icing

1 For streusel, in a medium mixing bowl combine graham cracker crumbs, pecans or walnuts, brown sugar, and cinnamon. Stir in the melted butter or margarine. Set aside.

2 In a large mixing bowl combine cake mix, water, cooking oil, and eggs. Beat on low speed with an electric mixer just until moistened. Beat on medium speed for 1½ minutes. Pour half of the batter into a greased 13×9×2-inch baking pan. Sprinkle batter with half of the streusel. Carefully spread the remaining batter over streusel; sprinkle with remaining streusel.

3 Bake in a 350° oven for 35 to 40 minutes or until a toothpick inserted near the center comes out clean. Cool slightly; drizzle with Powdered Sugar Icing. Serve warm. Makes 12 to 16 servings.

Powdered Sugar Icing: In a small bowl stir together 1 cup sifted *powdered sugar,* 1 teaspoon *vanilla,* and enough *water* to make icing of drizzling consistency.

Nutrition facts per serving: 497 calories, 25 g total fat (9 g saturated fat), 81 mg cholesterol, 461 mg sodium, 66 g carbohydrate, 1 g fiber, 4 g protein.

*H*eart-Healthy Apple Coffee Cake

1992

Nonstick spray coating
⅔ cup all-purpose flour
½ cup whole wheat flour
1 teaspoon baking soda
1 teaspoon ground cinnamon
¼ teaspoon salt
1½ cups peeled, cored, and finely chopped tart apple (such as Jonathan or Granny Smith)
¼ cup refrigerated or frozen egg product, thawed
¾ cup granulated sugar

¼ cup chopped walnuts or pecans
¼ cup applesauce
¼ cup packed brown sugar
1 tablespoon all-purpose flour
1 tablespoon whole wheat flour
½ teaspoon ground cinnamon
1 tablespoon margarine
¼ cup chopped walnuts or pecans

Kathleen Fishman of Scottsdale, Arizona, won the September 1992 coffee cake category of our Prize Tested Recipes contest with this apple-studded version. Not only is it scrumptious, but it has only 5 grams of fat per serving.

1 Spray a 9×1½-inch round baking pan with nonstick coating; set aside. In a medium mixing bowl combine the ⅔ cup all-purpose flour, the ½ cup whole wheat flour, the baking soda, the 1 teaspoon cinnamon, and the salt; set aside.

2 In a large mixing bowl toss together the chopped apple and egg product. Stir in the granulated sugar, ¼ cup nuts, and the applesauce. Add flour mixture and stir just until combined. Pour batter into prepared pan.

3 For topping, stir together the brown sugar, 1 tablespoon all-purpose flour, 1 tablespoon whole wheat flour, and ½ teaspoon cinnamon. Cut in margarine until crumbly. Stir in ¼ cup chopped nuts. Sprinkle topping over batter in pan. Bake in a 350° oven for 30 to 35 minutes or until a wooden toothpick inserted near the center comes out clean. Cool in pan for 10 minutes. Remove from pan and serve warm. Makes 10 servings.

♥*Nutrition information per serving: 196 calories, 5 g total fat (1 g saturated fat), 0 mg cholesterol, 207 mg sodium, 35 g carbohydrate, 2 g fiber, 3 g protein.*

Creamy Caramel-Pecan Rolls

1992

Cinnamon rolls have starred on the magazine's cover many times over the years. This recipe, which ran in October 1992, gets top billing because it's made with frozen bread dough, a real timesaver. The rolls can be made up ahead, refrigerated overnight, and baked in the morning.

1¼ cups sifted powdered sugar
½ cup whipping cream
1 cup coarsely chopped pecans
2 14- to 16-ounce loaves frozen sweet roll or white bread dough, thawed

3 tablespoons margarine or butter, melted
½ cup packed brown sugar
1 tablespoon ground cinnamon
¾ cup light or dark raisins (optional)

1 For topping, in a small mixing bowl stir together powdered sugar and whipping cream. Divide evenly between two 9×1½-inch round baking pans. Sprinkle pecans evenly over sugar mixture.

2 On a lightly floured surface, roll each loaf of dough into a 12×8-inch rectangle. Brush with melted margarine or butter.

3 In a small mixing bowl stir together brown sugar and cinnamon; sprinkle over dough. If desired, top with raisins. Roll up rectangles, jelly-roll style, starting from a long side. Pinch seam and ends to seal. Cut each roll into 10 to 12 slices. Place slices, seam sides down, on sugar mixture in pans. Cover with a towel. Let rise in a warm place until nearly double (about 30 minutes). (Or, cover with oiled waxed paper, then with plastic wrap. Refrigerate for 2 to 24 hours. Before baking, let chilled rolls stand, covered, 20 minutes at room temperature.) Puncture surface bubbles with a greased toothpick before baking.

4 Bake rolls, uncovered, in a 375° oven until golden brown, allowing 20 to 25 minutes for unchilled rolls and 25 to 30 minutes for chilled rolls. If necessary, cover rolls with foil the last 10 minutes of baking to prevent overbrowning. Cool in pans on a wire rack for 5 minutes. Invert onto a serving platter. Serve warm. Makes 20 to 24 rolls.

♥ *Nutrition facts per roll: 227 calories, 10 g total fat (3 g saturated fat), 31 mg cholesterol, 95 mg sodium, 31 g carbohydrate, 1 g fiber, 4 g protein.*

Swirl Breakfast Loaf

1984

3½ to 4 cups all-purpose flour
1 package active dry yeast
1 cup milk
2 tablespoons granulated sugar
¼ cup margarine or butter
1 teaspoon salt
2 eggs

1 cup dried currants
½ cup orange juice
⅓ cup packed brown sugar
½ teaspoon ground cinnamon
⅛ teaspoon ground cloves
2 tablespoons margarine or butter, melted
Pearl sugar

The dried fruit filling creates an attractive swirl in this even-textured bread accented with a hint of orange, cinnamon, and cloves. Serve it with a fresh fruit compote and your favorite style of eggs for a company-pleasing breakfast.

1 In a large mixing bowl combine *1½ cups* of the flour and the yeast. In a small saucepan combine milk, granulated sugar, the ¼ cup margarine or butter, and salt. Heat and stir until warm (120° to 130°) and margarine almost melts. Add to flour mixture; add eggs. Beat with an electric mixer on low speed for 30 seconds, scraping side of bowl. Beat 3 minutes at high speed. Stir in as much of the remaining flour as you can with a wooden spoon. Turn dough out onto floured surface. Knead in enough of the remaining flour to make a moderately soft dough that is smooth and elastic. Shape into a ball. Place in a greased bowl, turning once to grease surface. Cover and let rise in a warm place until double (1¼ to 1½ hours). Punch dough down. Let rest 10 minutes.

2 Meanwhile, in a small saucepan combine currants and orange juice; heat to boiling. Remove from heat and let stand 5 minutes. Drain, reserving liquid. Stir brown sugar, cinnamon, and cloves into currants.

3 Divide dough in half. On a lightly floured surface, roll half of dough to a 15×8-inch rectangle. Brush with half of the reserved liquid and sprinkle with half of the currant mixture. Roll up rectangle, jelly-roll style, starting from a short side. Pinch seam and ends to seal. Place, seam side down, in a greased 8×4×2-inch loaf pan. Repeat with remaining dough, remaining reserved liquid, and remaining currant mixture.

4 Cover; let rise in a warm place until nearly double (45 to 60 minutes). Brush the 2 tablespoons melted margarine or butter on loaves. Sprinkle with pearl sugar. Cut the top of each loaf ½ inch deep lengthwise. Bake in a 375° oven for 35 minutes or until bread sounds hollow when lightly tapped. If necessary, cover with foil the last 10 minutes of baking to prevent overbrowning. Remove from pans. Cool completely on wire racks. Makes 2 loaves (32 servings).

♥ *Nutrition facts per serving: 100 calories, 3 g total fat (1 g saturated fat), 14 mg cholesterol, 102 mg sodium, 17 g carbohydrate, 1 g fiber, 2 g protein.*

Super-Colossal Cinnamon-Pecan Ring

1989

This large brunch ring comes together even more quickly because you use frozen bread dough instead of making your own. The first refrigerated bread dough—for buttermilk biscuits—was not available in supermarkets until 1953, even though it was invented in the 1930s.

2 16-ounce loaves frozen white bread dough, thawed
⅓ cup margarine or butter, melted
⅓ cup granulated sugar
⅓ cup packed brown sugar
2 teaspoons ground cinnamon
½ cup chopped pecans
⅔ cups sifted powdered sugar
¼ teaspoon vanilla
Milk

1 Grease a 14-inch pizza pan; set aside. On a lightly floured surface, flatten thawed dough slightly. Cut each loaf of dough into 4 pieces (8 pieces total). Form each piece into a rope about 18 inches long. Brush entire surface of each rope with melted margarine or butter.

2 Stir together the granulated sugar, brown sugar, and cinnamon. Place mixture in shallow pan or on large sheet of foil.

3 Roll 1 rope in sugar mixture to coat evenly. Shape rope into coil in center of the prepared pan. Roll another rope in sugar mixture. Attach securely to end of first rope and coil around first coil. Continue coating remaining ropes with sugar mixture and attaching them to form a 10- to 11-inch circle. Sprinkle any remaining sugar mixture over ring. Sprinkle chopped pecans on top.

4 Cover and let rise in a warm place until nearly double (30 to 40 minutes). (Or, cover with plastic wrap and let rise overnight in the refrigerator. Before baking, remove from the refrigerator and let stand 15 to 20 minutes.)

5 Bake in a 350° oven for 25 to 30 minutes or until bread sounds hollow when lightly tapped. If necessary, cover with foil the last 10 minutes of baking to prevent overbrowning. Cool about 15 minutes.

6 Stir together powdered sugar, vanilla, and enough milk (about 2 teaspoons) to make a thick glaze. Spoon over ring. Serve warm, cut into wedges. Makes 12 servings.

♥ *Nutrition facts per serving: 317 calories, 8 g total fat (1 g saturated fat), 0 mg cholesterol, 62 mg sodium, 49 g carbohydrate, 0 g fiber, 6 g protein.*

Fruit Bran Muffins

1979

The late '70s and early '80s were the golden age of the muffin. Transformed from a plain, slightly sweet bread, the muffin became a large extravaganza of all sorts of ingredients—from apple bits to macadamia nuts and white chocolate. One of the most popular was the bran muffin. Our versatile 1979 recipe gives you a choice of nine fruits.

1½ cups whole bran cereal
1 cup milk
1 egg
¼ cup cooking oil
1 cup all-purpose flour
¼ to ⅓ cup sugar
2 teaspoons baking powder
½ teaspoon baking soda
½ teaspoon ground cinnamon
½ teaspoon finely shredded lemon peel

¼ teaspoon salt
1 cup fresh fruit (such as chopped, peeled apples, apricots, nectarines, peaches, or plums; halved dark sweet cherries; whole blueberries or raspberries; or chopped bananas)

1 Lightly grease 12 muffin cups or line with paper bake cups. In a small mixing bowl combine bran cereal and milk; let stand 3 minutes or until liquid is absorbed. Stir in egg and oil; set aside. In a separate bowl stir together flour, sugar, baking powder, soda, cinnamon, lemon peel, and salt. Add bran mixture all at once, stirring just until moistened (batter will be thick). Fold in fruit.

2 Fill prepared muffin cups two-thirds full of batter. Bake in a 400° oven 20 to 25 minutes or until golden brown. Makes 12 muffins.

Nutrition facts per muffin: 140 calories, 6 g total fat (1 g saturated fat), 19 mg cholesterol, 293 mg sodium, 22 g carbohydrate, 4 g fiber, 4 g protein.

Health Muffins

1936

1 cup whole bran cereal
¾ cup snipped pitted dates
⅔ cup boiling water
⅓ cup dark-colored corn
　 syrup
3 tablespoons cooking oil

1 beaten egg
1 cup all-purpose flour
2 tablespoons sugar
2 teaspoons baking powder
¼ teaspoon salt
½ cup chopped walnuts

1 Grease 12 muffin cups. In a large mixing bowl stir together bran cereal, dates, and boiling water. Let stand 5 minutes. Stir in corn syrup, oil, and egg. In a medium mixing bowl stir together flour, sugar, baking powder, and salt; stir in walnuts. Stir dry mixture into date mixture.

2 Fill prepared muffin cups two-thirds full of batter. Bake in a 400° oven for 20 minutes or until golden brown. Makes 12 muffins.

Nutrition facts per muffin: 187 calories, 7 g total fat (1 g saturated fat), 18 mg cholesterol, 198 mg sodium, 31 g carbohydrate, 4 g fiber, 3 g protein.

Cooks in the '30s were concerned about eating nutritiously, although they probably weren't quite as health-conscious as we are now. Modern research proved a relationship between fat and heart disease that changed our way of life. These muffins from that earlier era include only a little oil, so they're in line with today's low-fat standards.

Vintage Views
1945

Our War Effort

In 1945, the focus on fat was different from today. An article titled "Cooking Ways That Take Less Fat" shared tips with readers to help them reuse or use less "fat" during the war. "Jack Sprat has plenty of company these days. Neither Mrs. Sprat nor any of us is using fat with the abandon of preshortage days," wrote Test Kitchen director Myrna Johnston. "You can't get along without fat altogether. You need it for heat and energy, for meals that satisfy. So make every ounce you buy an ounce to use and save, and if possible, use again, then salvage." Interestingly, some of the techniques we've "discovered" today to lower fat in our diets were suggested in that 1945 article.

Nun's Puffs

1985

These delicate rolls are close cousins of cream puffs because they use the same classic French choux paste method of combining flour with boiling water, butter, and beaten eggs into a sticky, pastelike dough. During baking, the eggs give the pastry its hallmark irregular-shaped domes. How these light, tender morsels were named is a mystery—but they are heavenly.

½ **cup butter**
1 **cup milk**
¾ **cup all-purpose flour**
4 **eggs**

1 **tablespoon sugar**
Cinnamon-sugar or honey (optional)

1 Generously grease twelve 2½-inch muffin cups, covering the edge and around the top of each cup. In a 2-quart saucepan melt the butter. Add milk; bring to boiling. Add flour all at once; stir vigorously. Cook and stir until mixture forms a ball that does not separate. Remove from heat; cool slightly (about 5 minutes).

2 Add the eggs, 1 at a time, beating with a wooden spoon after each addition for 1 minute or until smooth. Fill the prepared muffin cups half full of dough; sprinkle with the sugar.

3 Bake puffs in a 375° oven about 40 minutes or until golden brown and puffy. Remove from pan.* If desired, sprinkle with cinnamon-sugar or serve with honey. Serve immediately. Makes 12 puffs.

*Note: The puffs will fall slightly when removed from the oven.

Nutrition facts per puff: 132 calories, 10 g total fat (5 g saturated fat), 93 mg cholesterol, 109 mg sodium, 8 g carbohydrate, 0 g fiber, 4 g protein.

Pear, Ginger, & Walnut Muffins

1993

2 cups all-purpose flour
¾ cup sugar
2 teaspoons baking soda
½ teaspoon salt
¼ teaspoon ground
    cardamom or 1 teaspoon
    ground cinnamon
2 beaten eggs

½ cup cooking oil
2 tablespoons milk
1 teaspoon grated gingerroot
2 medium pears, peeled,
    cored, and finely
    chopped (1½ cups)
¾ cup chopped walnuts
½ cup raisins

Fresh gingerroot and cardamom spice up these contest-winning muffins from Linda McPhee, a reader from Newport, Oregon. The pears and raisins make for a fruity on-the-go breakfast muffin.

1 In a large mixing bowl combine the flour, sugar, baking soda, salt, and cardamom or cinnamon. Make a well in the center. Combine the eggs, oil, milk, and gingerroot; add all at once to flour mixture. Stir just until moistened (batter will be thick). Fold in the chopped pears, walnuts, and raisins.

2 Lightly grease muffin cups or line with paper bake cups; fill each three-fourths full. Bake in a 350° oven for 20 to 25 minutes or until a toothpick inserted near the center of muffins comes out clean. Remove muffins from cups; serve warm. Makes 18 muffins.

Nutrition facts per muffin: 194 calories, 10 g total fat (4 g saturated fat), 24 mg cholesterol, 160 mg sodium, 25 g carbohydrate, 1 g fiber, 3 g protein.

Coffee Banana Smoothie

1995

With everyone running off to work or school in the morning, our fast-paced lives mandate something quick yet nutritious. For adults who have to have their morning coffee, this '90s breakfast in a glass is the answer. Keep frozen bananas on hand to plop into the blender with a few added ingredients for a quick morning starter.

2 small bananas, peeled, cut up, and frozen
1½ cups skim milk
1 8-ounce container low-fat coffee yogurt
¼ teaspoon ground cinnamon
   Dash ground nutmeg

1 In a blender container combine bananas, milk, yogurt, cinnamon, and nutmeg. Cover and blend until smooth. To serve, pour into glasses. Serve immediately. Makes 2 (1½-cup) servings.

♥ *Nutrition facts per serving: 280 calories, 2 g fat (1 g saturated fat), 9 mg cholesterol, 165 mg sodium, 52 g carbohydrate, 4 g fiber, 13 g protein.*

Fruited Granola

1970

Granola, the darling of the '70s health food craze, is a crunchy mixture of oats, peanuts, wheat germ, raisins, apricots, and brown sugar.

1½ cups quick-cooking rolled oats
½ cup chopped raw peanuts
½ cup chopped blanched almonds
½ cup toasted wheat germ
½ cup raisins
⅓ cup snipped dried apricots
⅓ cup packed brown sugar
   Milk, half-and-half, or light cream (optional)

1 Combine oats, peanuts, almonds, and wheat germ. Spread in a 15½×10½×1-inch baking pan.
2 Toast in 400° oven for 10 minutes; stir once. Stir in raisins, apricots, and brown sugar. Cool. If desired, serve with milk, half-and-half, or cream. Store in an airtight container. Makes 4½ cups (9 servings).

Nutrition facts per serving: 215 calories, 8 g total fat (1 g saturated fat), 0 mg cholesterol, 6 mg sodium, 30 g carbohydrate, 3 g fiber, 8 g protein.

For Starters

Shoyster Cocktail

1985

Shrimp cocktail is no little thing when it comes to American appetizers. You might think that something so simple couldn't be improved upon. Not so, thought Anthony Lamar Bierly from Winona, Minnesota, who submitted this newfangled adaptation in our 1985 Holiday Recipe contest. He called it Shoyster Cocktail because it combines shrimp and oysters in a zesty sauce.

12 fresh shucked oysters, halved
12 fresh or frozen medium shrimp, cooked, shelled and deveined, or one 6-ounce package frozen cooked shrimp, thawed
1 medium avocado, pitted, peeled, and chopped
½ cup seeded, chopped tomato
½ cup cocktail sauce

⅓ cup finely chopped onion
2 tablespoons snipped parsley
1 tablespoon lime juice
1 medium red or green fresh chili pepper, seeded and chopped
¼ teaspoon bottled hot pepper sauce
1 clove garlic, minced
Leaf lettuce (optional)
Assorted crackers (optional)
Lemon wedges (optional)

1 In a medium skillet cook oysters in simmering, *lightly salted water* for 1 to 2 minutes or until edges curl. Drain well. Cut the shrimp into bite-size pieces.

2 In a large bowl combine oysters, shrimp, avocado, tomato, cocktail sauce, onion, parsley, lime juice, chili pepper, hot pepper sauce, and garlic. Cover; refrigerate for several hours. If desired, serve in individual lettuce-lined dishes with crackers and lemon wedges. Makes 8 servings.

♥*Nutrition facts per serving: 83 calories, 4 g total fat, (1g saturated fat), 30 mg cholesterol, 216 mg sodium, 9 g carbohydrate, 1 g fiber, 4 g protein.*

*V*intage Views
1946

The Big Chill

Refrigerators were introduced in the 1930s, but the article "Here Are the 1946 Refrigerators" touted the newer models as being better: "Lessons learned in the manufacture of war equipment have been applied to refrigerator production. Sometimes it's highest precision building, sometimes refinement of detail or type of material used. But whatever the new models or changes, they're designed to give you better value, greater usability, lower operating cost—all of which spell economy for you."

Steamed Mussels Vinaigrette

1988

1 pound mussels, scrubbed
   (about 18)
12 cups cold water
6 tablespoons salt
½ cup finely chopped green
   sweet pepper
3 cloves garlic
2 tablespoons margarine or
   butter
½ cup dry white wine or
   chicken broth

1 medium tomato, seeded
   and chopped
2 tablespoons snipped fresh
   basil or 1½ teaspoons
   dried basil, crushed
1 teaspoon snipped fresh
   cilantro or 1 tablespoon
   snipped parsley
   Sliced French bread
   (optional)

In the '80s, improvements in shipping and transportation opened up American markets to all types of ingredients from around the world. This 1988 recipe was published to showcase New Zealand green-lipped mussels. Their luminous green color makes this appetizer especially attractive, but any variety of mussels will work.

1 Remove beards from mussels. In a large bowl or kettle combine *4 cups* of the cold water and *2 tablespoons* of the salt; add mussels. Soak mussels for 15 minutes; drain and rinse. Discard water; repeat soaking, draining, and rinsing two times more.

2 In a 3-quart saucepan cook sweet pepper and garlic in margarine until almost tender. Stir in wine, tomato, and basil. Add mussels. Bring to boiling; reduce heat. Simmer, covered, for 3 to 4 minutes or just until mussels open. Remove from heat. Discard any mussels that do not open.

3 Using a slotted spoon, transfer mussels and vegetables to a large serving bowl. Cover and set aside to keep warm.

4 If necessary, boil the cooking liquid gently, uncovered, about 4 minutes or until it has been reduced to ⅔ cup. Spoon sauce over the mussels. Sprinkle with cilantro. If desired, serve with French bread. Makes 3 or 4 appetizer servings.

Nutrition facts per serving: 213 calories, 10 g total fat (2 g saturated fat), 32 mg cholesterol, 393 mg sodium, 9 g carbohydrate, 1 g fiber, 14 g protein.

Jamaican Shrimp

2 pounds fresh or frozen large shrimp in shells
¼ cup salad oil
3 tablespoons white wine vinegar
2 tablespoons lime juice
1 jalapeño pepper, seeded and finely chopped
1 tablespoon honey

2 teaspoons Jamaican Jerk Seasoning
1 medium mango, peeled, pitted, sliced, and halved crosswise
1 small lime, halved lengthwise and sliced
1 small red onion, quartered and thinly sliced

Jamaican cooks usually use Scotch bonnet peppers instead of jalapeño peppers in their spicy dishes. Scotch bonnets, one of the hottest of the chili peppers, add fire to this recipe. Use them if they're available and you like your shrimp hot, hot, hot.

1 In a large saucepan cook fresh or frozen shrimp, uncovered, in *lightly salted boiling water* for 1 to 3 minutes or until shrimp turn pink. Drain immediately and cool. Peel shrimp, leaving tails intact; devein. Place shrimp in a heavy plastic bag. At this point, you can seal the bag and chill for up to 24 hours.

2 For marinade, in a screw-top jar combine salad oil, white wine vinegar, lime juice, jalapeño pepper, honey, and the Jamaican Jerk Seasoning. Cover and shake well to mix; pour over shrimp in plastic bag. Cover and chill for 1 hour, turning bag occasionally.

3 To serve, drain shrimp, reserving marinade. In a large serving bowl layer shrimp, mango, lime slices, and onion, repeating until all are used. Drizzle with reserved marinade. Makes 10 to 12 appetizer servings.

Jamaican Jerk Seasoning: In a small mixing bowl combine 2 teaspoons *onion powder,* 1 teaspoon *sugar,* 1 teaspoon *ground thyme,* 1 teaspoon *salt,* ½ teaspoon *ground allspice,* ¼ teaspoon *ground cinnamon,* and ¼ teaspoon *ground red pepper.*

♥ *Nutrition facts per serving: 128 calories, 6 g total fat (1 g saturated fat), 105 mg cholesterol, 174 mg sodium, 7 g carbohydrate, 1 g fiber, 11 g protein.*

Holiday Shrimp Rounds

1976

Pretty as you please and easy to make, these creamy little appetizers feature a dough of sour cream and sharp cheddar cheese. Part of our December 1976 holiday food story, they stand out on any buffet table.

1 cup butter
1½ cups all-purpose flour
½ cup dairy sour cream
½ cup shredded sharp
   cheddar cheese
   (2 ounces)
1 4½-ounce can small
   shrimp, drained

1 8-ounce package cream
   cheese, softened
¼ cup milk
1 teaspoon lemon juice
1 teaspoon Worcestershire
   sauce
¼ teaspoon dried dillweed
   Dash garlic powder
   Fresh herb sprigs (optional)

1 In a large mixing bowl cut butter into flour until mixture resembles coarse crumbs. Stir in sour cream and cheddar cheese. Divide mixture in half; wrap and refrigerate for 1 hour or until dough is firm (or, if desired, refrigerate overnight).

2 On a floured surface, roll out 1 portion of dough to ¹⁄₁₆-inch thickness. Using a 2-inch floured biscuit cutter, cut into 48 rounds. Using a round hors d'oeuvre cutter, cut a 1-inch circle out of the center of 32 of the dough rounds. Place remaining 16 rounds on an ungreased baking sheet; brush with *milk*. Top each with 2 dough rounds with centers removed, making 3 layers in all. Brush with additional *milk* between layers. Repeat with remaining dough and reroll center cutouts to make a total of 32 layered rounds. Bake in a 350° oven for 22 to 25 minutes or until golden brown. Remove and cool on wire racks.

3 Meanwhile, for the filling, set aside 32 shrimp for garnish. Chop remaining shrimp. Beat together cream cheese, the ¼ cup milk, lemon juice, Worcestershire, dillweed, and garlic powder; stir in the chopped shrimp. Cover and refrigerate.

4 Spoon filling into pastry rounds. Top with reserved shrimp. If desired, garnish with fresh herb sprigs. Makes 32 appetizers.

To make ahead: Prepare as directed. Cover filled rounds and refrigerate for up to 2 hours. Remove from refrigerator 10 minutes before serving and let stand at room temperature.

Nutrition facts per appetizer: 114 calories, 10 g total fat (6 g saturated fat), 32 mg cholesterol, 100 mg sodium, 5 g carbohydrate, 0 g fiber, 2 g protein.

Nutty Blue Cheese Rolls

1994

This winner of a Prize Tested Recipe category called Easy-to-Make Recipes is ideal for after-work get-togethers. The rolls, which take advantage of refrigerated piecrust, can be made up to 24 hours ahead. Then all you have to do is pop them into the oven for 15 minutes.

⅔ **cup finely chopped walnuts**
⅓ **cup crumbled blue cheese**
1 **tablespoon finely snipped parsley**
¼ **teaspoon pepper**

½ **of a 15-ounce package (1 crust) folded refrigerated unbaked piecrust**
1 **tablespoon milk**
2 **teaspoons grated Parmesan cheese**
Finely snipped parsley

1 For filling, in a medium mixing bowl stir together walnuts, blue cheese, the 1 tablespoon parsley, and the pepper. On a lightly floured surface, unfold piecrust according to package directions. Spread filling evenly over the crust. Cut the pastry circle into 12 wedges. Starting at wide ends, loosely roll up wedges. Place rolls, tip sides down, on a greased baking sheet.*

2 Brush rolls lightly with milk. Sprinkle with Parmesan cheese and additional parsley. Bake in a 425° oven about 15 minutes or until golden brown. Cool on a wire rack. Serve warm. Makes 12 rolls.

To make ahead: Prepare as directed to the asterisk (*). Cover and refrigerate for up to 24 hours. Continue as directed.

Nutrition facts per roll: 139 calories, 10 g total fat (1 g saturated fat), 8 mg cholesterol, 130 mg sodium, 9 g carbohydrate, 3 g fiber, 3 g protein.

Chicken-Spinach Phyllo Rolls

1995

1 5-ounce can chunk-style chicken, drained and flaked

1 cup shredded cheddar cheese

1 10-ounce package frozen chopped spinach, thawed and well drained

½ of an 8-ounce tub cream cheese with chives and onion

½ cup chopped walnuts

1 tablespoon dry sherry

½ teaspoon Worcestershire sauce

¼ teaspoon ground nutmeg

8 sheets frozen phyllo dough (about 17×12-inch rectangles), thawed

⅓ cup margarine or butter, melted

When you're talking about festive holiday appetizers, this one sent in by Marline Schindewolf of Granger, Indiana, is a winner. One of her personal favorites, the recipe won her $100—a fine way to greet the season.

1 For filling, in a large mixing bowl combine chicken, cheddar cheese, spinach, cream cheese, walnuts, sherry, Worcestershire sauce, and nutmeg. Set aside.

2 Unroll the phyllo dough; cover with plastic wrap. Remove 1 sheet phyllo; brush lightly with some of the melted margarine. Place another phyllo sheet on top; brush with more melted margarine.

3 Spoon one-fourth of the filling (about ½ cup) evenly down the long side of the phyllo, about 2 inches from a long side and 1 inch from a short side. Fold 2 inches of the long side over the filling; fold in the short sides. Loosely roll up, jelly-roll style, starting from the long side. Place roll, seam side down, on an ungreased baking sheet. Repeat with remaining phyllo, remaining margarine, and remaining filling.*

4 Brush tops with any remaining margarine. With a sharp knife, score rolls at 1½-inch intervals. Bake in a 400° oven about 15 minutes or until golden brown. Let stand for 5 minutes before slicing. Serve warm. Makes 36 appetizers.

To make ahead: Prepare as directed to asterisk (*). Cover and refrigerate for up to 6 hours. Continue as directed.

♥ *Nutrition facts per appetizer: 71 calories, 5 g total fat (2 g saturated fat), 9 mg cholesterol, 96 mg sodium, 3 g carbohydrate, 0 g fiber, 3 g protein.*

Greek Croustade

1983

1 10-ounce package frozen chopped spinach
¼ cup chopped onion
3 tablespoons butter or margarine
3 tablespoons all-purpose flour
¼ teaspoon dried tarragon, crushed
⅛ teaspoon pepper

¾ cup milk
2 beaten eggs
1 cup cream-style cottage cheese
½ cup crumbled feta cheese
10 sheets frozen phyllo dough (about 17×12-inch rectangles), thawed
½ cup butter or margarine, melted

French in origin, a croustade (kroo-STAHD) is any crisp container with a savory filling. Sheets of phyllo (meaning "leaf" in Greek) make up the crust in this version. The tissue-thin sheets traditionally were used in Greek foods, such as the dessert baklava *and hearty pie* spanakopita. *Today phyllo is found in the frozen foods section of the supermarket. Don't fret if the sheets tear or crumple when you try to form a rosette. Phyllo is ever-forgiving when baked. This recipe was sent to us as her favorite recipe from the magazine by Mrs. Lawrence Keon of Croton On Hudson, New York.*

1 For filling, cook spinach according to package directions; drain well, squeezing out excess liquid. In a saucepan cook onion in the 3 tablespoons butter or margarine until tender. Stir in the flour, tarragon, and pepper. Add milk all at once. Cook and stir until mixture is thickened and bubbly. Cook and stir for 1 minute more. Stir about half of the hot mixture into eggs; return all to saucepan. Stir in spinach, cottage cheese, and feta cheese. Remove from heat; set aside.

2 Unroll the phyllo dough; cover with plastic wrap. Remove 1 sheet phyllo; brush lightly with some of the melted butter or margarine. Fold into thirds lengthwise; brush top with melted butter. Place 1 end of folded sheet in center of a 12- or 14-inch pizza pan, extending sheet over the side of the pan. Repeat brushing and folding with remaining dough and remaining butter, arranging strips evenly in a spoke fashion around the pan (ends of each sheet will overlap at center and will be about 3 inches apart at outer ends).

3 Spread filling in an 8-inch circle at the center of phyllo on pan. Starting with the last sheet of phyllo placed in the pan, lift end of the folded sheet up and bring toward center of filling. Holding end with both hands, twist several times; coil and tuck end under to form a rosette. Lay rosette over filling, but allow filling to show at the center. Repeat with remaining strips in the reverse order they were placed on pan, leaving a 3-inch circle of filling showing at the center.

4 Drizzle any remaining melted butter over all. Bake in a 375° oven for 35 to 40 minutes or until golden brown. Serve warm, cut into wedges. Makes 16 appetizer servings.

Nutrition facts per serving: 163 calories, 12 g total fat (7 g saturated fat), 58 mg cholesterol, 303 mg sodium, 9 g carbohydrate, 0 g fiber, 5 g protein.

Chive Chip Dip

1958

Dips and chips were mighty hip as the ultimate in 1950s casual entertaining. Still a hit at parties today, they're often served with veggie nibbles instead of fatty chips. With the availability of reduced-fat dairy sour cream, these dips are even more welcome on the party scene.

1 8-ounce carton dairy sour cream
½ cup mayonnaise
¼ cup snipped chives

1 tablespoon herbed vinegar, such as tarragon
Dash white pepper
Potato chips or assorted vegetable dippers

1 In a medium mixing bowl stir together the sour cream, mayonnaise, chives, vinegar, white pepper, and ⅛ teaspoon *salt*. Cover and refrigerate for up to 48 hours. Serve with potato chips or vegetable dippers. Makes about 1⅓ cups (twenty-two 1-tablespoon servings).

For a lower-fat version: Substitute fat-free dairy sour cream and nonfat mayonnaise dressing for the regular sour cream and mayonnaise.

Nutrition facts per serving: 58 calories, 6 g total fat (2 g saturated fat), 7 mg cholesterol, 46 mg sodium, 1 g carbohydrate, 0 g fiber, 0 g protein.
♥Lower-fat version: 32 calories, 2 g total fat (1 g saturated fat), 1 mg cholesterol, 64 mg sodium, 2 g carbohydrate, 0 g fiber, 1 g protein.

Creamy Onion Dip

1956

Perhaps the most well known of the '50s dips, this recipe combines sour cream with a new product of the time—dry onion soup mix. We pepped up our version with a little crumbled blue cheese.

1½ cups dairy sour cream
2 tablespoons dry onion soup mix
½ cup crumbed blue cheese
Snipped parsley (optional)

Assorted vegetable dippers (such as carrot, zucchini, jicama, or red sweet pepper strips, and/or broccoli or cauliflower flowerets)

1 In a medium mixing bowl stir together the sour cream and dry onion soup mix until mixed. Stir in blue cheese. Cover and refrigerate for up to 48 hours. If desired, sprinkle with snipped parsley. Serve with vegetable dippers. Makes 1¾ cups (twenty-eight 1-tablespoon servings).

♥Nutrition facts per serving: 37 calories, 3 g total fat (2 g saturated fat), 7 mg cholesterol, 103 mg sodium, 1 g carbohydrate, 0 g fiber, 1 g protein.

Herb-Curry Dip

1968

1 cup mayonnaise or salad
  dressing
½ cup dairy sour cream
1 teaspoon mixed dried herbs
  (such as basil, thyme,
  and oregano), crushed,
  or 1 tablespoon snipped
  fresh herbs
⅛ teaspoon curry powder
1 tablespoon snipped parsley
1 tablespoon finely chopped
  onion

2 teaspoons drained capers
1½ teaspoons lemon juice
½ teaspoon Worcestershire
  sauce
  Assorted vegetable dippers
  (such as carrot or celery
  sticks, jicama or sweet
  pepper strips, and/or
  cauliflower or broccoli
  flowerets)

Piquant and tart on the tongue, this dip gains a lot of flavor from just a hint of curry. Jean LemMon, Better Homes and Gardens magazine's current editor in chief, reached back to the '60s to nominate this one as her favorite snack recipe.

1 In a blender container or food processor bowl, combine mayonnaise, sour cream, herbs, curry powder, parsley, onion, capers, lemon juice, and Worcestershire sauce. Cover and blend or process until combined. Cover and refrigerate for up to 24 hours. Serve with vegetable dippers. Makes 1¾ cups (twenty-eight 1-tablespoon servings).

Nutrition facts per serving: 66 calories, 7 g total fat (1 g saturated fat), 6 mg cholesterol, 52 mg sodium, 1 g carbohydrate, 0 g fiber, 0 g protein.

Artichoke Dip

1978

1 14-ounce can artichoke
  hearts
½ cup mayonnaise or salad
  dressing

¼ cup grated Parmesan cheese
1 clove garlic, minced
  Paprika (optional)
  Assorted vegetable dippers

Before the late 1930s, polite society frowned on artichokes because you had to use your hands to eat them. But fashion changed, and using your fingers became more acceptable. Convenience products such as canned and frozen artichoke hearts made cooking with the exotic vegetable popular.

1 Drain artichokes thoroughly, pressing to remove excess liquid. In a medium mixing bowl mash artichokes; stir in mayonnaise, Parmesan cheese, and garlic. Cover and refrigerate several hours. If desired, sprinkle with paprika. Serve with vegetable dippers. Makes about 1¼ cups (twenty 1-tablespoon servings).

♥ *Nutrition facts per serving: 52 calories, 5 g total fat (1 g saturated fat), 4 mg cholesterol, 24 mg sodium, 2 g carbohydrate, 1 g fiber, 1 g protein.*

Potted Pepper Dip

1978

2 tablespoons lemon juice
2 teaspoons olive oil or
   cooking oil
1 teaspoon sugar
¼ teaspoon salt
   Dash black pepper
1 small onion, cut up
4 large red, green, yellow, or
   orange sweet peppers,
   seeded and cut up*
1 8-ounce package cream
   cheese, softened

¼ cup mayonnaise or salad
   dressing
1 teaspoon prepared
   horseradish
   Few dashes bottled hot
   pepper sauce
2 medium red, yellow, and/or
   orange sweet peppers,
   tops removed and seeded
   Assorted vegetable dippers
   and/or breadsticks
   Fresh herbs (optional)

A rainbow of peppers lines grocery store produce bins everywhere today, unlike in 1978, when you rarely found anything but green peppers. Although they work just fine, an assortment of peppers has more eye appeal. The original version of this recipe suggested tortilla chips as an accompaniment, but we think assorted vegetables, breadsticks, and crackers taste great, too.

1 In a blender container or food processor bowl, combine the lemon juice, oil, sugar, salt, and black pepper. Add the onion and about *one-third* of the cut-up sweet peppers.

2 Cover and blend or process until smooth. Add the remaining cut-up sweet peppers; cover and blend until smooth. Transfer mixture to a mixing bowl. Let stand, covered, at room temperature at least 2 hours.

3 Place pureed vegetable mixture in sieve, pressing gently to drain off excess liquid. In a medium mixing bowl combine cream cheese, mayonnaise, horseradish, and hot pepper sauce.

4 Stir in pureed vegetable mixture. Cover and refrigerate for 2 to 3 hours. Spoon into the whole sweet pepper shells. Place filled peppers in the center of a serving platter; surround with vegetable dippers and/or breadsticks. If desired, garnish with fresh herbs. Makes about 2 cups dip (thirty-two 1-tablespoon servings).

For a lower-fat version: Use fat-free cream cheese and mayonnaise or salad dressing in place of regular.

*Note: To avoid getting tough pepper skins in the dip, blanch seeded, quartered peppers in boiling water for a few seconds. When cool enough to handle, peel off skins with a small knife and cut peppers into pieces.

♥ *Nutrition facts per serving: 46 calories, 4 g total fat (2 g saturated fat), 9 mg cholesterol, 50 mg sodium, 2 g carbohydrate, 0 g fiber, 1 g protein.*
♥ *Lower-fat version: 16 calories, 0 g total fat, 1 mg cholesterol, 43 mg sodium, 2 g carbohydrate, 0 g fiber, 1 g protein.*

Appetizer Cheesecake

1993

Remember this sophisticated savory cheesecake the next time you're planning an appetizer buffet. It boasts artichoke hearts, feta cheese, and Greek olives for flavor. Plus, you can make it up to 24 hours ahead, then cut it into thin wedges so guests easily can serve themselves.

¼ cup margarine or butter, melted

6 sheets frozen phyllo dough (about 18×14-inch sheets), thawed

½ of a 6-ounce jar marinated artichoke hearts

3 8-ounce packages cream cheese, softened

1¼ cups crumbled feta cheese (5 ounces)

½ teaspoon dried oregano, crushed

¼ teaspoon garlic powder

3 eggs

¼ cup sliced green onions

Plum tomato slices (optional)

Whole Greek or ripe olives (optional)

Fresh basil leaves (optional)

1 For crust, brush bottom and sides of a 9-inch springform pan with some of the melted margarine. Unroll phyllo dough; cover with plastic wrap. Remove 1 sheet of phyllo and cut into a 13-inch circle. Ease the circle into the prepared pan off-center so that phyllo extends 3 inches up side of pan. Brush with melted margarine. Repeat with remaining phyllo and remaining margarine, placing sheets off-center to cover bottom and side of pan. Make 2 slits in the center of phyllo for steam to escape.

2 Bake in a 400° oven 9 to 10 minutes or until light golden brown. Cool on a wire rack. Lower oven temperature to 325°.

3 Meanwhile, drain and chop artichokes, reserving 2 tablespoons of the marinade; set aside.

4 In a large mixing bowl beat cream cheese with an electric mixer until smooth. Add feta, oregano, and garlic powder. Beat well. Add eggs; beat just until combined. *Do not overbeat.* Stir in artichoke hearts, reserved marinade, and green onions. Pour into crust. Bake in a 325° oven 35 to 40 minutes or until center is soft-set and outside stays firm when gently shaken. Cool.

5 Cover; refrigerate for at least 2 hours or for up to 24 hours. To serve, remove from pan and, if desired, let stand to bring to room temperature or serve immediately. If desired, top with tomato slices, olives, and basil leaves. Cut into wedges. Makes 14 appetizer servings.

For a lower-fat version: Substitute fat-free cream cheese for the regular cream cheese.

Nutrition facts per serving: 273 calories, 24 g total fat (13 g saturated fat), 108 mg cholesterol, 368 mg sodium, 7 g carbohydrate, 0 g fiber, 7 g protein.
Lower-fat version: 144 calories, 7 g total fat (3 g saturated fat), 62 mg cholesterol, 223 mg sodium, 9 g carbohydrate, 0 g fiber, 10 g protein.

Cheese-Pesto Pâté

1½ cups firmly packed
    parsley
¾ cup grated Parmesan
    cheese
¼ cup hazelnuts or walnuts
¼ cup olive oil or cooking oil
2 tablespoons snipped fresh
    basil, marjoram, thyme,
    or dill, or 1 teaspoon
    dried basil, marjoram,
    thyme, or dillweed,
    crushed

1 8-ounce package cream
    cheese, softened
1 5-ounce container semisoft
    cheese with French onion
    or ½ of an 8-ounce tub
    cream cheese with chives
    and onion
2 tablespoons milk
    Crackers, pita wedges,
    and/or carrot or celery
    sticks

Most people think of a ground meat mixture (usually liver) when they hear pâté. But the word actually is French for "pie." Pâtés can be made from vegetables, fish, poultry, or meat. In this recipe, cheeses layered with pesto create a pretty pie— perfect for spreading on crackers.

1 Line a 3-cup bowl or mold with plastic wrap; set aside. In a blender container or food processor bowl combine parsley, Parmesan cheese, and nuts. Cover and blend or process with several on/off turns until mixture is crumbly, stopping frequently to scrape down side of container. With machine running slowly, add oil and blend or process until mixture is the consistency of soft butter. Add desired herb to the mixture, blending or processing until well mixed; set aside.

2 In a medium mixing bowl beat cream cheese and semisoft cheese with an electric mixer until smooth. Stir in milk.

3 Spread half of the herb mixture evenly into the prepared bowl. Top with half of the cheese mixture. Repeat layers. Cover and refrigerate for several hours or overnight.

4 To serve, invert onto a serving platter. Remove bowl and plastic wrap. Serve with crackers, pita wedges, and/or carrot or celery sticks. Makes 24 servings.

Nutrition facts per serving dip: 98 calories, 9 g total fat (4 g saturated fat), 19 mg cholesterol, 110 mg sodium, 1 g carbohydrate, 0 g fiber, 3 g protein.

Ratatouille Pizza

1992

Ready-made Italian bread shells make pizza preparation ever so easy. This garden-fresh version takes four different vegetables, arranges them atop a tongue-tingling tomato sauce, and sprinkles the entire concoction with feta and mozzarella cheeses.

1 small eggplant (12 ounces)
½ cup chopped onion
2 cloves garlic, minced
2 tablespoons olive oil or cooking oil
4 medium tomatoes, peeled, seeded, and chopped (about 2⅔ cups)
1 tablespoon snipped fresh oregano or thyme, or 1 teaspoon dried oregano or thyme, crushed
½ teaspoon sugar
¼ teaspoon salt
⅛ teaspoon pepper

1 16-ounce Italian bread shell (Boboli)
2 medium red and/or yellow tomatoes, halved lengthwise and thinly sliced
1 small zucchini, thinly sliced
1 small yellow summer squash, thinly sliced
⅓ cup crumbled feta cheese
2 tablespoons sliced pitted ripe olives
½ cup shredded mozzarella cheese (2 ounces)

1 Chop enough of the eggplant to make 1 cup. Halve remaining eggplant lengthwise and thinly slice; set aside. In a medium skillet cook onion and garlic in *1 tablespoon* of the oil until tender. Add chopped eggplant, chopped tomatoes, oregano or thyme, sugar, salt, and pepper. Cook, uncovered, over medium-low heat about 15 minutes or until liquid is evaporated and mixture is of spreading consistency, stirring occasionally during cooking.

2 Place the bread shell on a lightly greased baking sheet. Spread the warm tomato mixture onto bread shell. Arrange the eggplant and tomato slices around the outside edge of the bread shell. Arrange zucchini and yellow summer squash slices in the center. Brush vegetables with the remaining oil. Sprinkle with feta cheese and olives. Sprinkle with shredded mozzarella cheese.

3 Bake, uncovered, in a 400° oven for 12 to 15 minutes or until vegetables are warm and cheese is melted. Transfer the bread to a serving platter. Cut into wedges to serve. Makes 12 appetizer servings.

Nutrition facts per serving: 180 calories, 7 g total fat (2 g saturated fat), 11 mg cholesterol, 366 mg sodium, 23 g carbohydrate, 3 g fiber, 8 g protein.

Zesty Italian Peasant Bread

1988

When you need a quick snack, it's hard to beat this super-simple, super-good bread. It also works well as an accompaniment to soup or as a side dish with grilled or broiled steaks and chops.

1 16-ounce Italian bread shell (Boboli)
1 tablespoon olive oil or cooking oil
1 clove garlic
⅛ teaspoon pepper
1 medium tomato, peeled, seeded, and chopped

⅓ cup crumbled Gorgonzola, blue, or feta cheese
1 tablespoon snipped fresh rosemary, oregano, or basil, or 1 teaspoon dried rosemary, oregano, or basil, crushed
Fresh rosemary, oregano, or basil sprigs (optional)

1 Place bread shell on a lightly greased baking sheet. In a small mixing bowl stir together oil, garlic, and pepper; brush over bread shell. Sprinkle tomato, cheese, and snipped or crushed herb over bread shell. Bake in a 400° oven 10 to 15 minutes or until warm and cheese softens slightly. Cut into 12 wedges. If desired, garnish with herb sprigs. Serve hot. Makes 12 servings.

♥ *Nutrition facts per serving: 126 calories, 5 g total fat (1 g saturated fat), 4 mg cholesterol, 260 mg sodium, 17 g carbohydrate, 1 g fiber, 5 g protein.*

Vintage Views
1930

A Tricky Balancing Act

In May 1930, the editors bemoaned: "Without doubt the modern conscientious homemaker has an occasional pang of envy of the woman who knows nothing at all about proper diet. As knowledge of nutrition has increased we have had to add more and more factors to the list of things to be considered as we plan, cook, and serve the meals. … One minute we have been hearing a great deal about eating bran, or brown, or whole-wheat bread; the next minute we are advised to include more white bread in our diet again. One minute we are told to refrain from eating so much meat; the next we hear of people living on an exclusive meat diet. And so it goes." Sound familiar?

Olive Pizza Bread

1963

1 slightly beaten egg
2 cups shredded process
   American cheese or
   cheddar cheese
   (8 ounces)
1 cup pitted ripe olives,
   coarsely chopped
1 tablespoon dried minced
   onion

1 teaspoon Worcestershire
   sauce
   Dash bottled hot pepper
   sauce
3 cups packaged biscuit mix
1 cup milk
1 teaspoon caraway seed
   (optional)

Although it might seem that Americans have always loved pizza, it was really after World War II that our passion for the pie skyrocketed. Since then, cooks have been in a fever creating myriad variations on the pizza theme. One delightful example is this bread, accented with American cheese and olives, from the free-spirited '60s.

1 Combine egg, cheese, olives, onion, Worcestershire sauce, and hot pepper sauce; set aside.

2 In a medium mixing bowl combine biscuit mix and milk to make a soft dough. Spread in a greased 12-inch pizza pan.

3 Spoon cheese mixture over dough. If desired, sprinkle with caraway seed. Bake in a 425° oven about 20 minutes or until golden brown. Serve hot, cut into wedges. Makes 16 appetizer servings.

For a lower-fat version: Use reduced-fat cheese, reduced-fat packaged biscuit mix, and skim milk.

Nutrition facts per serving: 171 calories, 9 g total fat (4 g saturated fat), 28 mg cholesterol, 570 mg sodium, 16 g carbohydrate, 1 g fiber, 6 g protein.
♥ *Lower-fat version: 141 calories, 5 g total fat (2 g saturated fat), 21 mg cholesterol, 517 mg sodium, 18 g carbohydrate, 0 g fiber, 5 g protein.*

Monterey Jack Fondue

1960

Monterey Jack cheese could be called the American mozzarella. Long known in California, it became available across the nation in the late '60s. It's great shredded over Mexican foods, such as enchiladas, or used in a grilled cheese sandwich.

3 tablespoons margarine or butter
3 tablespoons all-purpose flour
1 teaspoon dried minced onion
⅛ teaspoon garlic powder
⅛ teaspoon ground red pepper
1 5-ounce can (⅔ cup) evaporated milk
½ cup chicken broth
1¼ cups shredded Monterey Jack cheese (5 ounces)
French bread cubes

1 In a small saucepan melt margarine; stir in flour, onion, garlic powder, and red pepper. Stir in milk and broth all at once. Cook and stir until thickened and bubbly. Gradually add cheese, stirring until cheese is melted. Transfer to a fondue pot; place over fondue burner.

2 Serve with bread cubes. (Add additional chicken broth, as necessary, for desired consistency.) Makes 6 servings.

Nutrition facts per ¼-cup serving of fondue and 1 cup bread cubes: 249 calories, 16 g total fat (7 g saturated fat), 28 mg cholesterol, 418 mg sodium, 18 g carbohydrate, 0 g fiber, 9 g protein.

Vintage Views
1930

Cause for Celebration

Throughout the years, food has been celebrated and exulted. In "Good Food in an English Chophouse" (June 1930), famous chef Jean Anthelme Brillat-Savarin waxed poetic on dinner:

"At the end of a good dinner, both body and soul enjoy a particular happiness. Physically, whilst the brain is enlivened, the physiognomy brightens, the color rises, the eyes sparkle, and a pleasant warmth is diffused in every limb.

"The true artist, the true connoisseur of art, will be as critical of a dinner as of a symphony, a statue, or a song."

Fondued Flank Steak

1960

1 pound beef flank steak
½ cup cooking oil
½ cup dry red wine
2 tablespoons catsup
2 tablespoons molasses
2 tablespoons finely chopped crystallized ginger

1 clove garlic, minced
½ teaspoon curry powder
¼ teaspoon salt
¼ teaspoon pepper
    Cooking oil
1 teaspoon salt

Many '60s newlyweds hoped to find a fondue pot among their wedding presents. The centerpiece of trendy parties, the fondue pot made hosting a gathering simple and fun with recipes like this one.

1 Bias-cut the flank steak into thin 3×1-inch strips. Place meat in a plastic bag set in a shallow bowl. Combine the ½ cup cooking oil, the wine, catsup, molasses, crystallized ginger, garlic, curry powder, the ¼ teaspoon salt, and pepper. Pour marinade over flank steak. Seal bag; marinate in refrigerator for 4 to 6 hours.

2 Drain meat well; pat dry with paper towels. Thread meat on metal fondue forks or bamboo skewers accordion-style. (Use 1 piece of meat per fork or skewer.) Place skewered meat strips on serving plate. Cover and refrigerate until needed. Pour cooking oil into metal fondue cooker to fill cooker about half full or to depth of 2 inches. Heat, uncovered, on range top until oil is 375°. Add the 1 teaspoon salt. Transfer cooker to fondue burner. Fry meat in hot oil until desired doneness, 15 to 20 seconds. Makes about 16 appetizer servings.

Nutrition facts per serving: 94 calories, 8 g total fat (2 g saturated fat), 13 mg cholesterol, 22 mg sodium, 1 g carbohydrate, 0 g fiber, 5 g protein.

Ginger-Pumpkin Bisque

1995

The Marsh Tavern in Manchester Village, Vermont, shared this recipe with Better Homes and Gardens readers in 1995. The historic tavern provided a brief refuge for the Green Mountain Boys during the American Revolution. Our magazine editors found the tavern's soup satisfying, saying, "It's like eating warm pumpkin pie with a spoon."

2 tablespoons walnut oil or cooking oil
¾ cup chopped shallots
½ cup chopped onion
2 teaspoons grated gingerroot
¼ cup all-purpose flour
4 cups chicken broth
½ cup apple cider
1 15- or 16-ounce can pumpkin
⅓ cup pure maple syrup

2 bay leaves
¼ teaspoon dried thyme, crushed
¼ teaspoon ground cinnamon
¼ teaspoon pepper
⅛ teaspoon ground cloves
1 cup half-and-half or whipping cream
½ teaspoon vanilla
Whipping cream (optional)
Fresh thyme (optional)

1 In a 3-quart saucepan heat oil over medium heat. Add the shallots, onion, and gingerroot and cook until tender. Stir in the flour. Carefully add the chicken broth and cider all at once. Cook and stir over medium heat until thickened and bubbly. Stir in the pumpkin, maple syrup, bay leaves, dried thyme, cinnamon, pepper, and cloves. Return to boiling; reduce heat. Simmer, covered, for 20 minutes.

2 Remove from heat. Discard bay leaves. Cool slightly. Pour one-fourth to one-third of mixture into a blender container or food processor bowl. Cover and blend or process until smooth. Pour into a bowl. Repeat with remaining mixture until all is processed.* Return the mixture to the saucepan. Stir in the 1 cup half-and-half or whipping cream and the vanilla. Heat through, but *do not boil.* If desired, swirl a little whipping cream into each serving; garnish with fresh thyme. Makes 8 to 10 appetizer servings.

To make ahead: Prepare as directed to the asterisk (*). Cover and refrigerate the blended mixture for up to 24 hours. To serve, transfer the soup to a saucepan and heat through. Stir in the whipping cream and vanilla; heat through, but *do not boil.*

Nutrition facts per serving: 178 calories, 8 g total fat (3 g saturated fat), 12 mg cholesterol, 407 mg sodium, 23 g carbohydrate, 2 g fiber, 5 g protein.

Crab Bisque

1964

Canned soups were an instant hit as soon as they hit the supermarket shelves. But they required some dressing up, and recipes that did that were especially popular in the '50s and '60s. This elegant '60s appetizer soup is outstanding enough to warm cooks of the '90s thanks to its convenience.

1 10¾-ounce can condensed cream of asparagus soup
1 10¾-ounce can condensed cream of mushroom soup
2¾ cups milk
1 cup half-and-half or light cream
1 6- to 7-ounce can crabmeat, drained, flaked, and cartilage removed
⅓ cup dry sherry or milk
Snipped parsley (optional)

1 In a large saucepan combine the cream of asparagus soup, cream of mushroom soup, milk, and half-and-half or light cream. Cook over medium heat just until boiling, stirring frequently. Stir in the crabmeat and sherry or milk; heat through. If desired, garnish with parsley. Makes 6 to 8 servings.

Nutrition facts per serving: 235 calories, 13 g total fat (6 g saturated fat), 46 mg cholesterol, 926 mg sodium, 16 g carbohydrate, 0 g fiber, 11 g protein.

Vintage Views
1940

"I Cook with a Can Opener"

A *Better Homes and Gardens* magazine editor was quite proud to be the proponent of cooking with a can opener. She relates her husband's reaction in a 1940 article: " 'Boy! You should taste the meal my wife can throw together in a jiffy! Give her 10 minutes and a can opener and she's got all the fancy chefs beaten to a frazzle!'

"That's my husband for you. And so I dash for my can opener and turn out something extra special by way of thanks for the build-up. But don't get us wrong. We're not claiming that a meal fit for the gods or the boss's wife results merely from jacking open a couple of cans, heating, and serving 'as is.' On the other hand, you certainly can dish up a good, satisfying meal this way.

"… [I]f you want breathless adjectives as your reward, season canned foods with a pinch of imagination and spice them with originality."

Chilled Cranberry Soup

1993

4 cups fresh cranberries
(1 pound)
3 cups water
1½ cups sugar
3 inches stick cinnamon
¼ teaspoon ground cloves

2 tablespoons lemon juice
1 tablespoon finely shredded
orange peel
Orange peel curl (optional)
Mint leaves (optional)

1 In a 3-quart saucepan combine cranberries, water, sugar, cinnamon stick, and cloves. Bring to boiling; reduce heat. Simmer, uncovered, about 5 minutes or until about half of the cranberries are popped.

2 Remove from heat. Stir in the lemon juice and orange peel. Cool. Cover and chill soup for 4 to 24 hours. Before serving, remove the cinnamon stick.

3 To serve, ladle into soup bowls. If desired, top each serving with an orange peel and mint. Makes 7 to 8 servings.

♥ *Nutrition facts per serving: 190 calories, 0 g total fat, 0 mg cholesterol, 4 mg sodium, 50 g carbohydrate, 3 g fiber, 0 g protein.*

A December story called "Delicious Memories" featured recipes from the magazine's readers that evoked images of the past. Pat Ward of Pennsauken, New Jersey, said in the letter accompanying her recipe: "Our family fell in love with this wonderful soup on a Massachusetts vacation several years ago. My kids now expect it as part of our celebration every year and call it their 'vacation soup.'"

Tomato-Basil Bisque

1995

3 cups tomatoes, peeled,
seeded, and coarsely
chopped
1 cup vegetable or chicken
broth

1 8-ounce can tomato sauce
2 tablespoons snipped fresh
basil or 1 teaspoon dried
basil, crushed

1 In a blender container or food processor bowl, combine the chopped tomatoes, broth, and tomato sauce. Cover and blend or process until smooth. Stir in basil. Cover; chill until serving time. Makes 4 servings.

♥ *Nutrition facts per serving: 56 calories, 1 g total fat (0 g saturated fat), 0 mg cholesterol, 591 mg sodium, 14 g carbohydrate, 3 g fiber, 2 g protein.*

What makes a soup a bisque? Food dictionaries tell us the word has been in use for centuries and that it has some connection with the Spanish province of Biscay. Originally, a bisque was a highly spiced boiled meat or game dish, but today the word generally refers to a puree of fish, wine, and cream. A bisque is sometimes made from pureed vegetables, as this one is. From the July 1995 issue, this soup is cool and easy. Just blend, chill, and serve.

Brie with Roasted Garlic

1991

When are two heads of garlic better than one? When they're roasted to a mellow, slightly sweet perfection as in this exquisite appetizer. If you like, heat one wheel of cheese at a time so the Brie always is warm and easy to spread on apples or bread.

2 whole heads garlic
¼ cup olive oil or cooking oil
4 4½-ounce Brie wheels or one 2-pound Brie wheel, well chilled

½ cup whole Greek olives or ripe olives, pitted and quartered
4 teaspoons finely snipped parsley
Apple wedges or warmed sourdough or French bread slices

1 Divide heads of garlic into cloves (should have 20 to 24 cloves); *do not peel.* Place garlic in a heavy 1-quart saucepan with the oil. Cook over medium heat for 5 minutes, stirring constantly. Cover and reduce heat to medium-low; continue cooking for 10 minutes or until garlic is soft. Remove garlic from oil; drain on paper towels. Reserve oil. When cool enough to handle, peel garlic.

2 To assemble Brie, carefully slice the thin rind off *one* of the flat sides of the wheel(s). Place Brie on an ovenproof serving platter, cut side up. With a small, sharp knife, slice garlic cloves lengthwise, being careful not to cut completely through end of clove. Gently press garlic cloves into fans. Arrange garlic fans and olive wedges atop Brie wheel(s). Drizzle top(s) with about 4 teaspoons of the reserved olive oil.*

3 Bake, uncovered, in a 400° oven for 8 to 10 minutes or until Brie is warm and slightly softened. Sprinkle with parsley. Serve immediately with apple wedges or bread. Makes 16 servings.

To make ahead: Prepare as directed to the asterisk (*). Wrap the assembled Brie wheel(s) in plastic wrap and refrigerate for up to 3 days. Before serving, bake as directed above.

Nutrition facts per serving: 148 calories, 13 g total fat (6 g saturated fat), 31 mg cholesterol, 220 mg sodium, 2 g carbohydrate, 0 g fiber, 7 g protein.

Smoky Cheese Ball

1970

2 8-ounce packages cream
   cheese
2 cups shredded smoky
   cheddar cheese
½ cup margarine or butter

2 tablespoons milk
2 teaspoons steak sauce
¾ cup finely chopped toasted
   almonds or pecans

1 Bring cream cheese, smoky cheddar cheese, and margarine or butter to room temperature. In a large mixing bowl combine the cream cheese, cheddar cheese, margarine or butter, milk, and steak sauce.

2 Beat on medium speed of an electric mixer until fluffy. Cover and refrigerate for 30 minutes or until slightly chilled. Shape cheese mixture into a ball; roll in almonds or pecans to coat, patting nuts onto ball to secure. Makes 1 large ball (eighty 1-tablespoon servings).

♥ *Nutrition facts per serving: 45 calories, 4 g total fat (3 g saturated fat), 12 mg cholesterol, 49 mg sodium, 0 g carbohydrate, 0 g fiber, 1 g protein.*

We found the distinct flavor of the smoked cheddar enticing, but you can make this cheese ball with regular cheddar if you prefer. If you're only serving a small group of people, shape the cheese mixture into two balls and only coat one with nuts. Freeze the uncoated ball for later. To serve it, thaw the ball and add the nuts.

Vintage Views
1930

Is Your Cupboard Bare?

A rule of thumb for impromptu meal preparation is to keep a few basic ingredients on hand. This is echoed in "Stocking a Guest Shelf" (April 1930) with this advice: "Today, in this age of fast and easy travel, it is almost imperative that the efficient homemaker keep a well-stocked pantry shelf containing foods that are easy to prepare on short notice. When the cousins from Humptyville drive in unannounced at 5 minutes to 6, or when Hubby brings home an old college friend without a phoned warning, what a comfort it is to be able to turn to the Emergency Shelf for inspiration and help."

Buffalo Wings

1992

The Anchor Bar in Buffalo, New York, is credited with this all-time hit. If you like your wings with extra heat, use the higher range of the bottled hot pepper sauce. In any case, blue cheese sauce is a necessity for dipping to cool the flame.

12 chicken wings (about
    2 pounds)
2 tablespoons margarine or
    butter, melted
2 to 3 tablespoons bottled
    hot pepper sauce

1 teaspoon paprika
   Salt (optional)
   Black pepper (optional)
1 recipe Blue Cheese Dip
   Celery sticks (optional)

1 Preheat broiler. Meanwhile, rinse chicken wings; pat dry with paper towels. Cut off and discard tips of chicken wings. Cut wings at joints to form 24 pieces. Place chicken wing pieces in a shallow, nonmetal pan.

2 For sauce, in a small mixing bowl stir together the melted margarine or butter, bottled hot pepper sauce, and paprika. Pour mixture over chicken wings, stirring to coat. Cover chicken and let stand at room temperature for 30 minutes.

3 Drain chicken, reserving sauce. Place the chicken wing pieces on the unheated rack of a broiler pan. If desired, sprinkle the chicken with salt and black pepper. Brush with some of the reserved sauce.

4 Broil chicken 4 to 5 inches from the heat about 10 minutes or until lightly browned. Turn the chicken pieces; brush again with the reserved sauce. Broil for 10 to 15 minutes more or until the chicken is tender and no longer pink. Serve with Blue Cheese Dip and, if desired, celery sticks. Makes 12 appetizer servings.

Blue Cheese Dip: In a blender container or a food processor bowl combine ½ cup *dairy sour cream;* ½ cup *mayonnaise* or *salad dressing;* ½ cup crumbled *blue cheese;* 1 clove *garlic,* minced; and 1 tablespoon *white wine vinegar* or *white vinegar.* Cover and blend or process dip until smooth. To store dip, cover and refrigerate for up to 2 weeks. If desired, top with additional crumbled *blue cheese* before serving. Makes 1¼ cups.

For a lower-fat version: Substitute fat-free dairy sour cream and nonfat mayonnaise dressing for the regular sour cream and mayonnaise.

Nutrition facts per serving plus 2 tablespoons dip: 225 calories, 19 g total fat (5 g saturated fat), 40 mg cholesterol, 197 mg sodium, 0 g carbohydrate, 0 g fiber, 10 g protein.
Lower-fat version: 155 calories, 10 g total fat (3 g saturated fat), 33 mg cholesterol, 273 mg sodium, 4 g carbohydrate, 0 g fiber, 11 g protein.

Soy Sauce Chicken Wings

1978

12 to 18 chicken wings (2 to 3 pounds)	1 tablespoon vinegar
2½ cups water	2 or 3 dried red chili peppers
1 10-ounce bottle (1⅓ cups) soy sauce	½ teaspoon Homemade Five-Spice Powder or purchased five-spice powder
4 slices gingerroot	
1 leek, cut up	2 cloves garlic, minced
1 tablespoon sugar	

Our make-it-yourself five-spice powder adds an intriguing Oriental accent to these wings. If you prefer, purchase bottled five-spice powder in the herb and spice section of your supermarket or at Asian food markets.

1 Rinse chicken wings; pat dry with paper towels. Cut off and discard tips of chicken wings. Cut wings at joints to form 24 to 36 pieces. In a kettle combine water, soy sauce, gingerroot, leek, sugar, vinegar, chili peppers, Homemade Five-Spice Powder, and garlic. Bring to boiling. Add chicken. Return to boiling; reduce heat. Simmer, covered, 20 to 25 minutes or until chicken is no longer pink. Remove chicken with a slotted spoon. Serve hot or chilled. Makes 12 to 18 appetizer servings.

Homemade Five-Spice Powder: In a small bowl combine 1 teaspoon *ground cinnamon;* 1 teaspoon *aniseed,* crushed; ¼ teaspoon *fennel seed,* crushed; ¼ teaspoon *Szechwan pepper,* crushed; and ⅛ teaspoon *ground cloves.* Store in a covered container. Makes about 1 tablespoon.

Nutrition facts per serving: 101 calories, 7 g total fat (2 g saturated fat), 28 mg cholesterol, 155 mg sodium, 0 g carbohydrate, 0 g fiber, 9 g protein.

Mexi Meatballs

1960

In the '60s, the original recipe of this dish called for frying the meatballs in oil as a fondue (readers were clamoring for recipes for their fondue pots). As we retested the recipe, however, we thought today's health-minded readers would prefer a baked version.

¾ cup soft bread crumbs
   (about 1 slice bread)
¼ cup bottled chili sauce
1 beaten egg
½ teaspoon dried minced
   onion
½ teaspoon salt
⅛ teaspoon garlic powder
1 pound ground beef
1 recipe Creamy Guacamole
   or 1 recipe Spicy
   Chili Sauce

1 In a medium mixing bowl combine the crumbs, chili sauce, egg, onion, salt, and garlic powder. Add ground beef and mix well. Shape meat mixture into 30 to 32 meatballs. Place the meatballs on a 15½×10½×1-inch baking pan. Bake in a 350° oven for 15 to 18 minutes or until juices are no longer pink. Drain. Serve warm with Creamy Guacamole Sauce or Spicy Chili Sauce. Makes 6 to 8 appetizer servings.

Nutrition facts per serving of meatballs (no sauce): 184 calories, 10 g total fat (4 g saturated fat), 83 mg cholesterol, 391 mg sodium, 5 g carbohydrate, 0 g fiber, 16 g protein.

Creamy Guacamole: Mix 1 cup mashed *avocado*, ½ cup *dairy sour cream*, 2 teaspoons *lemon juice*, ½ teaspoon grated *onion*, ¼ teaspoon *salt*, and ¼ teaspoon *chili powder*; refrigerate. Stir in 3 slices *bacon*, crisp-cooked and crumbled. Makes 1½ cups.

♥ *Nutrition facts per tablespoon: 29 calories, 3 g total fat (1 g saturated fat), 3 mg cholesterol, 38 mg sodium, 1 g carbohydrate, 0 g fiber, 1 g protein.*

Spicy Chili Sauce: In a medium saucepan combine 1 cup *bottled chili sauce;* ¼ cup chopped *onion;* 3 tablespoons *vinegar;* 1 teaspoon packed *brown sugar;* 1 clove *garlic,* crushed; ¼ teaspoon *dry mustard;* ¼ teaspoon *bottled hot pepper sauce,* and ⅛ teaspoon *salt.* Bring to boiling; reduce heat. Simmer, uncovered, 10 minutes, stirring often. Serve warm or cool. Makes 1¼ cups.

♥ *Nutrition facts per tablespoon: 14 calories, 0 g total fat, 0 mg cholesterol, 175 mg sodium, 3 g carbohydrate, 0 g fiber, 0 g protein.*

Super Salads

Pecan Rice & Feta Salad

1992

The dawning of the '90s brought a renewed interest in rice. Gourmet food shops and supermarkets no longer stock just one or two kinds. Shoppers can find everything from East Indian basmati to Italian Arborio and Thai jasmine varieties. This 1992 salad takes advantage of the nutty flavor and popcornlike aroma of wild pecan rice grown in Louisiana.

1 7-ounce package wild pecan long-grain rice
4 ounces feta cheese, crumbled
1 cup chopped green and/or red sweet pepper
½ cup chopped onion
⅓ cup pine nuts, toasted
1 2-ounce jar diced pimiento, drained
¼ cup olive oil or salad oil
2 tablespoons tarragon white wine vinegar*
⅛ teaspoon black pepper

1 Cook rice according to package directions, using 1 teaspoon *salt;* cool slightly. In a large mixing bowl stir together cheese, sweet pepper, onion, nuts, and pimiento; add cooled rice.

2 For dressing, stir together oil, vinegar, and black pepper; add to rice mixture. Toss gently to coat. Cover; refrigerate until chilled or for up to 24 hours. Makes 8 side-dish servings.

*Note: You can substitute 2 tablespoons white wine vinegar combined with ⅛ to ¼ teaspoon dried tarragon, crushed.

Nutrition facts per serving: 228 calories, 14 g total fat (4 g saturated fat), 12 mg cholesterol, 166 mg sodium, 23 g carbohydrate, 0 g fiber, 6 g protein.

Vintage Views
1936

The Spin on Lettuce

In the '30s, in a column called, "Confessions of Good Cooks," the magazine published cooking tips submitted by readers. Here, with the original illustration, is one such tip from March 1936:

"Being constitutionally lazy, the job of wiping lettuce leaves dry for salad bores me. I have a lot more fun with the whirl-dry method especially since I've learned to enlist the husband. The crisp wet lettuce goes in a clean towel or napkin, he rolls it loosely, seizes the corners, and whirls it over the sink. The water promptly flies off, leaving the lettuce dry."
—Mrs. Daisy

Curried Fruit & Nut Salad

1980

1 head red leaf lettuce or
   romaine, torn (about
   6 cups)
2 cups torn fresh spinach
1 11-ounce can mandarin
   orange sections, chilled
   and drained
1 cup seedless grapes, halved
½ cup slivered or sliced
   almonds, toasted
¼ cup salad oil
¼ cup white wine vinegar

2 tablespoons packed brown
   sugar
2 tablespoons snipped fresh
   chives or thinly sliced
   green onion tops
1 clove garlic, minced
1½ to 2 teaspoons curry
   powder
1 teaspoon soy sauce
1 avocado, peeled, seeded,
   and sliced (optional)

*This $250 winner in our
1980 Busy People's Recipe
Contest makes a great-tasting side
dish. To make it a hearty main
dish for four, just toss in 2 cups
of cubed cooked chicken. Curry
powder gives the salad its Indian-
style flavor. Use the lower range
to make it milder.*

1 In a large salad bowl toss together the lettuce, spinach, orange
sections, grapes, and almonds.

2 For the dressing, in a screw-top jar combine salad oil, vinegar,
brown sugar, chives or onion tops, garlic, curry powder, and soy sauce.
Cover and shake well.

3 Just before serving, toss some of the dressing with the salad. If
desired, garnish with avocado slices. Pass remaining dressing. Makes
8 side-dish servings.

*Nutrition facts per serving: 152 calories, 10 g total fat (1 g saturated fat),
0 mg cholesterol, 62 mg sodium, 15 g carbohydrate, 2 g fiber, 3 g protein.*

Cobb Salad

1964

Made famous at the Brown Derby restaurant in Hollywood, this salad appeared in our magazine in 1964. To make it a little easier to prepare, we suggest you use your favorite purchased French salad dressing instead of the original Brown Derby dressing that was included with the recipe in 1964.

½ large head lettuce, shredded (about 6 cups)
4 medium skinless, boneless chicken breast halves, cooked, chilled, and cubed, or 3 cups diced cooked chicken
2 medium tomatoes, diced
3 hard-cooked eggs, chopped
6 slices bacon, crisp-cooked and crumbled

¾ cup crumbled blue cheese (3 ounces)
1 or 2 medium avocados, halved, peeled, and cut in wedges
1 small Belgian endive
1 tablespoon snipped chives or thinly sliced green onion tops (optional)
½ cup purchased French salad dressing

1 On 4 individual salad plates or on a large platter arrange the shredded lettuce. On top of the lettuce, arrange a row each of chicken, tomatoes, eggs, bacon, and cheese.

2 Just before serving, tuck avocado wedges and endive leaves around the edges of the plates or platter. If desired, sprinkle with chives or green onion tops. Serve with dressing. Makes 4 to 6 main-dish servings.

For a lower-fat version: Use a low-fat or low-calorie French salad dressing in place of regular salad dressing and omit the bacon and avocado.

Nutrition facts per serving: 648 calories, 43 g total fat (14 g saturated fat), 289 mg cholesterol, 1,038 mg sodium, 18 g carbohydrate, 4 g fiber, 48 g protein.
♥ *Lower-fat version: 292 calories, 5 g total fat (3 g saturated fat), 266 mg cholesterol, 628 mg sodium, 14 g carbohydrate, 4 g fiber, 44 g protein.*

Salad Pizza

1986

Streamline this pizza (and cut the fat by almost 8 grams per serving) just by using an Italian bread shell. Try the complete lower-fat version of the recipe and reduce the fat even more.

½ of a 17-ounce package (1 sheet) frozen puff pastry
3 cups torn mixed greens
½ of a 14-ounce can (¾ cup) artichoke hearts, coarsely chopped
6 cherry tomatoes, quartered
½ cup sliced pitted ripe olives

1 4-ounce container semisoft cheese with herbs or ½ of an 8-ounce tub cream cheese with chives and onion
2 teaspoons Dijon-style mustard
1 to 2 tablespoons milk
1½ cups shredded mozzarella cheese (6 ounces)
1 medium avocado, halved, seeded, peeled, and sliced (optional)

1 For crust, thaw pastry according to package directions. On a lightly floured surface roll pastry to a 12-inch square; cut out a 12-inch circle of pastry. Place pastry circle on a large baking sheet or a 12-inch pizza pan; generously prick bottom. Bake in a 375° oven 15 to 18 minutes or until golden brown. Cool.

2 In a large mixing bowl combine greens, artichoke hearts, tomatoes, and olives. In a small mixing bowl stir together semisoft cheese or cream cheese, mustard, and enough milk to make of drizzling consistency; drizzle over greens mixture. Toss to coat well.

3 Preheat broiler. Sprinkle *1 cup* of the mozzarella cheese evenly over crust. Broil 3 inches from heat for 1 to 1½ minutes or until cheese is melted. Spoon salad mixture evenly over cheese. Sprinkle remaining mozzarella cheese on top. Broil for 1 to 2 minutes more or just until cheese starts to melt. If desired, arrange avocado slices on top. Cut pizza into wedges. Serve at once. Makes 6 main-dish servings.

For a lower-fat version: Omit the puff pastry and use one 16-ounce Italian bread shell (Boboli) for the crust. Instead of the semisoft cheese, use 4 ounces reduced-fat cream cheese (Neufchâtel) mixed with 1 tablespoon snipped fresh chives. Reduce the mozzarella cheese to 1 cup (4 ounces) and omit the avocado.

Nutrition facts per serving: 353 calories, 25 g total fat (6 g saturated fat), 36 mg cholesterol, 499 mg sodium, 21 g carbohydrate, 2 g fiber, 12 g protein.
♥ *Lower-fat version: 332 calories, 14 g total fat (5 g saturated fat), 29 mg cholesterol, 724 mg sodium, 38 g carbohydrate, 3 g fiber, 17 g protein.*

Garden-Fresh Couscous Salad

1990

2 cups water

2 teaspoons instant chicken
   bouillon granules

1 10-ounce package (about
   1⅓ cups) couscous

1 large carrot, shredded

1 large green sweet pepper,
   cut into ½-inch squares

1 large zucchini, halved
   lengthwise and
   thinly sliced

1 large yellow summer
   squash, halved
   lengthwise and
   thinly sliced

1 cup cherry tomatoes,
   halved

1 8-ounce bottle clear Italian
   salad dressing (about
   1 cup)

This summery salad features a recently introduced grain product, couscous, a staple in North African cooking. It's terrific for crowd-size picnics and family reunions. But when you want to serve fewer folks, all you have to do is halve the recipe. Also, if Italian dressing isn't your favorite, substitute any vinaigrette-type dressing you like.

1 In a medium saucepan combine water and bouillon granules; bring to boiling. Add couscous. Remove from heat; cover and let stand for 5 minutes or until liquid is absorbed. Transfer to an extra-large bowl.

2 Add carrot, sweet pepper, zucchini, yellow summer squash, and cherry tomatoes; mix well. Drizzle with salad dressing; toss to coat. Cover and refrigerate for 6 to 24 hours. Makes 15 side-dish servings.

For a lower-fat version: Use low-calorie clear Italian salad dressing.

Nutrition facts per serving: 157 calories, 8 g total fat (1 g saturated fat), 0 mg cholesterol, 242 mg sodium, 19 g carbohydrate, 4 g fiber, 3 g protein
♥*Lower-fat version: 102 calories, 2 g total fat (0 g saturated fat), 1 mg cholesterol, 242 mg sodium, 19 g carbohydrate, 4 g fiber, 3 g protein.*

Vegetables

PLUS IMAGINATION

By Meta Given

1992

Taco Salad

American cooks looked south of the border to Mexican cooking in the '80s and early '90s and discovered the tomatillo as a key ingredient in authentic dishes. This green fruit with a papery brown husk looks like a small, firm tomato, and the tomatillo's refreshing tartness makes one think of lemon and apple. The zesty guacamole served with our taco salad —a makeover of a reader's favorite recipe—is accented with the great flavor of the tomatillo in the guacamole. Using it also cuts down on fat because you don't need to use as much avocado.

1 recipe Tortilla Cups
8 ounces lean ground beef
3 cloves garlic, minced
1 15-ounce can dark red kidney beans, drained
¾ cup frozen whole kernel corn
1 8-ounce jar taco sauce
1 tablespoon chili powder
1 small head lettuce, torn into pieces (about 8 cups)

2 medium tomatoes, chopped
1 large green sweet pepper, chopped
¾ cup shredded reduced-fat sharp cheddar cheese (3 ounces)
4 green onions, thinly sliced
1 recipe Tomatillo Guacamole
Salsa (optional)

1 Prepare Tortilla Cups; set aside. In a medium skillet cook beef and garlic until beef is brown. Drain well. Stir in kidney beans, corn, taco sauce, and chili powder. Bring to boiling; reduce heat. Simmer, covered, for 10 minutes.

2 Meanwhile, in a large bowl combine lettuce, tomatoes, sweet pepper, cheese, and green onions. Add beef mixture; toss to mix. To serve, divide lettuce mixture among Tortilla Cups. Top with Tomatillo Guacamole. If desired, serve with salsa. Makes 6 main-dish servings.

Tortilla Cups: Lightly brush 1 side of each of six 9- or 10-inch *flour tortillas* with a small amount of *water* or spray with *nonstick spray coating.* Spray nonstick coating into 6 small oven-safe bowls or 16-ounce individual casseroles. Press tortillas, coated sides up, into casseroles. Place a ball of foil in each tortilla cup to help hold its shape. Bake in a 350° oven for 15 to 20 minutes or until light brown. Remove foil. Cool; remove Tortilla Cups from bowls or casseroles. If desired, cups can be made ahead and stored in an airtight container for up to 5 days.

Tomatillo Guacamole: Rinse, drain, and finely chop 4 *canned tomatillos* (about ⅓ cup). (Or, simmer 2 husked *tomatillos,* about 3½ ounces total, in *boiling water* for 10 minutes. Drain and chop.) In a small mixing bowl combine tomatillos; half of a small seeded, peeled, and chopped *avocado* (about ½ cup); 2 tablespoons chopped *canned green chili peppers;* and ⅛ teaspoon *garlic salt.* Cover and refrigerate until chilled or for up to 24 hours. Makes about ¾ cup.

Nutrition facts per serving: 459 calories, 16 g total fat (4 g saturated fat), 34 mg cholesterol, 981 mg sodium, 62 g carbohydrate, 7 g fiber, 24 g protein.

Mexican Chef's Salad

6 cups torn mixed greens
1 cup shredded carrot
1 cup chopped celery
1 cup cooked ham cut in
    thin matchsticks
1 cup cooked chicken cut in
    thin matchsticks
2 cups red and/or yellow
    cherry tomatoes, cut in
    quarters
3 tablespoons thinly sliced
    green onions

2 cups shredded sharp
    process American or
    cheddar cheese
    (8 ounces)
⅔ cup milk
1 4½-ounce can diced green
    chili peppers, drained
3 tablespoons sliced pitted
    ripe olives
2 cups corn chips (optional)

When retesting this 22-year-old recipe, our current arbiters of taste in the Test Kitchen thought it needed more zip. So, instead of using just one Anaheim pepper as the original recipe called for, we used a whole can of chili peppers. This salad is probably the forerunner of what we now know as the taco salad.

1 In a large salad bowl toss together greens, carrot, and celery. Arrange ham, chicken, tomatoes, and green onions on the greens.

2 In a heavy medium saucepan combine cheese and milk. Cook and stir over low heat until cheese is melted and mixture is smooth. Stir in chili peppers and olives.

3 Just before serving, drizzle the cheese mixture over salad. Toss lightly to coat. Serve at once. If desired, serve with corn chips. Makes 6 main-dish servings.

Nutrition facts per serving: 281 calories, 17 g total fat (9 g saturated fat), 73 mg cholesterol, 970 mg sodium, 10 g carbohydrate, 3 g fiber, 24 g protein.

Apple & Sweet Pepper Slaw

1992

Who says we have to give up our favorites? Although this lightened slaw is made with lower-fat products, the flavor is not sacrificed. Ranch-style dressing and honey give it up-to-date taste.

⅓ cup plain nonfat yogurt or nonfat mayonnaise dressing or salad dressing

¼ of a 0.4-ounce package buttermilk ranch salad dressing mix (about 1 teaspoon)

1 teaspoon honey

2 cups shredded red and/or green cabbage

1 small red or green sweet pepper, cut into thin strips (about ½ cup)

1 carrot, shredded

¼ cup thinly sliced celery

1 small apple, chopped

1 For dressing, in a small bowl stir together the yogurt or mayonnaise, dressing mix, and honey until blended. Thin with a little *water,* if necessary. Cover; refrigerate until ready to serve.

2 In a large bowl combine cabbage, pepper, carrot, celery, and apple. Pour dressing over cabbage mixture. Toss to coat. Makes 3 to 4 servings.

♥ *Nutrition facts per serving: 70 calories, 0 g total fat, 1 mg cholesterol, 109 mg sodium, 16 g carbohydrate, 3 g fiber, 2 g protein.*

Orange-Walnut Cabbage Slaw

1996

5 cups packaged shredded cabbage with carrot (coleslaw mix)
1 small orange, peeled, sliced crosswise, and quartered
2 green onions, thinly sliced
3 tablespoons vinegar
3 tablespoons salad oil
2 tablespoons sugar

1½ teaspoons finely shredded orange peel
2 tablespoons orange juice
1 teaspoon walnut oil (optional)
⅛ teaspoon salt
¼ cup chopped walnuts, toasted

These are truly the salad days of convenience at supermarkets. Salad bars sell salad ingredients you can select by the pound. You'll also find cut-up veggies, such as cauliflower and broccoli, as well as washed and torn greens in prepackaged bags just waiting to be opened and tossed in a bowl. This nutty slaw easily fixes up one such product, a preshredded coleslaw mix.

1 In a large bowl combine shredded cabbage mix, orange pieces, and onions. For dressing, in a screw-top jar combine vinegar, salad oil, sugar, orange peel, orange juice, walnut oil (if using), and salt. Cover and shake well. Pour dressing over cabbage mixture; toss gently to coat.

2 Cover and refrigerate for 2 to 4 hours or until chilled. Before serving, add chopped walnuts and toss again. Makes 6 side-dish servings.

Nutrition facts per serving: 142 calories, 10 g total fat (1 g saturated fat), 0 mg cholesterol, 61 mg sodium, 13 g carbohydrate, 2 g fiber, 2 g protein.

Vintage Views
1934

Oldest Cooking Club

It seems that way back in 1732, a group of young Philadelphia men who liked to fish and cook organized The Colony in Schuylkill (pronounced SCHOOL-kill), a mythical 14th colony. The group was actually the first cooking club in America and had a long history. Our February 1934 issue featured the men's favorite recipes, most of which were for pan-fried fish, and noted that these men, known as "Citizens" and outfitted in "broad-brimmed fishing hats and great aprons with cavernous pockets," would "go about their kitchen, practicing the art of preparing fine food."

Sizzling Cheese Salad

1984

Simple American cheese was considered a luxury in eras gone by, but today we have so many options it is staggering. Gjetost cheese (pronounced YEHT-ohst) is a Norwegian cheese made from a combination of goat's- and cow's-milk whey. It is lightly sweet in flavor and caramel in color. The color and flavor are attributed to the slow cooking of the milk until the milk sugar caramelizes. Look for mysost (or primost) cheese if gjetost is unavailable. This Scandinavian cheese is made from cow's milk in the same way as gjetost and has the same flavor.

6   cups torn mixed greens
¼   cup pitted ripe olives
1   small tomato, cut into wedges, or 6 oil-packed dried tomatoes, drained and cut into slivers
¼   cup salad oil
¼   cup tarragon vinegar
2   teaspoons finely chopped green onion
1   teaspoon Dijon-style mustard
1   teaspoon walnut oil (optional)
1   egg

1   tablespoon water
2   tablespoons cornmeal
1   tablespoon fine, dry bread crumbs
1   tablespoon sesame seed, toasted
2   teaspoons grated Parmesan cheese
½   of an 8-ounce package reduced-fat cream cheese (Neufchâtel), cut up
1   cup shredded gjetost cheese (4 ounces)
2   tablespoons margarine or butter, melted

1 On a serving platter arrange greens, olives, and tomatoes. Cover and refrigerate. In a screw-top jar combine salad oil, vinegar, green onion, mustard, and walnut oil (if using). Cover and shake well; refrigerate.

2 In a small bowl combine egg and water; use a fork to beat together. In a shallow bowl combine cornmeal, bread crumbs, sesame seed, and Parmesan cheese.

3 Place cream cheese and gjetost in a medium mixing bowl. Beat with an electric mixer until combined. Shape into 1-inch balls; flatten to form patties. Dip cheese patties into egg mixture; coat both sides with the cornmeal mixture. Cover; refrigerate patties for 1 hour or until thoroughly chilled.

4 To fry cheese patties, in a large skillet heat margarine or butter. Add cheese patties; cook on medium heat for 6 to 8 minutes or until golden brown, turning once.

5 Shake dressing; drizzle over greens mixture. Arrange cheese patties on salad. Makes 6 side-dish servings.

Nutrition facts per serving: 312 calories, 26 g total fat (9 g saturated fat), 51 mg cholesterol, 332 mg sodium, 15 g carbohydrate, 1 g fiber, 7 g protein.

Two-Bean & Rice Salad

1990

To halve this potluck-size recipe, use one 15-ounce can of pinto or black beans instead of a combination of 3 cans of beans. Reduce the amount of peas to 1 cup and cut the remaining ingredient amounts in half. For the dressing, reduce the white wine vinegar to 3 tablespoons and use only half the amounts of the remaining ingredients.

3 cups chilled cooked rice
1 15-ounce can pinto beans, rinsed and drained
1 15-ounce can black beans, rinsed and drained
1 10-ounce package frozen peas, thawed
1 cup sliced celery
½ cup chopped red onion
2 4½-ounce cans diced green chili peppers, drained
¼ cup snipped fresh cilantro or parsley
1 recipe Garlic Dressing or ¾ cup bottled Italian salad dressing

1 In a large bowl combine rice, beans, peas, celery, onion, chili peppers, and cilantro. Pour dressing over rice mixture; toss to coat. Cover; chill until serving time or for up to 24 hours. Makes 16 servings.

Garlic Dressing: In a screw-top jar combine ⅓ cup *white wine vinegar,* ¼ cup *olive oil* or *cooking oil,* 2 tablespoons *water,* ½ teaspoon *salt,* ½ teaspoon *garlic powder,* and ½ teaspoon *pepper.* Cover and shake well. Makes about ¾ cup.

♥ *Nutrition facts per serving: 124 calories, 4 g total fat (1 g saturated fat), 0 mg cholesterol, 301 mg sodium, 19 g carbohydrate, 3 g fiber, 5 g protein.*

Vintage Views
1934

The Misunderstood Tomato

A February 1934 article educated readers: "Not more than one hundred years ago it was the general belief that the tomato was poisonous because botanists said it was a member of the Deadly Nightshade family. Even tho they thought it was poisonous the people of Europe so admired its beautiful red and yellow fruits that they planted it in their front yards for decoration on a trellis. They called it the love-apple.

"One day physicians and chemists discovered that the tomato contained some of the vitamins, the food essentials most needed by the body. Won't you appreciate more your next bowl of delicious tomato soup, now that you know how long it took the poor tomato to be appreciated?"

New Layered Salad

1994

4 cups torn mixed greens
1 15-ounce can garbanzo
   beans, drained
1 cup red and/or yellow
   cherry tomatoes,
   quartered or halved
1 cup thinly sliced fennel
   bulb or celery
1 cup chopped yellow and/or
   red sweet pepper
   (1 large)
1 cup diced cooked turkey
   ham (6 ounces)

¼ cup thinly sliced green
   onions
1 cup light mayonnaise
   dressing or salad dressing
2 tablespoons milk
1 tablespoon snipped fresh
   fennel tops or 1 teaspoon
   fennel seed, crushed
⅛ teaspoon ground white or
   black pepper
¾ cup shredded reduced-fat
   or smoked cheddar
   cheese

This pretty, tiered salad is ideal for making a day ahead because the salad dressing on top seals in freshness. What makes it new? The lighter dressing, lower-fat cheeses, and delicate licoricelike flavor twist from the fennel bulb.

1 Place mixed greens in the bottom of a 2½-quart clear salad bowl. Layer in the following order: garbanzo beans, tomatoes, sliced fennel or celery, sweet pepper, turkey ham, and green onions.

2 For dressing, stir together mayonnaise dressing or salad dressing, milk, snipped fennel tops or fennel seed, and white or black pepper. Spread the dressing over the top of the salad, sealing to the edge of the bowl. Cover tightly with plastic wrap. Refrigerate for 4 to 24 hours.

3 Before serving, top salad with shredded cheese; toss gently to mix. Makes 8 to 10 side-dish servings.

Nutrition facts per serving: 283 calories, 11 g total fat (2 g saturated fat), 30 mg cholesterol, 345 mg sodium, 7 g carbohydrate, 1 g fiber, 8 g protein.

Avocado Pontchartrain With Shrimp Rémoulade

1964

A tangy tarragon-vinegar dressing brings out the best in the greens, shrimp, and avocado in this elegant main dish with its French sauce. Serve it to evoke the flavor of New Orleans and nearby Lake Pontchartrain. When it comes to torn mixed greens, select several varieties to give you a contrast in flavors and textures. Mix soft and buttery Bibb or Boston lettuce with crisp, mild iceberg or romaine. Or, toss together tender, sweet leaf lettuce with more pungent greens, such as spinach, escarole, or radicchio.

¼ cup tarragon vinegar
2 tablespoons catsup
1 tablespoon horseradish mustard
¾ teaspoon paprika
⅛ teaspoon ground red pepper
¼ cup cooking oil
2 tablespoons finely chopped celery
2 tablespoons finely chopped green onion

1 pound fresh or frozen shrimp in shell, peeled, deveined, and cooked
4 cups torn mixed greens
2 medium avocados
Sliced cooked beets (optional)
Hard-cooked egg wedges (optional)
Lemon peel strips (optional)

1 For rémoulade, in a small bowl combine vinegar, catsup, horseradish mustard, paprika, and ground red pepper. Slowly add oil while beating with a whisk or fork; beat until combined. Stir in celery and green onion.

2 Place cooked shrimp in a plastic bag set into a bowl. Pour rémoulade over the shrimp. Seal bag. Turn bag to coat shrimp. Marinate in the refrigerator for 1 to 2 hours, turning occasionally.

3 To serve, drain shrimp, reserving marinade. Divide greens among 4 dinner plates. Halve, peel, and seed avocados. Slice avocados and arrange on torn greens. Arrange shrimp over avocados. If desired, garnish with beets, hard-cooked egg, and lemon peel. Stir and pass reserved marinade. Makes 4 main-dish servings.

Nutrition facts per serving: 362 calories, 30 g total fat (4 g saturated fat), 129 mg cholesterol, 303 mg sodium, 11 g carbohydrate, 4 g fiber, 17 g protein.

1927

Asheville Salad

Tomato aspic has a checkered history in American cooking. Over the decades, cooks have either loved it or hated it. A must according to many turn-of-the-century cookbooks, the molded salad was quite fashionable in the late '20s when packaged gelatin was new. Since then, many cooks have dismissed it as passé, but we found this 1927 recipe refreshing, as did the reader who sent it in as a favorite.

1 envelope unflavored
  gelatin
⅓ cup cold water
1 10¾-ounce can condensed
  tomato soup
1 8-ounce package cream
  cheese, cut up

½ cup mayonnaise or salad
  dressing
½ cup chopped green sweet
  pepper
½ cup chopped celery
¼ cup sliced green onions
¼ cup chopped ripe olives
  Lettuce leaves (optional)

1 In a small bowl stir together gelatin and water; let stand 5 minutes. Meanwhile, in a medium saucepan bring soup just to boiling. Stir in the gelatin mixture and cream cheese. Cook and stir over medium-low heat until gelatin is dissolved and cream cheese is melted. (If necessary, whisk until smooth.) Remove the mixture from heat. Cool slightly.

2 Stir the mayonnaise into cream cheese mixture until smooth. Stir in sweet pepper, celery, green onions, and olives. Pour mixture into small individual molds or an 8×4×2½-inch loaf pan. Cover and refrigerate until set. If desired, line salad plates or a platter with lettuce leaves. Unmold individual molds or loaf pan onto lettuce-lined plates or a platter. Makes 10 to 12 side-dish servings.

For a lower-fat version: Use reduced-fat cream cheese (Neufchâtel) in place of regular cream cheese and plain fat-free yogurt or nonfat mayonnaise dressing instead of mayonnaise.

Nutrition facts per serving: 192 calories, 18 g total fat (6 g saturated fat), 31 mg cholesterol, 366 mg sodium, 6 g carbohydrate, 1 g fiber, 3g protein.
Lower-fat version: 102 calories, 6 g total fat (3 g saturated fat), 18 mg cholesterol, 238 mg sodium, 7 g carbohydrate, 1 g fiber, 4g protein.

During the '40s, the Campbell soup kids were familiar icons in the giant food company's ads and helped make soups popular in all kinds of recipes.

Penne Salad with Italian Green Beans

1996

6 ounces packaged dried penne, ziti, elbow macaroni, or other short pasta

8 ounces fresh Italian green beans, trimmed and bias-sliced into 1-inch pieces, or one 9-ounce package frozen Italian green beans, thawed

⅓ cup bottled fat-free Italian salad dressing

1 tablespoon snipped fresh tarragon or 1½ teaspoons dried tarragon, crushed

½ teaspoon freshly ground pepper

2 cups torn radicchio or 1 cup finely shredded red cabbage

4 cups fresh sorrel or spinach leaves, cleaned, trimmed, and shredded (optional)

½ cup crumbled Gorgonzola or blue cheese (2 ounces)

Pasta is everywhere in the '90s. You'll find it served at fancy restaurants, casual take-out places, formal dinner parties, and cozy family gatherings. One reason it's so popular is its versatility. You can serve it dressed down with a simple sauce or dressed up as in this exotic salad with fresh green beans, tarragon, radicchio, and sorrel.

1 Cook pasta according to package directions, adding fresh green beans to pasta for the last 5 to 7 minutes of cooking. (Or, add frozen and thawed beans for the last 3 to 4 minutes.) Rinse pasta and beans well under cold running water; drain thoroughly.

2 In a large mixing bowl combine the Italian dressing, tarragon, and pepper. Add pasta mixture and radicchio or cabbage; toss gently to coat.

3 If desired, serve salad on a bed of shredded sorrel or spinach. Top salad with the Gorgonzola cheese. Makes 8 side-dish servings.

♥ *Nutrition facts per serving: 126 calories, 3 g total fat (2 g saturated fat), 6 mg cholesterol, 259 mg sodium, 20 g carbohydrate, 1 g fiber, 5 g protein.*

Fresh Vegetable Pasta Salad

1995

Team this tasty pasta mixture with broiled fish or chicken for a side dish. For a main dish, serve a hearty bowlful with crusty Italian bread. To speed up cutting the matchstick strips, first cut the carrot, turnip, and zucchini into slices about 2 inches long and ¼ inch thick. Stack the slices and cut them lengthwise into thinner strips of about ⅛ to ¼ inch wide.

¼ cup loosely packed parsley sprigs
2 tablespoons salad oil
2 tablespoons wine vinegar
2 tablespoons water
1 to 2 cloves garlic
½ teaspoon dry mustard
¼ teaspoon salt
¼ teaspoon black pepper
4 ounces fresh or refrigerated linguine, cut into 4-inch pieces, or 2 ounces packaged dried linguine, broken

1 large carrot, cut into thin matchsticks
1 small turnip, cut into thin matchsticks
1 small zucchini, cut into thin matchsticks
½ cup chopped red sweet pepper
½ cup frozen peas, thawed
2 ounces mozzarella, Gruyère, or Swiss cheese, cubed

1 For dressing, in a blender container or food processor bowl, combine the parsley sprigs, salad oil, wine vinegar, water, garlic cloves, dry mustard, salt, and black pepper. Cover and blend or process until combined; set aside.

2 In a large saucepan cook the fresh or refrigerated linguine, carrot, and turnip in a large amount of boiling water for 3 to 4 minutes or until pasta and vegetables are tender. (Or, if using dried linguine, cook according to package directions, adding carrot and turnip for the last 3 to 4 minutes of cooking.) Drain. Rinse with cold water; drain again.

3 In a large salad bowl combine the cooked pasta mixture, zucchini, sweet pepper, peas, and cheese. Add the dressing and toss to coat. Makes 6 side-dish or 3 main-dish servings.

Nutrition facts per side-dish serving: 155 calories, 7 g total fat (1 g saturated fat), 27 mg cholesterol, 166 mg sodium, 18 g carbohydrate, 2 g fiber, 6 g protein.

*I*talian-Style Pasta Salad

1983

4 ounces packaged dried
   spaghetti or vermicelli
1 6-ounce jar marinated
   artichoke hearts
1 small zucchini, halved and
   sliced lengthwise
1 carrot, sliced
2 ounces sliced salami, cut
   in strips
1 cup shredded mozzarella
   cheese

2 tablespoons grated
   Parmesan cheese
2 tablespoons salad oil
2 tablespoons white wine
   vinegar
¾ teaspoon dry mustard
½ teaspoon dried oregano,
   crushed
½ teaspoon dried basil,
   crushed
1 clove garlic, minced

The picnic salads category of our Prize Tested Recipes contest in 1983 inspired tasty entries. None was better than this full-flavored salad sent in by winner Mary Kowinsky of Petaluma, California. It's sensational with grilled Italian sausage, brats, pork chops, or chicken.

1 Break pasta in half. Cook pasta according to package directions; drain and set aside.

2 Drain artichoke hearts, reserving marinade; coarsely chop artichoke hearts. In a large bowl combine the cooked pasta, artichokes, zucchini, carrot, salami, mozzarella cheese, and Parmesan cheese.

3 In a screw-top jar combine the reserved artichoke marinade, salad oil, vinegar, mustard, oregano, basil, and garlic. Cover and shake well. Pour dressing over pasta mixture; toss to coat evenly. Transfer salad to a covered container; refrigerate several hours or until thoroughly chilled. Makes 8 to 10 side-dish servings.

Nutrition facts per serving: 183 calories, 10 g total fat (3 g saturated fat), 15 mg cholesterol, 325 mg sodium, 16 g carbohydrate, 0 g fiber, 8 g protein.

Oriental Vegetable & Pasta Salad

1993

Cooks are reaping the benefits of the '90s global economy as the number of ethnic food markets increase and supermarket sections for international foods expand. The Asian ingredients of plum sauce, soy sauce, and sesame oil make this pasta salad truly exceptional. For the best flavor, make sure you purchase toasted sesame oil, which is darker and more robust than the light-colored variety.

8 ounces packaged dried pasta (such as vermicelli, angel hair, rotini, or bow tie)

8 ounces fresh asparagus spears, trimmed and cut into 1-inch pieces (1 cup)

⅓ cup bottled plum sauce

2 tablespoons water

1 to 2 tablespoons soy sauce

½ teaspoon toasted sesame oil

⅛ teaspoon crushed red pepper

1 medium red or green sweet pepper, cut into bite-size strips

1 11-ounce can mandarin orange sections, drained

1 cup fresh or frozen sugar snap peas, halved crosswise

⅓ cup sliced green onions

⅓ cup slivered almonds, toasted

1 Cook pasta according to package directions, adding asparagus the last 5 minutes of cooking. Rinse well under cold running water; drain thoroughly. Cover and refrigerate until thoroughly chilled.

2 For dressing, in a small mixing bowl stir together plum sauce, water, soy sauce, sesame oil, and crushed red pepper.

3 In a large bowl combine pasta mixture, sweet pepper, oranges, sugar snap peas, green onions, and almonds. Add dressing; toss to coat. Serve immediately. Makes 8 to 10 side-dish servings.

♥*Nutrition facts per serving: 187 calories, 3 g total fat (0 g saturated fat), 0 mg cholesterol, 123 mg sodium, 34 g carbohydrate, 2 g fiber, 7 g protein.*

Salade Flan

1973

2 3-ounce packages lemon-flavored gelatin	**½ of a 6-ounce can (⅓ cup) frozen lemonade concentrate**
3 cups boiling water	**2 cups sliced fresh strawberries (1 pint)**
½ cup mayonnaise or salad dressing	**1 small banana, sliced diagonally**
1 3-ounce package cream cheese	

1 Dissolve gelatin in the boiling water. Remove ¾ cup gelatin mixture and let stand at room temperature. Pour remaining gelatin into a blender container. Add the mayonnaise, cream cheese, and lemonade concentrate. Cover and blend just until smooth. Refrigerate until partially set (consistency of unbeaten egg whites).

2 Pour the mixture into a 9-inch springform pan or a 2-quart square or rectangular dish. Refrigerate until almost firm (30 to 45 minutes). Meanwhile, chill reserved ¾ cup gelatin until slightly thickened.

3 Arrange the strawberries and banana over the cream cheese layer. Spoon the reserved gelatin over the fruit to glaze. Refrigerate at least 2 hours or until set. Makes 10 to 12 side-dish servings.

Nutrition facts per serving: 155 calories, 12 g total fat (3 g saturated fat), 16 mg cholesterol, 96 mg sodium, 12 g carbohydrate, 1 g fiber, 1 g protein.

Flavored gelatin didn't gain in popularity until advertising paid off around the 1840s when a young child named Elizabeth King became the "Jell-O Girl." The ads assured moms that Jell-O was easy to make and was good for kids, too. By 1900, flavored gelatin set well with most everyone, especially when fruit was added, as in this '70s gelatin salad.

Vintage Views
1924

First of Many Winners

A salad was one of the recipes to win the first contest held by our magazine in 1924. Back then, the contest was called Cook's Round Table. The winner was Perfection Salad, a gelatin concoction with cabbage, tart cherries, and pimiento. Although it was born during the same era, the salad didn't resemble the famous salad by the same name—a creation containing ginger ale that is credited to Fannie Farmer.

Zesty Fiesta Corn Salad

1971

Come summertime, serve this sassy salad with grilled chicken or burgers. In winter, try it with roast turkey or broiled chops.

½ **envelope (about 2 tablespoons) taco seasoning mix**
¼ **cup water**
¼ **cup cooking oil**
¼ **cup vinegar**

1 **15¼-ounce can whole kernel corn, drained**
1½ **cups diced tomatoes**
½ **cup sliced ripe olives**
¼ **cup diced green sweet pepper**

1 In a large bowl stir together taco seasoning mix and water until well mixed; stir in oil and vinegar. Add corn, diced tomatoes, olives, and sweet pepper; toss lightly to coat. Cover and refrigerate several hours or overnight, stirring mixture occasionally. Serve with a slotted spoon. Makes 8 side-dish servings.

Nutrition facts per serving: 116 calories, 9 g total fat (1 g saturated fat), 0 mg cholesterol, 383 mg sodium, 11 g carbohydrate, 1 g fiber, 2 g protein.

Dill-Artichoke Potato Salad

1992

3 pounds whole tiny new
   potatoes
1 cup mayonnaise or salad
   dressing
2 tablespoons red wine
   vinegar
2 tablespoons Dijon-style
   mustard
1 tablespoon lemon-pepper
   seasoning

1 tablespoon snipped fresh
   dill or 2 to 3 teaspoons
   dillweed, crushed
4 hard-cooked eggs, chopped
2 6-ounce jars marinated
   artichoke hearts, drained
   and sliced
¾ cup chopped onion
2 tablespoons chopped dill
   pickle

One of the only two potato salads we published in the first edition of the 1930 Better Homes and Gardens cookbook used French dressing; the other had a dressing made with cream and vinegar. Later, potato salads with mayonnaise or vinaigrettes were more popular. Still later, cooks began dressing up potato salad with such ingredients as artichokes and Dijon-style mustard, as in this 1992 recipe.

1 Scrub potatoes with a vegetable brush under running water. In a covered kettle cook unpeeled potatoes in *boiling lightly salted water* about 20 minutes or just until tender. Drain. Cool potatoes; cut into bite-size pieces.

2 In a very large bowl stir together mayonnaise or salad dressing, vinegar, mustard, lemon-pepper seasoning, and dill. Gently fold in cooked potatoes, eggs, artichoke hearts, onion, and pickle. Cover and refrigerate for 4 to 24 hours. Stir the mixture gently before serving. Makes 16 side-dish servings.

For a lower-fat version: Use light mayonnaise dressing or salad dressing in place of regular.

Nutrition facts per serving: 215 calories, 13 g total fat (2 g saturated fat), 61 mg cholesterol, 400 mg sodium, 21 g carbohydrate, 1 g fiber, 4 g protein.
Lower-fat version: 166 calories, 7 g total fat (1 g saturated fat), 53 mg cholesterol, 431 mg sodium, 22 g carbohydrate, 1 g fiber, 4 g protein.

No-Chop Potato Salad

1986

Take the work out of potato salad by starting with frozen hash brown potatoes with peppers and onions. You'll find it hard to believe that potato salad can be so easy yet so delectable.

1 24-ounce package frozen diced hash brown potatoes with onions and peppers
1½ cups thinly sliced celery
1 8-ounce container dairy sour cream dip with chives
⅔ cup mayonnaise or salad dressing
1 tablespoon sugar
1 tablespoon white wine vinegar
1 tablespoon prepared mustard
½ teaspoon salt
3 hard-cooked eggs, coarsely chopped
   Lettuce leaves (optional)
   Celery leaves (optional)
   Pimiento strips (optional)

1 In a large covered saucepan cook hash brown potatoes in boiling water for 6 to 8 minutes or until tender; drain well. In a large mixing bowl combine the potatoes and celery. Set aside.

2 In a small mixing bowl combine sour cream dip, mayonnaise or salad dressing, sugar, vinegar, mustard, and salt. Add mayonnaise mixture to potato mixture; toss lightly to coat. Gently fold in eggs. Cover and refrigerate thoroughly until chilled.

3 If desired, garnish with lettuce leaves, celery leaves, and/or pimiento strips. Makes 20 side-dish servings.

For a lower-fat version: Use light sour cream dip with onion and light mayonnaise dressing or salad dressing.

Nutrition facts per serving: 119 calories, 8 g total fat (1 g saturated fat), 36 mg cholesterol, 220 mg sodium, 9 g carbohydrate, 1 g fiber, 2 g protein.
♥*Lower-fat version: 85 calories, 4 g total fat (1 g saturated fat), 33 mg cholesterol, 159 mg sodium, 9 g carbohydrate, 1 g fiber, 2 g protein.*

Creamy Potato Salad

1955

3 cooked medium potatoes
   (about 1 pound), peeled,
   quartered, and sliced
1 teaspoon sugar
1 teaspoon vinegar
½ cup sliced celery
⅓ cup finely chopped onion

¼ cup chopped sweet pickle
¼ teaspoon salt
1 teaspoon celery seed
¾ cup mayonnaise or salad
   dressing
2 hard-cooked eggs, sliced

1 In medium mixing bowl sprinkle potatoes with sugar and vinegar. Add celery, onion, sweet pickle, salt, and celery seed; toss gently to mix.

2 Add mayonnaise or salad dressing; toss gently to coat. Carefully fold in sliced eggs. Refrigerate until chilled. Makes 6 side-dish servings.

For a lower-fat version: Use nonfat mayonnaise or salad dressing in place of regular.

Nutrition facts per serving: 308 calories, 24 g total fat (4 g saturated fat), 87 mg cholesterol, 355 mg sodium, 21 g carbohydrate, 1 g fiber, 4 g protein.
♥*Lower-fat version: 135 calories, 2 g total fat (1 g saturated fat) 71 mg cholesterol, 578 mg sodium, 26 g carbohydrate, 1 g fiber, 4 g protein.*

During the '50s, backyard barbecues and patio picnics were in vogue across the country. And what better side dish to go along with a giant juicy steak or hot dog than potato salad? This classic recipe was called Perfect Potato Salad when it first ran in the magazine in 1955. Although we think it's perfectly scrumptious, we changed the name to fit its creamy consistency.

Fresh Fruit Medley With Frosty Melon Dressing

1993

By the early '90s, once-exotic fruits such as kiwifruit, yellow watermelon, and papaya were more readily available in supermarkets. We began creating recipes to take advantage of their wonderful flavors. The frozen sorbetlike dressing on this salad makes it deliciously different.

¼ cup orange juice
1 teaspoon unflavored gelatin
1½ cups very ripe cantaloupe chunks
1 tablespoon honey
2 teaspoons white wine vinegar
⅛ teaspoon ground cinnamon

Kale and/or romaine leaves (optional)
5 to 6 cups assorted fresh fruit (such as peeled and sliced nectarines, peeled and sliced kiwifruit, sliced pears, strawberries, seedless grapes, cherries, sliced plums, papaya chunks, and/or assorted melon chunks)

1 In a small saucepan combine the orange juice and gelatin; let stand for 5 minutes to soften. Cook over low heat, stirring constantly, until gelatin is dissolved; set aside.

2 In blender container or food processor bowl combine the 1½ cups cantaloupe, the honey, vinegar, and cinnamon. Cover and blend or process until smooth. Add the orange juice mixture; blend or process until combined.

3 Transfer melon mixture to an 8×4×2-inch or 9×5×3-inch loaf pan. Cover; freeze for 4 hours or until firm. Break frozen mixture into small chunks. Transfer melon mixture to a chilled mixing bowl. Beat with an electric mixer on medium-low speed until smooth, but not melted. Rinse and dry the pan; line pan with plastic wrap. Return mixture to loaf pan. Cover and freeze until firm or for up to 2 weeks.

4 To serve, if desired, arrange kale and/or romaine on a serving platter or on 6 salad plates. Arrange fruit on the greens.

5 For dressing, use a melon baller or scrape a spoon across the top of the frozen melon mixture to make small scoops. (If too frozen to scoop or scrape, let frozen mixture stand at room temperature for 5 to 10 minutes to soften.) Place frozen scoops of dressing on top of fruit and serve immediately. Makes 6 side-dish servings.

♥ *Nutrition facts per serving: 85 calories, 1 g total fat (0 g saturated fat), 0 mg cholesterol, 7 mg sodium, 21 g carbohydrate, 2 g fiber, 2 g protein.*

Winter Fruit Bowl

★ 1976

3 **medium grapefruit**
½ **cup sugar**
½ **cup orange marmalade**

2 **cups cranberries (8 ounces)**
3 **medium bananas, sliced**

When she cast her vote for this dish as her favorite from past issues of the magazine, Connie Stutterheim of Salina, Kansas, told us: "This tasty, colorful fruit combination has been a must for our family holiday gatherings for many years."

1 Cut a thin slice from each end of each grapefruit. Using a very sharp utility knife or a serrated knife and cutting from the top of the fruit down, cut off the grapefruit peel and the white membrane. (Or, cut around the fruit in a spiral.) Working over a bowl to catch the juices, cut between one fruit section and the membrane. Cut to the center of the fruit. Turn the knife and slide it up the other side of the section next to the membrane; repeat to make sections. Remove any seeds from the fruit sections. Set grapefruit sections aside (should have about 3 cups).

2 Add enough *water* to the reserved grapefruit juice to measure 1 cup. In a medium saucepan combine the 1 cup grapefruit juice, the sugar, and marmalade. Heat to boiling, stirring to dissolve sugar. Add cranberries; cook and stir for 5 to 8 minutes or until skins pop. Remove from heat; cool. Stir grapefruit into cranberry mixture. Cover and refrigerate until thoroughly chilled.

3 Just before serving, stir sliced bananas into chilled grapefruit mixture. Makes 10 side-dish servings.

♥ *Nutrition facts per serving: 144 calories, 0 g total fat, 0 mg cholesterol, 3 mg sodium, 38 g carbohydrate, 3 g fiber, 1 g protein.*

Ginger Marinated Fruit

1993

This beautiful fruit salad comes from "A Taste of Romance from Historic Inns," a February 1993 article that featured recipes from three of what we deemed to be the country's "most charming historic inns." From coast to coast, they were the Hotel Hershey in Hershey, Pennsylvania; the St. James Hotel in Red Wing, Minnesota; and The Majestic in San Francisco. This salad is served at the St. James Hotel.

½ **cup water**
4 **teaspoons finely shredded orange peel**
1 **tablespoon sugar**
1 **teaspoon grated gingerroot**
½ **cup orange liqueur or**
 ½ **cup orange juice plus**
 1 **tablespoon sugar**
⅓ **cup orange juice**

¼ **cup honey**
6 **cups cut-up assorted fruit, such as kiwifruit, apples, oranges, cantaloupe, honeydew melon, pineapple, pears, and/or red seedless grapes**
 Fresh mint (optional)

1 In a small saucepan combine water, orange peel, sugar, and gingerroot. Bring to boiling; reduce heat. Cover; simmer over low heat 5 minutes. Remove saucepan from heat. Stir in liqueur, orange juice, and honey. Cool thoroughly.

2 Pour cooled ginger mixture over fruit. Cover and marinate fruit for at least 1 hour or up to 12 hours in the refrigerator. To serve, spoon fruit and marinade into individual dishes. If desired, garnish with fresh mint. Makes 8 to 10 servings.

♥*Nutrition facts per serving: 158 calories, 0 g total fat, 0 mg cholesterol, 3 mg sodium, 38 g carbohydrate, 5 g fiber, 1 g protein.*

The Bakery

Old-Fashioned Popovers

1992

Brides of the 1930s were advised by the editors, "The time to eat a popover is when it has just popped over." These quick and easy batter breads from the '90s are similar to, but smaller than, the Yorkshire puddings the English serve with roast beef.

1 tablespoon shortening or
  nonstick spray coating
2 eggs
1 cup milk
1 tablespoon cooking oil
¾ cup all-purpose flour
½ teaspoon salt
Margarine or butter
  (optional)

1 Using *½ teaspoon* shortening for each cup, grease the bottom and sides of 6 cups of a popover pan or five 6-ounce custard cups. (Or, generously spray with nonstick coating.) Place the custard cups, if using, on a 15×10×1-inch baking pan. Set aside.

2 In a medium mixing bowl use a wire whisk or a rotary beater to beat eggs; beat in milk and cooking oil. Add flour and salt; beat until mixture is combined but still slightly lumpy. Fill the prepared popover or custard cups half full.

3 Bake popovers in a 400° oven about 40 minutes or until the crusts are very firm.

4 Turn off oven. Using the tines of a fork, *immediately* prick each popover to let steam escape. Return the popovers to the oven for 5 to 10 minutes more or until of desired crispness. (Be sure the oven is turned off.) Serve immediately. If desired, serve with margarine or butter. Makes 5 or 6 popovers.

Eggnog Popovers: Prepare popovers as directed, except add 1 tablespoon *instant eggnog milk flavoring powder*, 1 tablespoon *rum* or ¼ teaspoon *rum extract*, and ¼ teaspoon *ground nutmeg* to batter.

Caraway Rye Popovers: Prepare popovers as directed, except decrease all-purpose flour to *½ cup*. Add ¼ cup *rye* or *whole wheat flour* and ½ teaspoon *caraway seed* with the all-purpose flour.

Nutrition facts per popover: 164 calories, 8 g total fat (2 g saturated fat), 89 mg cholesterol, 263 mg sodium, 16 g carbohydrate, 0 g fiber, 6 g protein.

Graham Popovers

1 **tablespoon shortening or nonstick spray coating**	1 **cup milk**
⅔ **cup all-purpose flour**	2 **eggs**
⅓ **cup whole wheat flour**	1 **teaspoon cooking oil**
½ **teaspoon salt**	**Margarine or butter (optional)**

1 Using *½ teaspoon* shortening for each cup, grease the bottom and sides of 6 cups of a popover pan or six 6-ounce custard cups. (Or, generously spray with nonstick coating.) Place the custard cups on a 15×10×1-inch baking pan. Set aside.

2 In a medium mixing bowl stir together the all-purpose flour, whole wheat flour, and salt until combined.

3 Add the milk, eggs, and oil; beat with an electric mixer or rotary beater about 30 seconds or until smooth.

4 Fill the prepared popover or custard cups half full.

5 Bake in a 400° oven about 40 minutes or until crusts are very firm.

6 Remove from the oven. Using the tines of a fork, *immediately* prick each popover to let steam escape. Serve immediately. If desired, serve with margarine or butter. Makes 6 popovers.

♥ *Nutrition facts per popover: 121 calories, 3 g total fat (1 g saturated fat), 74 mg cholesterol, 220 mg sodium, 17 g carbohydrate, 1 g fiber, 6 g protein.*

Graham flour (named after the Rev. Sylvester Graham, a 19th-century temperance leader and self-proclaimed nutrition expert) was a term originally used to describe a coarse grind of whole wheat flour. Over the years, the term has been applied to any whole wheat flour, which is how this 1931 popover recipe was named.

Vintage Views
1935

Important News Cash Awards!

This call to readers in the January 1935 issue of the magazine was the beginning of a tradition. Every month readers still are invited to send in recipes for cash. Originally, $5 was the cash award for the winning recipe, and runner-ups were awarded $1.

Today, the top prizewinner receives $200 plus kitchen products. At the end of 1996, all top winners vied for the grand prize: $5,000 worth of new kitchen appliances.

Onion-Cheese Supper Bread

1953

Time seemed to speed up in the 1950s as innovations and products promised us more leisure hours. Cooks, too, started looking for ways to make time fly in the kitchen. This 1953 bread was considered a convenience recipe because it's based on packaged biscuit mix.

½ cup chopped onion	1 cup shredded sharp process
2 tablespoons margarine or	American cheese or
butter	cheddar cheese
½ cup milk	(4 ounces)
1 slightly beaten egg	1 tablespoon poppy seed
1½ cups packaged biscuit mix	Cooked, thinly sliced onion
	(optional)

1 Grease an 8×1½-inch round baking pan. Set aside.

2 Cook chopped onion in *1 tablespoon* of the margarine or butter until onion is tender.

3 Stir together the milk and egg. Add to biscuit mix; stir just until moistened. Add the onion mixture, *half* of the cheese, and *half* of the poppy seed to biscuit mix mixture. Spread batter in prepared pan. Sprinkle with the remaining cheese and the remaining poppy seed. If desired, arrange cooked onion on top.

4 Melt remaining margarine; drizzle over mixture in pan. Bake in a 400° oven about 20 minutes or until a wooden toothpick inserted near the center comes out clean. Serve warm. Makes 8 servings.

Nutrition facts per serving: 182 calories, 10 g total fat (4 g saturated fat), 43 mg cholesterol, 498 mg sodium, 17 g carbohydrate, 1 g fiber, 5 g protein.

1993

Festive Holiday Brioches

From what our magazine editors said about hot baked bread in 1930, you'd think one could live by bread alone: "Hot bread crisp and fragrant from the oven, popped onto the table at that strategic moment when the members of the family are hungry and expectant; yellow butter melting over delectable morsels that disappear with the speed of the proverbial hotcakes! No matter how plain the fare, nor how elaborate, if accompanied by a delicious hot bread, the homemaker may know that the success of her meal is assured." No doubt your success also will be assured with these 1993 prizewinning rich bread rolls.

1 package active dry yeast
¼ cup warm water (105° to 115°)
½ cup butter or margarine, softened
⅓ cup sugar
1 teaspoon salt
4 cups all-purpose flour
½ cup milk
4 eggs
½ cup dried cranberries or dried cherries
½ cup chopped candied citron
¼ cup dried currants
1 tablespoon sugar

1 Soften yeast in the warm water. In a mixing bowl beat the butter or margarine, the ⅓ cup sugar, and the salt until fluffy. Add *1 cup* of the flour and the milk to the sugar mixture. Separate *one* of the eggs. Add the egg yolk and the remaining whole eggs to the beaten mixture. (Refrigerate remaining egg white.) Add softened yeast to flour mixture and beat well. Stir in cranberries or cherries, citron, and currants. Stir in remaining flour. Place in a greased bowl. Cover; let rise in a warm place until double in size (about 2 hours), then refrigerate dough for 6 hours. (Or, omit 2-hour rise and refrigerate dough overnight.)

2 Generously grease twenty-four 2½-inch muffin cups. Stir dough. Turn out onto a floured surface. Divide dough into 4 equal portions; set 1 portion aside. Divide remaining 3 portions into 8 pieces each (24 pieces total). Roll pieces into balls. Place dough balls in prepared muffin cups. Divide remaining dough into 24 pieces; shape into small balls. With thumb, make an indentation in middle of each large ball. Press a small ball into each indentation.

3 Using a fork, beat together reserved egg white and the 1 tablespoon sugar. Brush over rolls. Cover; let rise in a warm place until nearly double in size (about 45 minutes). Bake in a 375° oven 15 minutes or until golden brown. Remove from pans. Cool on racks. Makes 24 rolls.

♥ *Nutrition facts per brioche: 155 calories, 5 g total fat (3 g saturated fat), 46 mg cholesterol, 142 mg sodium, 24 g carbohydrate, 1 g fiber, 3 g protein.*

Honey-Aniseed Bread

1992

5¼ to 5¾ cups all-purpose
    flour
  2 packages active dry yeast
2¼ cups water
  ½ cup honey
  3 tablespoons margarine or
    butter

1 teaspoon salt
1 cup whole wheat flour
½ cup cracked wheat cereal
3 tablespoons aniseed,
  crushed

Rendi A. Hahn of Grand Prairie, Texas, entered this recipe in the yeast breads and rolls category of our March 1992 Prize Tested Recipes contest. We liked her home-style bread with just a whisper of licorice flavor so well that it won first prize.

1 In a mixing bowl combine *2 cups* of the all-purpose flour and the yeast. In a medium saucepan heat and stir water, honey, margarine or butter, and salt just until warm (120° to 130°) and margarine almost melts. Add to dry mixture in mixing bowl. Beat with an electric mixer on low speed 30 seconds, scraping side of bowl constantly. Beat on high speed for 3 minutes. Using a wooden spoon, stir in whole wheat flour, cracked wheat cereal, and aniseed. Stir in as much of the remaining all-purpose flour as you can.

2 Turn out onto a floured surface. Knead in enough of the remaining all-purpose flour to make a moderately stiff dough (6 to 8 minutes total). Shape into a ball. Place in a lightly greased bowl; turn once to grease surface of dough. Cover; let rise in a warm place until double in size (about 45 minutes).

3 Punch the dough down. Turn out onto a floured surface; divide the dough in half. Cover and let rest 10 minutes. Meanwhile, lightly grease two 8×4×2-inch or 9×5×3-inch loaf pans.

4 Shape dough into loaves; place in prepared pans. Cover; let rise in a warm place until nearly double in size (30 to 40 minutes).

5 Bake in a 375° oven 40 to 45 minutes or until bread sounds hollow when lightly tapped. If necessary, cover with foil the last 15 minutes of baking to prevent overbrowning. Immediately remove from pans. Cool on wire racks. Makes 2 loaves (32 servings).

♥ *Nutrition facts per serving: 115 calories, 1 g total fat (0 g saturated fat), 0 mg cholesterol, 81 mg sodium, 23 g carbohydrate, 1 g fiber, 3 g protein.*

Dilly Bread

2 cups all-purpose flour
1 package active dry yeast
2 teaspoons dillseed
¼ teaspoon baking soda
2 tablespoons chopped onion
1 tablespoon margarine or
  butter

1 cup cream-style cottage
  cheese
¼ cup water
2 tablespoons sugar
½ teaspoon salt
1 egg

This no-knead bread gets its subtle tang from cottage cheese and its mild herb essence from dillseed. Serve it with your favorite main dish soup or salad.

1 Generously grease a 1½-quart soufflé dish or casserole or a 9×1½-inch round baking pan. In a large mixing bowl combine ¾ *cup* of the flour, the yeast, dillseed, and baking soda. Set aside.

2 In a medium saucepan cook onion in the margarine or butter until tender. Add cottage cheese, water, sugar, and salt to onion mixture; heat and stir just until warm (120° to 130°). Add to dry mixture in mixing bowl; add egg. Beat with an electric mixer on low speed for 30 seconds, scraping side of bowl constantly. Beat on high speed for 3 minutes. Using a wooden spoon, stir in the remaining flour.

3 Spread batter into the prepared pan or casserole. Cover; let rise in warm place until nearly double in size (50 to 60 minutes).

4 Bake in a 375° oven about 25 minutes or until golden brown. If necessary, cover with foil the last 10 minutes of baking to prevent overbrowning. Immediately remove from pan or casserole. Serve warm, or allow to cool on wire rack. Makes 1 loaf (8 servings).

♥*Nutrition facts per serving: 171 calories, 4 g total fat (1 g saturated fat), 31 mg cholesterol, 305 mg sodium, 27 g carbohydrate, 1 g fiber, 8 g protein.*

Hazelnut-Amaretto Loaf

1995

Bread machines rose to baking prominence in the '90s. With this timesaving appliance, families could enjoy fresh baked bread with little effort. Here's one of our 1995 bread machine loaves that's chock-full of hazelnuts and drizzled with an appealing amaretto glaze.

1-Pound Loaf	1½-Pound Loaf
2 cups bread flour	3 cups bread flour
⅔ cup milk	1 cup milk
½ cup chopped hazelnuts or almonds, toasted	¾ cup chopped hazelnuts or almonds, toasted
1 egg	1 egg
2 tablespoons sugar	3 tablespoons sugar
2 tablespoons margarine or butter	3 tablespoons margarine or butter
4 teaspoons amaretto or hazelnut liqueur	2 tablespoons amaretto or hazelnut liqueur
¾ teaspoon active dry yeast	1 teaspoon active dry yeast
½ teaspoon salt	¾ teaspoon salt
1 recipe Amaretto Glaze Toasted chopped hazelnuts or almonds (optional)	1 recipe Amaretto Glaze Toasted chopped hazelnuts or almonds (optional)

1 Select loaf size. Add the flour, milk, nuts, egg, sugar, margarine or butter, liqueur, yeast, and salt to a bread machine pan, according to the manufacturer's directions. Bake and cool as directed. Drizzle cooled bread with Amaretto Glaze. If desired, top with additional nuts. Makes one 1- or 1½-pound loaf (16 or 24 servings).

Amaretto Glaze: In a small bowl stir together ½ cup sifted *powdered sugar,* 1 tablespoon *amaretto* or *hazelnut liqueur* or ½ teaspoon *almond extract,* and enough *milk* (1 to 2 teaspoons) to make a glaze consistency.

♥ *Nutrition facts per serving: 131 calories, 4 g total fat (1 g saturated fat), 14 mg cholesterol, 93 mg sodium, 19 g carbohydrate, 1 g fiber, 3 g protein.*

Light Bread

1973

½ cup sugar
½ cup shortening
2 teaspoons salt
1 cup warm milk
    (105° to 115°)
2 beaten eggs

2 packages active dry yeast
1 cup warm water
    (105° to 115°)
6¼ to 6¾ cups all-purpose
    flour

The original name of this bread was "Shug Geter's Light Bread." It was one of several recipes in a 1973 story featuring Shug Geter, of Georgia, and her best recipes. Lillian R. Arnold, of Oregon, remembered it and sent it in, saying the bread is "a delicious, melt-in-your-mouth, light bread so far surpassed by none."

1 In a large mixing bowl place sugar, shortening, and salt. Add warm milk and stir to soften shortening; cool. Beat in eggs. Soften yeast in the warm water; stir into shortening mixture.

2 Add *4 cups* of the flour. Using a wooden spoon, beat until smooth. Stir in as much of the remaining flour as you can.

3 Shape into ball. Turn out onto floured surface. Knead in enough of the remaining flour to make a moderately soft dough that is smooth and elastic (8 to 10 minutes total). Place in greased bowl, turning once to grease surface of dough. Cover; let rise in warm place until double in size (about 1¼ hours).

4 Punch dough down.* Grease two 9×5×3-inch or three 8×4×2-inch loaf pans. Divide dough into halves or thirds. Cover; let rest 10 minutes. Shape dough into loaves. Place in prepared pans. Let rise in warm place until double in size (45 to 60 minutes).

5 Bake in a 375° oven about 25 minutes or until bread sounds hollow when lightly tapped. If necessary, cover with foil the last 5 to 10 minutes of baking to prevent overbrowning. Immediately remove from pans. Cool on wire racks. Makes 2 or 3 loaves (32 servings).

For pan rolls: Prepare as directed to asterisk (*). Shape dough into 36 rolls. Place in 2 greased 13×9×2-inch baking pans. Let rise in a warm place until double in size (45 to 60 minutes). Bake in a 375° oven for 15 to 20 minutes or until golden brown. Makes 36 rolls.

♥ *Nutrition facts per serving: 132 calories, 4 g total fat (1 g saturated fat), 14 mg cholesterol, 142 mg sodium, 21 g carbohydrate, 1 g fiber, 3 g protein.*

Sunflower Seed Bread

1970

Homemade bread was the rage in the '70s, and plain bread was considered out of style. After years of bleaching flour, milling companies began marketing an unbleached product, too. Sunflower seeds, wheat germ, and other seeds or nuts often were stirred into the dough for special flavor and a nutritional boost. This bread has a wonderful hint of orange flavor.

3½ to 4 cups all-purpose flour
1 package active dry yeast
½ cup milk
3 tablespoons sugar
2 tablespoons margarine or butter
½ teaspoon salt
1 egg
1 tablespoon finely shredded orange peel (set aside)
½ cup orange juice
⅔ cup shelled sunflower seeds
Melted margarine or butter (optional)
Honey (optional)

1 In a large mixing bowl combine *1½ cups* of the flour and the yeast.

2 In a small saucepan heat and stir milk, sugar, the 2 tablespoons margarine or butter, and the salt just until warm (120° to130°) and margarine almost melts. Add to dry mixture in mixing bowl; add egg and orange juice. Beat with an electric mixer on low speed for 30 seconds, scraping side of bowl constantly. Beat on high speed for 3 minutes. Using a wooden spoon, stir in sunflower seeds, orange peel, and as much of the remaining flour as you can.

3 Turn the dough out onto a lightly floured surface. Knead in enough of the remaining flour to make a moderately stiff dough that is smooth and elastic (6 to 8 minutes total). Shape into a ball. Place in a lightly greased bowl, turning once to grease the surface of dough. Cover; let rise in warm place until double in size (1¼ to1½ hours).

4 Punch dough down. Cover; let rest 10 minutes. Meanwhile, grease an 8×4×2-inch loaf pan. Shape dough into loaf; place in prepared pan. Cover; let rise in warm place until double in size (30 to 45 minutes). If desired, brush top with melted margarine or butter.

5 Bake in a 375° oven for 35 to 40 minutes or until bread sounds hollow when lightly tapped. If necessary, cover with foil the last 15 minutes of baking to prevent overbrowning. Immediately remove from pan. Cool on wire rack. If desired, serve with honey. Makes 1 loaf (16 servings).

♥ *Nutrition facts per serving: 161 calories, 5 g total fat (1 g saturated fat), 14 mg cholesterol, 92 mg sodium, 24 g carbohydrate, 1 g fiber, 5 g protein.*

Honey-Oatmeal Bread

1959

Although this recipe was first published in 1959, the tantalizing combination of whole wheat flour, rolled oats, and honey fits right in with today's renewed interest in whole grains and natural sweeteners.

4¾ to 5¼ cups whole wheat flour
3 packages active dry yeast
2 cups milk
⅓ cup honey
¼ cup cooking oil
2 teaspoons salt
½ cup quick-cooking rolled oats
Quick-cooking rolled oats
1 beaten egg white
1 tablespoon water

1 In a large mixing bowl combine *2 cups* of the flour and the yeast. In saucepan heat milk, honey, oil, and salt just until warm (120° to 130°). Add to dry mixture in mixing bowl. Beat with an electric mixer on low speed for 30 seconds, scraping side of bowl constantly. Beat on high speed for 3 minutes. Using a wooden spoon, stir in the ½ cup oats and as much of the remaining flour as you can.

2 Turn out onto a lightly floured surface. Knead in enough of any remaining flour to make a moderately stiff dough that is smooth and elastic (5 to 6 minutes total). Shape into a ball. Place in lightly greased bowl, turning once to grease surface of dough. Cover; let rise in warm place until double in size (45 to 60 minutes).

3 Punch dough down. Turn out onto a lightly floured surface. Divide dough in half. Cover; let rest 10 minutes. Meanwhile, generously grease two 8×4×2-inch loaf pans. Sprinkle each pan with *2 tablespoons* oats. Shape dough into loaves. Place in prepared pans. Cover; let rise in warm place until double in size (35 to 45 minutes).

4 Using a fork, beat together egg white and water; brush over loaves. Sprinkle loaves lightly with oats.

5 Bake in a 375° oven for 35 to 40 minutes or until bread sounds hollow when lightly tapped. If necessary, cover with foil the last 15 minutes of baking to prevent overbrowning. Immediately remove from pans. Cool on wire racks. Makes 2 loaves (32 servings).

♥ *Nutrition facts per serving: 102 calories, 2 g total fat (1 g saturated fat), 1 mg cholesterol, 144 mg sodium, 18 g carbohydrate, 3 g fiber, 4 g protein.*

Banana Bread with Mango Curd

4 **cups all-purpose flour**	1¼ **cups cooking oil**
1⅓ **cups packed brown sugar**	4 **eggs**
1 **tablespoon baking powder**	⅔ **cup chopped macadamia**
1 **teaspoon baking soda**	**nuts or walnuts, toasted**
½ **teaspoon salt**	1 **recipe Nut 'n' Streusel**
½ **teaspoon ground cloves**	**Topping**
2 **cups mashed ripe banana**	1 **recipe Mango Curd**
(about 4 medium)	

This '90s quick bread is a sophisticated adaptation of the old-fashioned banana favorite. Featuring macadamia nuts instead of old-time pecans or walnuts, it is spread with an elegant mango curd rather than simple butter.

1 Grease two 8×4×2-inch or 9×5×3-inch loaf pans. Set aside.

2 In a very large mixing bowl combine *1½ cups* of the flour, the brown sugar, baking powder, baking soda, salt, and cloves. Add the banana and oil. Beat with an electric mixer on low speed until combined. Beat on high speed for 2 minutes. Add the eggs; beat until combined. Stir in the remaining flour and the nuts.

3 Pour batter into prepared pans. Sprinkle with Nut 'n' Streusel Topping. Bake in a 350° oven for 60 to 65 minutes or until wooden toothpicks inserted near the centers come out clean. Cool in pans on a wire rack for 10 minutes. Remove from pans and cool completely. Wrap bread and store overnight at room temperature before slicing. Serve with Mango Curd. Makes 2 loaves (32 servings).

Nut 'n' Streusel Topping: In a small mixing bowl stir together ⅓ cup packed *brown sugar* and ¼ cup *all-purpose flour*. With a pastry blender or 2 forks, cut in 2 tablespoons *butter* or *margarine* until mixture resembles coarse crumbs. Stir in ⅓ cup toasted *chopped macadamia nuts* or *walnuts*.

Mango Curd: In a large saucepan stir together ¾ cup *granulated sugar* and 2 tablespoons *cornstarch*. Stir in 1 cup pureed *mango*, ¼ cup *margarine* or *butter*, 2 tablespoons *lemon juice*, and 1 tablespoon finely shredded *orange peel*. Cook and stir over medium heat until thickened and bubbly. Slowly stir about half of the mixture into 6 beaten *egg yolks*. Return all of the egg yolk mixture to the mixture in saucepan. Bring to a gentle boil. Cook and stir for 2 minutes more. Cover surface with plastic wrap. Refrigerate at least 2 hours or until serving time. Makes 2 cups.

Nutrition facts per serving with 1 tablespoon Mango Curd: 272 calories, 16 g total fat (3 g saturated fat), 68 mg cholesterol, 144 mg sodium, 31 g carbohydrate, 1 g fiber, 3 g protein.

Finnish Braids

1974

his eye-catching braid blends the spicy-sweet flavor of cardamom with just a hint of orange. To give it as an extra-special present, wrap the loaf in plastic wrap, tie it with a bow, and place it in an attractive bread basket.

5¼ to 5¾ **cups all-purpose
   flour**
2 **packages active dry yeast**
½ **teaspoon ground
   cardamom**
1 **cup milk**
½ **cup margarine or butter**
½ **cup sugar**

1 **teaspoon salt**
2 **eggs**
1 **tablespoon finely shredded
   orange peel**
⅓ **cup orange juice**
1 **egg yolk**
1 **tablespoon milk**

1 In a large mixing bowl combine *2½ cups* of the flour, the yeast, and ground cardamom. In a saucepan heat and stir the 1 cup milk, the margarine or butter, sugar, and salt just until warm (120° to 130°) and margarine almost melts. Add to dry mixture in mixing bowl; add eggs, orange peel, and orange juice. Beat with an electric mixer on low speed for 30 seconds, scraping sides of bowl constantly. Beat on high speed for 3 minutes. Using a wooden spoon, stir in as much of remaining flour as you can.

2 Turn the dough out onto a floured surface. Knead in enough of the remaining flour to make a moderately soft dough (3 to 5 minutes total). Shape dough into a ball. Place in greased bowl, turning once to grease surface of the dough. Cover; let dough rise in a warm place until double in size (about1 hour).

3 Punch dough down. Divide dough in half. Divide each half in thirds; shape into 6 balls. Cover; let rest 10 minutes. Meanwhile, grease 2 baking sheets.

4 Roll each ball to a 16-inch-long rope. Lay 3 ropes, side by side and about 1 inch apart, on a prepared baking sheet. Starting in the middle, loosely braid by bringing the left rope under the center rope. Next bring right rope under new center rope. Repeat to end. Braid other end by bringing alternate ropes over center rope. Press ends together to seal; tuck under. Repeat with remaining ropes. Cover; let rise in warm place until nearly double in size (30 to 40 minutes).

5 Using a fork, beat together the egg yolk and the 1 tablespoon milk. Brush braids with egg yolk mixture.

6 Bake bread in a 350° oven for 25 to 30 minutes or until bread sounds hollow when lightly tapped. If necessary, cover loaves with foil the last 5 to 10 minutes of baking to prevent overbrowning. Makes 2 loaves (32 servings).

♥ *Nutrition facts per serving: 119 calories, 4 g total fat (1 g saturated fat), 21 mg cholesterol, 104 mg sodium, 18 g carbohydrate, 1 g fiber, 3 g protein.*

Herb Focaccia

1994

Focaccia is one of the most popular ethnic breads of the '90s. This round, flat Italian bread is ideal as a base for pizza. Or, you can cut the bread in wedges to serve as a savory accompaniment to almost any main dish. We've made it easy—use a timesaving hot roll mix instead of starting from scratch.

1 **16-ounce package hot roll mix**
1 **egg**
2 **tablespoons olive oil**
⅓ **cup finely chopped onion**

½ **teaspoon dried rosemary, crushed**
3 **tablespoons olive oil or cooking oil**

1 Lightly grease two 9×1½-inch round baking pans or one 12- or 13-inch pizza pan. Set aside.

2 Prepare hot roll mix according to package directions for basic dough, using the 1 egg and substituting the 2 tablespoons olive oil for the margarine called for on the package. Knead dough; allow to rest as directed. If using round baking pans, divide dough in half; roll each half into a 9-inch round. If using a pizza pan, roll dough into a 12-inch round. Place in prepared pan(s).

3 In a skillet cook onion and rosemary in the 3 tablespoons oil until onion is tender. With fingertips, press indentations every inch or so in dough round(s). Top dough evenly with onion mixture. Cover; let rise in a warm place until nearly double in size (30 to 40 minutes).

4 Bake in a 375° oven for 15 to 20 minutes or until golden brown. Remove from pan to a wire rack; cool. Makes 6 to 8 servings.

Nutrition facts per serving: 413 calories, 17 g total fat (3 g saturated fat), 40 mg cholesterol, 322 mg sodium, 56 g carbohydrate, 0 g fiber, 10 g protein.

Feather Rolls

5 cups all-purpose flour
1 package active dry yeast
1½ cups warm water (105° to 115°)
½ cup mashed, cooked potatoes (about 2 small or 1 medium)

⅓ cup margarine or butter, melted
¼ cup sugar
1 teaspoon salt

A Sunday dinner standby during the '30s, these no-knead pan rolls made with mashed potatoes are as light as feathers.

1 In a large mixing bowl combine *2 cups* of the flour and the yeast. In a small mixing bowl combine warm water, potatoes, margarine or butter, sugar, and salt. Add to dry mixture in mixing bowl. Beat with an electric mixer on low speed for 30 seconds, scraping side of bowl constantly. Beat on high speed for 3 minutes. Using a wooden spoon, stir in remaining flour. Cover; refrigerate for 2 to 24 hours.

2 Punch dough down. Turn out on a lightly floured surface. Cover; let rest 10 minutes. Meanwhile, grease a 13×9×2-inch baking pan. With lightly floured hands, shape dough into 24 rolls. Place rolls in prepared pan. Cover; let rise in a warm place until nearly double in size (about 40 minutes). Bake in a 400° oven for 16 to 20 minutes or until golden brown. Makes 24 rolls.

♥ *Nutrition facts per roll: 129 calories, 3 g total fat (0 g saturated fat), 0 mg cholesterol, 111 mg sodium, 23 g carbohydrate, 1 g fiber, 3 g protein.*

Sugar-Cinnamon Loaf

1951

The cinnamon swirl in the center of each slice makes this bread special enough for company. It's exceptionally tasty served with honey butter.

3¾ to 4¼ cups all-purpose
    flour
1 package active dry yeast
1¼ cups milk
¼ cup sugar
¼ cup shortening, margarine,
    or butter
1 teaspoon salt

1 egg
¼ cup sugar
1 teaspoon ground cinnamon
2 teaspoons milk
1 tablespoon sugar
½ teaspoon ground cinnamon
1 tablespoon margarine or
    butter, melted

1 In a large mixing bowl combine *1½ cups* of the flour and the yeast. In a saucepan heat and stir the 1¼ cups milk, ¼ cup sugar, the shortening, and salt just until warm (120° to 130°) and shortening almost melts. Add to dry mixture in mixing bowl; add egg. Beat with an electric mixer on low speed for 30 seconds, scraping side of bowl constantly. Beat on high speed for 3 minutes. Using a wooden spoon, stir in as much of the remaining flour as you can.

2 Turn dough onto a lightly floured surface. Knead in enough of the remaining flour to make a moderately soft dough that is smooth and elastic (3 to 5 minutes total). Shape into a ball. Place in greased bowl, turning once to grease surface of the dough. Cover; let rise in warm place until nearly double in size (about 1¼ hours).

3 Punch dough down. Turn out onto floured surface. Cover; let rest 10 minutes. Meanwhile, grease a 9×5×3-inch loaf pan.

4 Roll dough to 18×7-inch rectangle. In a small bowl stir together the ¼ cup sugar and the 1 teaspoon cinnamon. Brush dough with the 2 teaspoons milk; sprinkle with the sugar-cinnamon mixture. Roll up, jelly-roll style, starting from a short side. Seal seam. Place in prepared pan. Let rise in a warm place until nearly double in size (45 minutes).

5 In a small bowl stir together the 1 tablespoon sugar and the ½ teaspoon cinnamon. Brush loaf with the 1 tablespoon melted margarine or butter; sprinkle with the sugar-cinnamon mixture. Bake in a 375° oven for 30 minutes or until bread sounds hollow when lightly tapped. If necessary, cover with foil the last 15 minutes of baking to prevent overbrowning. Makes 1 loaf (16 servings).

♥ *Nutrition facts per serving: 176 calories, 5 g total fat (1 g saturated fat), 15 mg cholesterol, 156 mg sodium, 29 g carbohydrate, 1 g fiber, 4 g protein.*

1950

Up-&-Down Biscuits

Mrs. Allen Medus of Jennings, Louisiana, submitted this recipe as her favorite from past issues of the magazine. She said in her letter, "My children, six in all, loved these biscuits. They took a little extra effort [to make], but were so good and never failed in quality, that it was worth the effort." She still makes this recipe today for her grandchildren and herself.

2 cups all-purpose flour
3 tablespoons sugar
4 teaspoons baking powder
½ teaspoon cream of tartar
½ teaspoon salt
½ cup shortening

⅔ cup milk
¼ cup margarine or butter, melted
¼ cup sugar
2 to 3 teaspoons ground cinnamon

1 Grease twelve 2½-inch muffin cups. Set aside.

2 In a medium mixing bowl stir together flour, the 3 tablespoons sugar, baking powder, cream of tartar, and salt. Cut in shortening until mixture resembles coarse crumbs. Make a well in the center of dry mixture. Add milk all at once. Using a fork, stir just until moistened.

3 Turn dough out onto a lightly floured surface. Quickly knead dough by gently folding and pressing for 10 to 12 strokes or until nearly smooth. Divide dough in half. Roll half of dough to a 12×10-inch rectangle. Brush dough with *half* of the melted margarine or butter. In a small bowl stir together the ¼ cup sugar and the cinnamon; sprinkle half over the dough. Cut rectangle into five 12×2-inch strips. Stack the 5 strips on top of each other. Cut stack into six 2×2-inch squares. Place squares, cut sides down, in prepared muffin cups. Repeat with remaining dough, remaining margarine, and remaining cinnamon mixture.

4 Bake biscuits in a 450° oven for 10 to 12 minutes or until golden brown. Serve warm. Makes 12 biscuits.

Nutrition facts per biscuit: 216 calories, 13 g total fat (3 g saturated fat), 1 mg cholesterol, 262 mg sodium, 23 g carbohydrate, 1 g fiber, 2 g protein.

*V*intage Views
1936
Ode to the Mixer

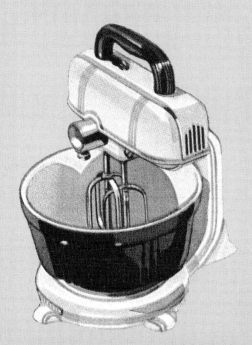

*T*he editors sang the praises of a new appliance in the December 1936 story titled "Merry Mixers": "Among all pieces of modern kitchen equipment, the electric mixer is the one most likely to call forth arias from the busy but imaginative cook. Delightfully practical, it saves just that element of labor in tedious 'little jobs' that tends to route songs into sighs. Withal it has a romantic side, shoving tricky occasionals, such as cream puffs, meringues, and frostings, out of the I'd-like-to-make-them-but-haven't-time group into the truly emergency or everyday class.

"There are things, to be sure, that the modern food mixer will not do. It will not, for instance, spread the frosting, measure the cake flour, bake your angel cake. It will not even satisfactorily cream very stiff butter, within a limited time. (Moral: leave butter out of the refrigerator to soften.) The food mixer in most general use is the one which retails for around $20.

"With the treasure once inside your kitchen, see that it is properly oiled, give it a prominent and permanent place on your workshelf, and prepare to trill your gayest notes [in song]."

Almond Twirl Bread

1974

3¾ to 4¼ cups all-purpose
    flour
1 package active dry yeast
1 cup milk
⅓ cup granulated sugar
⅓ cup margarine or butter
½ teaspoon salt

2 eggs
1 recipe Almond Filling
½ cup sifted powdered sugar
½ teaspoon vanilla
1 to 2 teaspoons milk
¼ cup sliced almonds,
    toasted

When we retested this 1974 recipe, our taste panel was delighted with the luscious results. One panel member described the bread as "cinnamon rolls in a ring."

1 In a large mixing bowl combine *2 cups* of the flour and the yeast. In a small saucepan heat and stir milk, sugar, margarine or butter, and salt just until warm (120° to 130°) and margarine almost melts. Add to dry mixture in mixing bowl; add eggs. Beat with an electric mixer on low speed for 30 seconds, scraping the side of the bowl constantly. Beat on high speed for 3 minutes. Using a wooden spoon, stir in as much of the remaining flour as you can.

2 Turn the dough out onto a lightly floured surface. Knead in enough of the remaining flour to make a moderately soft dough that is smooth and elastic (3 to 5 minutes total). Shape dough into a ball. Place dough in a lightly greased bowl, turning once to grease surface of dough. Cover; let rise in a warm place until double in size (about 1 hour).

3 Punch dough down. Turn dough out onto a lightly floured surface. Cover; let rest 10 minutes. Meanwhile, lightly grease a large baking sheet.

4 Roll dough to an 18×12-inch rectangle. Sprinkle with Almond Filling. Roll up, jelly-roll style, starting from a long side. Seal seam. Place, seam side down, on prepared baking sheet. Shape into a ring; press ends together to seal. Using kitchen scissors, snip at 1-inch intervals, making each cut two-thirds of the way to center. Gently turn each section slightly to a side. Cover and let rise in warm place until nearly double in size (about 30 minutes).

5 Bake in a 350° oven for 20 to 25 minutes or until bread sounds hollow when lightly tapped. Transfer to a wire rack and let cool.

6 For icing, in a small bowl combine the powdered sugar, vanilla, and enough of the 1 to 2 teaspoons milk to make of drizzling consistency. Drizzle over bread. Top with sliced almonds. Makes 1 ring (18 servings).

Almond Filling: In a small mixing bowl beat ⅓ cup *granulated sugar* and 2 tablespoons *margarine* or *butter* with an electric mixer on medium speed until well combined. Stir in ½ cup *ground almonds.*

Nutrition facts per serving: 203 calories, 8 g total fat (0 g saturated fat), 25 mg cholesterol, 128 mg sodium, 28 g carbohydrate, 1 g fiber, 5 g protein.

*V*intage Views

1933

RECIPE ENDORSED

BETTER HOMES & GARDENS
TASTING-TEST KITCHEN

*I*n 1933, *Better Homes and Gardens* magazine introduced the logo that would symbolize its Test Kitchen's satisfaction with recipes sent in from readers. The famous recipe endorsement had been in place for more than a year when the editors wrote:

"[T]he stamp of recipe endorsement has become known and recognized as the mark of an accurate, dependable recipe by homemakers in suburbs and cities from coast to coast. Since the beginning of cookery, the evils in housewives' recipes have been the words 'scant,' 'heaping,' 'rounding,' and 'pinch.' Unless a recipe is accurate as to measurements and clear as to method, it is not dependable for other women to follow. Even the best of food products will produce an inferior dish—if the recipe is wrong! By awarding Certificates of Endorsement for recipes which pass The Tasting-Test Kitchen's tests for dependability, *Better Homes & Gardens* rewards homemakers for their care in making recipes accurate."

Rosemary Pound Cake

1995

1 cup butter, softened
1 cup sugar
¼ cup honey
5 eggs
2 cups sifted cake flour
1 teaspoon baking powder
1 tablespoon snipped fresh
    rosemary or 1 teaspoon
    dried rosemary, crushed

1½ teaspoons orange flower
    water or ¼ teaspoon
    orange extract
1¼ teaspoons finely shredded
    orange peel
1½ teaspoons orange juice
1 recipe Orange Juice Glaze
    Fresh rosemary sprigs
    (optional)

Ordinary pound cake is transformed into something new with the addition of the fragrant herb rosemary. Top each serving off with a swirl of orange-flavored yogurt for a dessert special enough for company. With its 1 cup of butter, pound cake is certainly decadent by today's standards but just too good to be forbidden.

1 Grease and flour two 8×4×2-inch loaf pans. Set aside.

2 In a medium mixing bowl beat butter and sugar with an electric mixer on medium speed about 6 minutes or until light and creamy. Beat in honey. Add eggs, 1 at a time, beating for 1 minute after each addition. (Batter may look slightly curdled.) Stir together cake flour and baking powder. Gradually add the dry mixture to the beaten mixture, beating on low speed just until combined. Gently stir in the snipped or crushed rosemary, the orange flower water or extract, orange peel, and juice.

3 Pour batter into prepared pans. Bake in a 325° oven about 45 minutes or until wooden toothpicks inserted near the centers come out clean. Cool in pans for 10 minutes. Remove and cool on wire racks. Drizzle with Orange Juice Glaze. If desired, top with rosemary sprigs. Makes 2 loaves (20 servings).

Orange Juice Glaze: Stir together ⅔ cup sifted *powdered sugar* and 1 tablespoon *orange juice.*

To make ahead: Prepare cakes as directed, except do not glaze. Place in a freezer container and freeze for up to 3 months. To serve, thaw at room temperature. Glaze as directed above.

Nutrition facts per serving: 204 calories, 10 g total fat (6 g saturated fat), 78 mg cholesterol, 127 mg sodium, 26 g carbohydrate, 0 g fiber, 3 g protein.

1946

Orange Bowknots

In our 25th anniversary issue, we featured our all-time best recipes, including the one for these rich rolls. It was a top winner in a 1946 Cook's Round Table, submitted by Mrs. Elinor Loatman, of Randolph, Massachusetts. The recipe has kept up with our tastes so well that our current staff chose it as a favorite. The pleasant citrus flavor comes from orange peel and juice. When shredding the peel, be careful to shred only the orange part of the peel, as the white part will make the dough bitter.

5½ to 6 cups all-purpose flour
  1 package active dry yeast
1¼ cups milk
  ½ cup shortening
  ⅓ cup sugar
  1 teaspoon salt

2 eggs
2 tablespoons finely shredded
   orange peel (set aside)
¼ cup orange juice
1 recipe Orange Icing

1 In a large mixing bowl combine *2 cups* of the flour and the yeast. In a saucepan heat and stir the milk, shortening, sugar, and salt just until warm (120° to 130°) and shortening almost melts. Add to flour mixture along with eggs and orange juice. Beat with an electric mixer on low speed for 30 seconds, scraping side of bowl constantly. Beat on high speed for 3 minutes. Using a wooden spoon, stir in the shredded orange peel and as much of the remaining flour as you can.

2 Turn dough out onto a lightly floured surface. Knead in enough of the remaining flour to make a moderately stiff dough that is smooth and elastic (6 to 8 minutes total). Shape dough into a ball. Place dough in a greased bowl, turning once to grease surface of dough. Cover; let rise in a warm place until double in size (about 1 hour).

3 Punch dough down. Turn out onto a lightly floured surface. Divide dough in half. Cover; let rest for 10 minutes. Meanwhile, lightly grease baking sheets.

4 Roll each half of dough to a 10×6-inch rectangle. Cut each rectangle into twelve 10×½-inch strips. Tie each strip into a loose knot. Place knots 2 to 3 inches apart on prepared baking sheets. Cover and let rise in a warm place until nearly double in size (about 30 minutes).

5 Bake in a 375° oven for 12 to 15 minutes or until golden brown. Drizzle with Orange Icing. Makes 24 rolls.

Orange Icing: In a small mixing bowl stir together 1 cup sifted *powdered sugar*, 1 teaspoon finely shredded *orange peel*, and enough *orange juice* (3 to 4 teaspoons) to make of spreading consistency.

♥ *Nutrition facts per serving: 176 calories, 5 g total fat (1 g saturated fat), 19 mg cholesterol, 101 mg sodium, 28 g carbohydrate, 1 g fiber, 4 g protein.*

Pear-Buttermilk Scones

1993

If you have too many scones to enjoy at once, wrap the leftovers in heavy foil. Then, store them at room temperature for 2 to 3 days or in the freezer for up to 3 months. To reheat, place the wrapped, room-temperature scones in a 300° oven for 10 to 12 minutes. Heat the wrapped, frozen scones for 20 to 25 minutes.

1¾ **cups all-purpose flour**
⅓ **cup sugar**
2 **teaspoons baking powder**
¼ **teaspoon baking soda**
¼ **teaspoon salt**
¼ **teaspoon ground cardamom, nutmeg, or allspice**
⅓ **cup butter or margarine**

2 **eggs**
¼ **cup buttermilk**
½ **cup chopped, peeled fresh pear, patted dry**
Powdered sugar
Whipped cream (optional)
Orange marmalade and/or strawberry preserves (optional)

1 In a large mixing bowl stir together flour; sugar; baking powder; baking soda; salt; and cardamom, nutmeg, or allspice. Using a pastry blender, cut in butter or margarine until mixture resembles coarse crumbs. Make a well in the center of the dry mixture.

2 In a small mixing bowl beat eggs slightly; stir in buttermilk. Add the buttermilk mixture all at once to the dry mixture. Using a fork, stir just until moistened. Fold in pear.

3 Turn dough out onto a floured surface. Quickly knead dough by gently folding and pressing for 10 to 12 strokes or until nearly smooth. Pat or lightly roll the dough to ½-inch thickness. Cut with a 2½-inch-round biscuit cutter, dipping cutter into flour between cuts.

4 Place dough rounds 1 inch apart on an ungreased baking sheet. Bake in a 375° oven for 10 to 12 minutes or until golden brown. Cool on the baking sheet for 5 minutes, then transfer scones to a wire rack. Sift powdered sugar over tops. If desired, serve warm with whipped cream and marmalade or preserves. Makes 12 to 14 scones.

Nutrition facts per scone: 149 calories, 6 g total fat (3 g saturated fat), 49 mg cholesterol, 199 mg sodium, 21 g carbohydrate, 1 g fiber, 3 g protein.

Gingerbread Scones

2 cups all-purpose flour
3 tablespoons brown sugar
2 teaspoons baking powder
1 teaspoon ground ginger
½ teaspoon baking soda
½ teaspoon salt
½ teaspoon ground cinnamon

¼ cup butter or margarine
1 beaten egg yolk
⅓ cup molasses
¼ cup milk
1 slightly beaten egg white
   Coarse sugar (optional)
1 recipe Nutmeg Whipped
   Cream (optional)

Cooks today have rediscovered European baked goods of all kinds. A particular favorite from the British Isles is the buttery, rich scone. This spicy, molasses-flavored version from our February 1995 issue is a top-notch variation of the biscuitlike classic. (Pictured on page 138.)

1 In a large mixing bowl combine flour, brown sugar, baking powder, ginger, baking soda, salt, and cinnamon. Using a pastry blender, cut in butter or margarine until mixture resembles coarse crumbs. Make a well in the center of the dry mixture.

2 In a small mixing bowl stir together the egg yolk, molasses, and milk. Add molasses mixture all at once to the dry mixture. Using a fork, stir until combined (mixture may seem dry).

3 Turn dough out onto a lightly floured surface. Quickly knead dough by gently folding and pressing for 10 to 12 strokes or until nearly smooth. Pat or lightly roll dough to a 7-inch circle. Using a knife, cut into 8 wedges. Arrange wedges on an ungreased baking sheet about 1 inch apart. Brush wedges with egg white. If desired, sprinkle wedges with coarse sugar.

4 Bake in a 400° oven for 12 to 15 minutes or until light brown. Transfer to a wire rack; cool for 20 minutes. Serve warm. If desired, serve with Nutmeg Whipped Cream. Makes 8 scones.

Nutmeg Whipped Cream: In a chilled mixing bowl combine ½ cup *whipping cream,* 1 tablespoon *granulated sugar,* ¼ teaspoon finely shredded *orange peel,* ¼ teaspoon *vanilla,* and ⅛ teaspoon *ground nutmeg.* Beat with chilled beaters of an electric mixer on low speed until soft peaks form (tips curl). Serve immediately, or cover and refrigerate for up to 2 hours. Makes 1 cup.

To make ahead: Cool baked scones completely. Wrap cooled scones tightly in foil and place in freezer bags. Freeze for up to 3 months. Place frozen, foil-wrapped scones in a 300° oven and heat for 15 to 20 minutes or until warm (10 to 15 minutes, if thawed). Serve as above.

Nutrition facts per scone: 223 calories, 7 g total fat (4 g saturated fat), 43 mg cholesterol, 286 mg sodium, 37 g carbohydrate, 1 g fiber, 4 g protein.

1975

Chocolate Cream Cheese Cake

This cake is different from the rest: You mix up the cake and reserve some of the mixture for the frosting. It's versatile, too. White chocolate fans can substitute white chocolate for the unsweetened chocolate. No wonder this cake was picked as a reader favorite.

1 **8-ounce package cream cheese, softened**	1 **to 2 cups sifted powdered sugar**
⅔ **cup butter or margarine, softened**	3 **eggs**
1 **teaspoon vanilla**	2½ **cups all-purpose flour**
5 **ounces unsweetened chocolate, melted and cooled**	1½ **teaspoons baking powder**
	½ **teaspoon baking soda**
	¼ **teaspoon salt**
8 **cups sifted powdered sugar**	1 **cup milk**
⅓ **cup milk**	½ **cup seedless red raspberry preserves**

1 In a large mixing bowl beat together the cream cheese, butter or margarine, and vanilla with an electric mixer on medium speed until fluffy. Blend in chocolate. Alternately beat in the 8 cups powdered sugar and the ⅓ cup milk. Reserve 3½ cups of the mixture to use in the cake; set aside.

2 To the remaining mixture (you should have 2 to 3 cups mixture), beat in enough of the additional 1 to 2 cups sifted powdered sugar to make of spreading consistency. Cover and refrigerate the frosting.

3 In a large mixing bowl place the reserved 3½ cups of cream cheese mixture. Add eggs; beat 1 minute at medium speed. Stir together the all-purpose flour, baking powder, baking soda, and salt. Beat into egg mixture alternately with the 1 cup milk, beating at low speed after each addition just until combined. Divide batter among three greased and floured 8×1½- or 9×1½-inch cake pans.

4 Bake in a 350° oven for 25 to 30 minutes for 8-inch pans or 22 to 25 minutes for 9-inch pans, or until a toothpick inserted near the center comes out clean. Cool in pans for 10 minutes. Remove cakes from pans; cool on racks.

5 Remove frosting from refrigerator about 30 minutes before frosting the cake. Place one cake layer on a serving plate; spread with *half* of the raspberry preserves. Top with second layer of cake; spread with remaining preserves. Top with third cake layer. Spread top and sides with frosting. Makes 12 servings.

White Chocolate Cream Cheese Cake: Prepare the cake as directed above, except substitute 5 ounces *white chocolate* for the unsweetened chocolate. If desired, garnish with *fresh raspberries, white chocolate curls,* and *powdered sugar.*

Nutrition facts per serving: 660 calories, 25 g total fat (14 g saturated fat), 103 mg cholesterol, 334 mg sodium, 109 g carbohydrate, 2 g fiber, 8 g protein.

Gingered Carrot Cake

1995

2 **cups all-purpose flour**	¾ **cup mixed dried fruit bits**
2 **cups sugar**	2 **teaspoons grated gingerroot**
2 **teaspoons baking powder**	**or ¾ teaspoon ground**
½ **teaspoon baking soda**	**ginger**
4 **beaten eggs**	1 **recipe Cream Cheese**
3 **cups finely shredded carrot**	**Frosting**
¾ **cup cooking oil**	1 **cup finely chopped pecans,**
	toasted (optional)

Moist and tender with a creamy frosting, carrot cake has been clamored for in restaurants and homes ever since the '60s. This 1995 recipe updates the classic by including mixed dried fruit bits and fresh gingerroot.

1 Grease and flour two 9×1½-inch round baking pans.* Set aside.

2 In a large mixing bowl stir together the flour, sugar, baking powder, and baking soda.

3 In a medium mixing bowl combine the eggs, carrot, oil, dried fruit bits, and gingerroot or ground ginger. Stir the egg mixture into the dry mixture. Pour into prepared pans.

4 Bake in a 350° oven 30 to 35 minutes or until wooden toothpicks inserted near centers come out clean. Cool in pans on wire racks for 10 minutes. Remove cakes from pans. Cool completely on wire racks.

5 Frost the top of 1 cake layer with some of the Cream Cheese Frosting. Top with remaining cake layer. Frost the top and side with the remaining frosting. If desired, press nuts onto the side of the cake. Cover loosely and store cake or any leftovers in the refrigerator (for up to 2 days). Makes 12 to 15 servings.

Cream Cheese Frosting: Beat together two 3-ounce packages *cream cheese*, ½ cup softened *butter* or *margarine*, and 1 tablespoon *apricot brandy* or *orange juice*. Gradually beat in enough sifted *powdered sugar* (4½ to 4¾ cups) to make frosting of spreading consistency. Stir in ½ teaspoon finely shredded *orange peel*. Makes about 2¾ cups frosting.

*Note: The 9-inch round baking pans need to be at least 1½ inches deep or the batter could flow over the sides of the pans during baking. If your round pans aren't deep enough, use 1 greased 13×9×2-inch baking pan. Prepare batter as directed above; turn into prepared pan. Bake in a 350° oven about 40 minutes or until a wooden toothpick inserted near the center comes out clean. Place pan on wire rack; cool completely. Frost with Cream Cheese Frosting. (There may be some leftover frosting if using the rectangular pan.) If desired, sprinkle with nuts. Makes 12 to 15 servings.

Nutrition facts per serving: 581 calories, 28 g total fat (7 g saturated fat), 87 mg cholesterol, 282 mg sodium, 79 g carbohydrate, 1 g fiber, 6 g protein.

Pineapple Chiffon Cake

1948

Chiffon cake, when introduced in May 1948, was the biggest cake news in a hundred years. Introducing a new method, this airy cake was beaten not creamed because it used cooking oil instead of butter or shortening. Flavors varied, but none surpassed those made with fruit juice, such as this Pineapple Chiffon Cake.

2¼ cups sifted cake flour	¾ cup unsweetened
1½ cups sugar	pineapple juice
1 tablespoon baking powder	1 cup egg whites (8 large)
¼ teaspoon salt	½ teaspoon cream of tartar
½ cup cooking oil	1 recipe Pineapple Topping
5 egg yolks	

1 In a large mixing bowl sift together cake flour, sugar, baking powder, and salt. Make well in center of dry mixture. Add oil, egg yolks, and pineapple juice. Beat with an electric mixer on low speed until combined. Beat on high speed for 5 minutes or until satin smooth.

2 Thoroughly wash beaters. In a very large mixing bowl beat egg whites and cream of tartar until stiff peaks form (tips stand straight). Pour batter in thin stream over entire surface of egg whites; fold in gently. Pour into an ungreased 10-inch tube pan.

3 Bake in a 325° oven for 65 to 70 minutes or until the top springs back when lightly touched. Immediately invert the cake (leave in pan); cool completely.

4 Remove cake from pan. Split cake horizontally into 2 layers. Fill and frost with Pineapple Topping. Makes 10 servings.

Pineapple Topping: Thoroughly drain one 20-ounce can *crushed pineapple (juice pack)*. Set aside. In a large mixing bowl beat 2 cups *whipping cream* with an electric mixer on high speed just until stiff peaks form (tips stand straight). Fold in drained pineapple.

Nutrition facts per serving: 557 calories, 31 g total fat (13 g saturated fat), 172 mg cholesterol, 230 mg sodium, 64 g carbohydrate, 1 g fiber, 8 g protein.

Vintage Views
1934

Budget Wise

The cost of food was a concern for cooks in 1934 just as today. One advertisement broke down the cost of making a cake from scratch; it came to 34 cents. Today, 63 years later, the cost would be more than 6 times greater at $2.14.

Caramel Angel Food Cake

1936

1½ cups egg whites (10 to 12 large)	2 cups sugar
¼ teaspoon cream of tartar	1½ cups sifted cake flour
1 teaspoon vanilla	1 recipe Burnt-Sugar Syrup
	1 recipe Burnt-Sugar Frosting

1 In a large mixing bowl beat together egg whites, cream of tartar, and vanilla until stiff peaks form (tips stand straight).

2 Sift together sugar and cake flour twice. Sift sugar mixture, one-fourth at a time, over beaten egg whites; fold in. Carefully fold in ¼ cup of the Burnt-Sugar Syrup. Spoon into ungreased 10-inch tube pan.

3 Bake in a 375° oven about 40 minutes or until top springs back when lightly touched. Immediately invert the cake (leave in pan); cool completely. Remove cake from pan. Frost with Burnt-Sugar Frosting. Makes 12 servings.

Burnt-Sugar Syrup: In a heavy skillet cook ¾ cup *sugar* over medium-high heat until sugar begins to melt, shaking the skillet occasionally to heat the sugar evenly. *Do not stir.* Once the sugar starts to melt, reduce heat to low and cook about 5 minutes more or until all of the sugar is melted and golden brown, stirring as needed with a wooden spoon. When a deep golden brown, remove syrup from heat. Slowly add 1 cup *boiling water.* Cook and stir over medium heat about 7 minutes more or until sugar dissolves and syrup is reduced to ½ cup. Cool.

Burnt-Sugar Frosting: In the top of a double boiler (not over boiling water) place 1¼ cups *sugar,* 2 *egg whites,* ¼ cup *Burnt-Sugar Syrup,* ¼ cup *cold water,* ¼ teaspoon *cream of tartar,* and dash *salt.* Beat with an electric mixer on low speed for 30 seconds or until combined. Place the mixture over, *but not touching,* boiling water. Cook, beating constantly with the electric mixer on high speed, about 7 minutes or until frosting forms stiff peaks (tips stand straight).

♥ *Nutrition facts per serving: 325 calories, 0 g total fat (0 g saturated fat), 0 mg cholesterol, 68 mg sodium, 78 g carbohydrate, 0 g fiber, 5 g protein.*

When we first published this recipe, Caramel Angel Food Cake was already a Sigma Nu legend as the cake that housemothers made for homesick college boys. Our instructions included the admonition that making angel food cake takes a gentle touch.

Italian Crème Cake

1991

½ cup butter or margarine, softened	¼ teaspoon baking soda
⅓ cup shortening	¾ cup buttermilk
1¾ cups sugar	¾ cup finely chopped pecans
4 egg yolks	4 egg whites
1 teaspoon vanilla	1 recipe Cream Cheese Frosting
1¾ cups all-purpose flour	½ cup coconut, toasted
1½ teaspoons baking powder	Pecan halves (optional)

Kitty Crider of Austin, Texas, sent us this pecan cake in 1991 when we solicited the best-loved potluck recipes in America. She says it's a surefire hit at her family's O'Kelly/Therrell reunion. A magazine staff editor voted it as tops, too.

1 Grease and flour three 8×1½-inch or 9×1½-inch round baking pans.* Set aside.

2 In a large mixing bowl beat butter or margarine and shortening with an electric mixer until combined. Add sugar; beat on medium speed until mixture is light and fluffy. Add egg yolks and vanilla; beat well.

3 In a medium mixing bowl combine flour, baking powder, and soda. Add dry mixture and buttermilk alternately to beaten mixture, beating on low speed after each addition just until combined. Stir in pecans.

4 Thoroughly wash the beaters. In a medium mixing bowl beat egg whites with an electric mixer on high speed until stiff peaks form (tips stand straight). Stir about one-third of the egg whites into the cake batter. Fold in remaining whites. Pour batter evenly into prepared pans.

5 Bake in a 350° oven for 25 to 30 minutes for 8-inch pans (or 18 to 22 minutes for 9-inch pans) or until wooden toothpicks inserted near centers come out clean. Cool on wire racks for 10 minutes. Remove from pans. Cool completely on wire racks.

6 Frost the top of 1 cake layer with Cream Cheese Frosting. Top with another layer, frost, and then top with the last layer. Frost top and side of cake with remaining frosting. Sprinkle top with toasted coconut. If desired, garnish with pecan halves. Cover loosely and store cake or any leftovers in the refrigerator for up to 2 days. Makes 14 servings.

Cream Cheese Frosting: In a medium bowl beat together 12 ounces *cream cheese*, 6 tablespoons *butter* or *margarine*, and 1½ teaspoons *vanilla* until smooth. Gradually add enough *powdered sugar* (6 to 7 cups) to make of spreading consistency, beating until smooth. Makes 4 cups.

*Note: If desired, the cake may be baked in 1 greased 13×9×2-inch baking pan instead of the round pans. Prepare batter as directed above; turn into prepared pan. Bake in a 350° oven for 35 to 40 minutes or until cake tests done. Place pan on wire rack; cool completely. Frost cake with a *half* recipe of the Cream Cheese Frosting. Sprinkle with toasted coconut. If desired, garnish with pecan halves. Makes 14 servings.

Nutrition facts per serving: 623 calories, 31 g total fat (15 g saturated fat), 119 mg cholesterol, 287 mg sodium, 83 g carbohydrate, 1 g fiber, 6 g protein.

Sugar-Saving Semisweets

1942

Due to rationing during the war in the 1940s, sugar was scarce. Recipes were found in the magazine at that time to help cut back on the amount of sugar used so sweets wouldn't be forgotten. Over the years, our Test Kitchen has developed dozens of tricks for making first-class cookies. To keep slice-and-bake cookies, such as these, perfectly round, they suggest sliding the wrapped log of dough into a round drinking glass before chilling it in the refrigerator. As you slice the chilled log, rotate it to avoid cookies with flat sides.

½ cup shortening
⅓ cup sugar
1 egg
1½ teaspoons finely shredded orange peel
1 tablespoon orange juice or water

1⅓ cups all-purpose flour
⅛ teaspoon baking soda
⅛ teaspoon salt
3 ounces semisweet chocolate, finely shredded
¼ cup finely chopped walnuts

1 In a large mixing bowl beat shortening and sugar until light. Beat in egg, orange peel, and orange juice or water.

2 In a small mixing bowl combine flour, soda, and salt; add to beaten mixture. Mix well. Stir in chocolate and nuts. Shape into a 10-inch-long log. Wrap and refrigerate for 1 hour or until firm enough to slice.

3 Using a thin-bladed knife, cut dough into ¼-inch-thick slices. Place on ungreased cookie sheets. Bake in a 350° oven 10 to 12 minutes or until edges are firm. Cool on wire racks. Makes 40 cookies.

♥ *Nutrition facts per cookie: 60 calories, 4 g total fat (1 g saturated fat), 5 mg cholesterol, 6 mg sodium, 6 g carbohydrate, 0 g fiber, 1 g protein.*

Vintage Views
1922

Recipes from Yesteryear

In 1922, *Better Homes and Gardens* magazine was known as *Fruit, Garden and Home*. Recipes weren't plentiful on our pages during the early years, and those that were included appeared as mere nuggets of ideas, as this recipe illustrates:

"Oatmeal cookies are especially popular with children and a good addition to luncheon dishes. To one cupful of sugar, add one-half cupful of butter, one-half cupful of drippings, two eggs, five tablespoonfuls of sour milk in which one teaspoonful of soda has been dissolved, two cupfuls of oatmeal and two cupfuls of flour. Roll until one-eighth inch in thickness, cut into rectangles, and bake upon a baking sheet until a light brown."

Fudge 'n' Nut Brownies

1995

1¾ cups sugar
1 cup butter or margarine, softened
4 eggs
2 teaspoons vanilla
1 13½-ounce jar (1¼ cups) fudge ice cream topping
2 cups chopped pecans or walnuts
1½ cups all-purpose flour
⅓ cup sifted unsweetened cocoa powder
¼ teaspoon baking powder

1 Grease a 13×9×2-inch baking pan. Set aside.

2 In a large mixing bowl combine the sugar, butter or margarine, eggs, and vanilla. Beat with a wooden spoon or with an electric mixer on medium speed until thoroughly combined. (Mixture will look curdled.) Stir in fudge topping. Stir in nuts, flour, cocoa powder, and baking powder until combined. Pour into prepared pan.

3 Bake in a 350° oven about 50 minutes or until a wooden toothpick inserted near the center comes out clean. Cool on a wire rack. Cut into bars. Makes 48 brownies.

Nutrition facts per serving: 140 calories, 8 g total fat (3 g saturated fat), 28 mg cholesterol, 52 mg sodium, 15 g carbohydrate, 0 g fiber, 2 g protein.

Brownies, the nutty chocolate cookies adored throughout this country, evolved from cocoa scones, a variation of Scottish tea cakes. But in Australia, a brownie isn't a cookie at all. It's a raisin bread traditionally served on cattle ranches at a "smoke oh," or morning break.

Trilevel Brownies

1963

In 1989, our magazine selected the 30 best recipes from our Test Kitchen's first 60 years. This moist brownie with two layers of chocolate over a chewy oat base was selected as one of the all-time greatest recipes from 1963 (pictured on page 149 on leaf-shaped plate).

1	cup quick-cooking rolled oats
½	cup all-purpose flour
½	cup packed brown sugar
¼	teaspoon baking soda
½	cup margarine or butter, melted
1	egg
¾	cup granulated sugar
⅔	cup all-purpose flour
¼	cup milk
¼	cup margarine or butter, melted

1	ounce unsweetened chocolate, melted and cooled
1	teaspoon vanilla
¼	teaspoon baking powder
½	cup chopped walnuts
1	ounce unsweetened chocolate
2	tablespoons margarine or butter
1½	cups sifted powdered sugar
½	teaspoon vanilla
	Walnut halves (optional)

1 For bottom layer, stir together oats, the ½ cup flour, the brown sugar, and baking soda. Stir in the ½ cup melted margarine or butter. Pat mixture into the bottom of an ungreased 11×7×1½-inch baking pan. Bake in a 350° oven for 10 minutes.

2 Meanwhile, for middle layer, stir together egg, granulated sugar, the ⅔ cup flour, the milk, the ¼ cup melted margarine or butter, 1 ounce melted chocolate, the 1 teaspoon vanilla, and the baking powder until smooth. Fold in chopped walnuts. Spread batter over baked layer in pan. Bake about 25 minutes more or until a wooden toothpick inserted in center comes out clean. Set on a wire rack while preparing top layer.

3 For top layer, in a medium saucepan heat and stir the 1 ounce chocolate and the 2 tablespoons margarine or butter until melted. Stir in the powdered sugar and the ½ teaspoon vanilla. Stir in enough *hot water* (1 to 2 tablespoons) to make a mixture that is almost pourable. Spread over brownies. If desired, garnish with walnut halves. Cool completely on wire rack. Cut into bars. Makes 32 brownies.

Nutrition facts per brownie: 141 calories, 7 g total fat (2 g saturated fat), 7 mg cholesterol, 76 mg sodium, 18 g carbohydrate, 1 g fiber, 2 g protein.

Pictured clockwise from glass container: **Double Chocolate Chunk Biscotti,** *recipe on page 156;* **Chocolate Revel Bars,** *recipe on page 151;* **Toffee Triangles,** *recipe on page 150;* **Trilevel Brownies,** *recipe above*

Toffee Triangles

1995

These coffeehouse pleasures from our February 1995 issue are perfect when you want to take treats to work, school, or a potluck, or give them as a gift during the holiday. Not only are they quick to fix, but the four layers of toffee and chocolate make the bars irresistible to all ages (pictured on page 149).

¾ **cup butter or margarine**
¾ **cup packed brown sugar**
1 **egg yolk**
1½ **cups all-purpose flour**
¼ **teaspoon salt**
1 **14-ounce can (1¼ cups) sweetened condensed milk**

2 **tablespoons butter or margarine**
2 **teaspoons vanilla**
1 **12-ounce package (2 cups) semisweet chocolate pieces**
1 **cup almond brickle pieces or toasted chopped pecans**

1 Grease a 13×9×2-inch baking pan. Set aside.

2 In a large mixing bowl beat the ¾ cup butter or margarine and the brown sugar with an electric mixer on medium speed until combined. Add the egg yolk; beat well. Using a spoon, stir in the flour and salt until well mixed. Using floured hands, press the dough into the bottom of the prepared pan. Bake in a 350° oven about 20 minutes or until light brown. Set on a wire rack while preparing the filling.

3 For filling, in a heavy medium saucepan heat and stir the sweetened condensed milk and the 2 tablespoons butter or margarine over medium heat until bubbly. Cook and stir for 5 minutes more. (Mixture will thicken and become smooth.) Stir in the vanilla. Spread filling over the baked layer. Bake for 12 to 15 minutes more or until top layer is golden brown.

4 Sprinkle the baked layers evenly with semisweet chocolate pieces. Bake for 1 to 2 minutes more or until chocolate pieces are shiny and melted. Remove from oven; set on a wire rack. Using a flexible spatula, immediately spread the chocolate evenly over baked layers. Sprinkle with brickle pieces or pecans. Cool completely on wire rack. Cover and refrigerate until chocolate is set.

5 To cut triangles, cut into rectangles (about 3×2 inches each), then cut each rectangle diagonally. Cover and store any leftover triangles in the refrigerator for up to 1 week. Makes about 36 triangles.

To make ahead: Place uncut or cut cookies in a freezer container; freeze for up to 3 months. Thaw at room temperature before serving.

Nutrition facts per triangle: 177 calories, 10 g total fat (3 g saturated fat), 23 mg cholesterol, 95 mg sodium, 22 g carbohydrate, 0 g fiber, 2 g protein.

Chocolate Revel Bars

★
1971

1 cup butter or margarine
2 cups packed brown sugar
2 eggs
2 teaspoons vanilla
2½ cups all-purpose flour
1 teaspoon baking soda
3 cups quick-cooking
   rolled oats

1 14-ounce (1¼ cups) can
   sweetened condensed
   milk
1 12-ounce package (2 cups)
   semisweet chocolate
   pieces
1 cup chopped walnuts
2 teaspoons vanilla

These bars are an all-time favorite of many people on the Better Homes and Gardens staff. Karen Pollock, editorial assistant for the magazine's food editors, submitted this cookie as her favorite recipe of all (pictured on page 149).

1 Set aside *2 tablespoons* of the butter or margarine. In a large mixing bowl beat the remaining butter or margarine with an electric mixer on medium speed for 30 seconds. Add brown sugar; beat until well mixed. Beat in eggs and 2 teaspoons vanilla. In another large bowl stir together flour and baking soda; stir in oats. Gradually stir dry mixture into beaten mixture. Set aside.

2 In a medium saucepan combine the reserved butter or margarine, the sweetened condensed milk, and chocolate pieces. Cook over low heat until chocolate melts, stirring occasionally. Remove from heat. Stir in walnuts and the 2 teaspoons vanilla.

3 Press two-thirds (about 3⅓ cups) of the oat mixture into the bottom of an ungreased 15×10×1-inch baking pan. Spread chocolate mixture over the oat mixture. Using your fingers, dot remaining oat mixture over the chocolate.

4 Bake in a 350° oven about 25 minutes or until top is lightly browned (chocolate mixture will still look moist). Cool on a wire rack. Cut into 2×1-inch bars. Makes about 75 bars.

Nutrition facts per bar: 117 calories, 6 g total fat (2 g saturated fat), 14 mg cholesterol, 52 mg sodium, 16 g carbohydrate, 0 g fiber, 2 g protein.

1981

Chocolate-Cherry Cookies

Mabel L. Leishman of Traverse City, Michigan, submitted this recipe as her first-choice cookie from over the years. She wrote to tell us, "My family and friends have enjoyed this cookie for the holidays as well as all year long." What makes them so different is that they're frosted before they're baked.

1½ cups all-purpose flour
½ cup unsweetened cocoa
    powder
½ cup butter or margarine
1 cup sugar
¼ teaspoon salt
¼ teaspoon baking powder
¼ teaspoon baking soda
1 egg

1½ teaspoons vanilla
48 undrained maraschino
    cherries (about one
    10-ounce jar)*
1 6-ounce package semisweet
    chocolate pieces**
½ cup sweetened condensed
    milk

1 In a medium mixing bowl combine flour and cocoa powder. Set aside. In a large mixing bowl beat butter or margarine with an electric mixer on medium speed for 30 seconds. Add sugar, salt, baking powder, and baking soda. Beat until well mixed. Add egg and vanilla; beat well. Gradually beat in dry mixture.

2 Shape dough into 1-inch balls; place on ungreased cookie sheets. Press down center of each ball with thumb. Drain maraschino cherries, reserving juice. Place one cherry in the center of each cookie.

3 For frosting, in a small saucepan combine chocolate pieces and sweetened condensed milk. Heat and stir over medium heat until chocolate is melted. Stir in 4 teaspoons of the reserved cherry juice. Spoon about 1 teaspoon frosting over each cherry, spreading to cover cherry. (If necessary, frosting may be thinned with additional cherry juice.)

4 Bake in a 350° oven about 10 minutes or until edges are firm. Transfer to wire racks and let cool. Makes 48 cookies.

*Note: Depending on size of cherries, you might need more than 1 jar.

**Note: Use only the real semisweet chocolate pieces.

♥ *Nutrition facts per cookie: 82 calories, 3 g total fat (1 g saturated fat), 11 mg cholesterol, 45 mg sodium, 13 g carbohydrate, 0 g fiber, 1 g protein.*

Brown Sugar Hazelnut Rounds

1993

½ cup shortening
½ cup butter or margarine
2½ cups all-purpose flour
1¼ cups packed brown sugar
1 egg
1 teaspoon vanilla
½ teaspoon baking soda
¼ teaspoon salt
¾ cup ground hazelnuts or pecans, toasted

⅓ cup finely chopped hazelnuts or pecans, toasted (optional)
1 recipe Confectioners' Icing (optional)
Finely chopped hazelnuts or almonds, toasted (optional)
Milk chocolate, melted (optional)

This versatile recipe can be decorated in any of several ways. You can coat the logs with nuts, dip the cookies in melted chocolate, and/or drizzle the rounds with Confectioners' Icing.

1 In a large mixing bowl beat shortening and butter or margarine with an electric mixer on medium speed for 30 seconds. Add *about 1 cup* of the flour to the shortening mixture. Add brown sugar, egg, vanilla, baking soda, and salt. Beat until well mixed, scraping side of bowl occasionally. Beat or stir in the remaining flour and the ¾ cup ground hazelnuts or pecans.

2 Divide the dough in half. On waxed paper, shape each half of the dough into a 10-inch-long log. (Lift and smooth the waxed paper to help shape the roll.) If desired, roll 1 of the logs in the ⅓ cup chopped nuts. Wrap each roll in waxed paper or plastic wrap. Refrigerate for 4 to 48 hours or until firm enough to slice. (Or, wrap dough in foil and freeze for up to 3 months; thaw in the refrigerator before slicing and baking.)

3 Using a thin-bladed knife, cut dough into ¼-inch-thick slices. Place slices 1 inch apart on ungreased cookie sheets. Bake in a 375° oven for 10 minutes or until edges are firm. Transfer to wire racks and let cool.

4 If desired, decorate some of the cookies with Confectioners' Icing by drizzling icing over cookies; sprinkle with chopped nuts. Or, if desired, dip cookies without nuts on the edges in melted chocolate, dipping about half of each cookie; sprinkle with chopped nuts, or pipe or drizzle Confectioners' Icing over cookies. Makes about 60 cookies.

Confectioners' Icing: In a small mixing bowl stir together 1 cup sifted *powdered sugar*, ½ teaspoon *vanilla* or ¼ teaspoon *maple flavoring*, and enough *milk* (4 to 5 teaspoons) to make of drizzling consistency.

♥ *Nutrition facts per cookie: 70 calories, 4 g total fat (1 g saturated fat), 8 mg cholesterol, 37 mg sodium, 7 g carbohydrate, 0 g fiber, 1 g protein.*

Big Soft Ginger Cookies

1989

Winnifred Jardine of Salt Lake City, a grandmother herself, shared her special Christmas recipes with Better Homes and Gardens readers in a holiday baking story called "Holiday Sweets—With Love from Grandma's Kitchen." Winnifred's recipe for these flavorful cookies also is popular with our Test Kitchen director Sharon Stilwell.

2¼ cups all-purpose flour	¾ cup butter, margarine, or shortening
2 teaspoons ground ginger	
1 teaspoon baking soda	1 cup sugar
¾ teaspoon ground cinnamon	1 egg
	¼ cup molasses
½ teaspoon ground cloves	2 tablespoons sugar

1 In a medium mixing bowl combine flour, ginger, baking soda, cinnamon, and cloves. Set aside.

2 In a large mixing bowl beat butter, margarine, or shortening with an electric mixer on low speed for 30 seconds. Gradually add the 1 cup sugar; beat until fluffy. Add the egg and molasses; beat well. Stir dry mixture into egg mixture.

3 Shape dough into 1½-inch balls (1 heaping tablespoon dough each). Roll balls in the 2 tablespoons sugar and place on ungreased cookie sheets about 2½ inches apart.

4 Bake in a 350° oven about 10 minutes or until light brown but still puffed. *(Do not overbake.)* Let stand on cookie sheets for 2 minutes; transfer to a wire rack and let cool. Makes 24 cookies.

Nutrition facts per cookie: 138 calories, 6 g total fat (4 g saturated fat), 24 mg cholesterol, 114 g sodium, 20 g carbohydrate, 0 g fiber, 1 g protein.

Baking with Margarine

For decades, we used butter or margarine interchangeably in our recipes for baked goods. But in the '90s, the proliferation of dozens of margarine-type products has made the situation a bit more complicated. Not all margarine-type products are an acceptable substitute for butter in baked items. For best results when using margarine, choose stick margarine that contains at least 60-percent vegetable oil. Spreads with less than 60-percent vegetable oil have a high water content and do not give satisfactory results. Also, avoid spreads labeled diet, whipped, liquid, or soft. They're intended for table use not for baking.

Frosted Butterscotch Cookies

1938

2½ cups all-purpose flour
½ teaspoon salt
1 teaspoon baking soda
½ teaspoon baking powder
1½ cups packed brown sugar
½ cup shortening
2 eggs
1 teaspoon vanilla
1 8-ounce carton dairy
   sour cream
⅔ cup chopped walnuts
1 recipe Browned Butter
   Frosting
   Chopped walnuts or
   walnut halves (optional)

Our taste panelists described these cookies, submitted as a favorite by reader Maurine Miller Welch of Florida, as "wonderful." Maurine wrote, "I have had many requests for this recipe. Even recently, a granddaughter phoned from Maryland wanting the recipe. She had remembered this cookie from her childhood when she spent time with us."

1 Grease cookie sheets. Set aside.

2 In a medium mixing bowl stir together flour, salt, baking soda, and baking powder. Set aside. In large mixing bowl beat the brown sugar and shortening with an electric mixer on medium speed until well mixed. Add eggs and vanilla. Beat until well mixed. Add dry mixture and sour cream alternately to beaten mixture, beating after each addition. Stir in nuts.

3 Drop dough by rounded teaspoons 2 inches apart onto prepared cookie sheets. Bake in a 375° oven for 10 to 12 minutes or until edges are lightly browned. Transfer to a wire rack and let cool. Spread cooled cookies with Browned Butter Frosting. If desired, top with additional chopped walnuts or walnut halves. Makes about 60 cookies.

Browned Butter Frosting: In a medium saucepan heat and stir ½ cup *butter (no substitutes)* over medium-low heat until golden brown. *(Do not scorch.)* Remove from heat. Stir in 3½ cups sifted *powdered sugar*, 5 teaspoons *boiling water*, and 1½ teaspoons *vanilla*. Beat until frosting is easy to spread. Immediately spread on cookies. If frosting begins to set up, stir in a small amount of additional *boiling water*. Makes about 1⅓ cups frosting.

♥ *Nutrition facts per cookie: 105 calories, 5 g total fat (2 g saturated fat), 13 mg cholesterol, 63 mg sodium, 14 g carbohydrate, 0 g fiber, 1 g protein.*

Double Chocolate Chunk Biscotti

1995

A traditional Italian treat, biscotti are popular today in coffeehouses across the country. They're baked twice, which makes them extra crisp and crunchy—perfect for dipping into coffee. Some consider them the adult cookie of the '90s (pictured on page 149).

⅓ cup butter or margarine
⅔ cup sugar
¼ cup unsweetened cocoa powder
2 teaspoons baking powder
2 eggs

1¾ cups all-purpose flour
4 ounces white baking bar, coarsely chopped
3 ounces semisweet chocolate, chopped

1 Lightly grease a large cookie sheet. Set aside.

2 In a large mixing bowl beat butter or margarine with an electric mixer on medium speed for 30 seconds. Add the sugar, cocoa powder, and baking powder; beat until combined. Beat in the eggs. Beat in as much of the flour as you can. Using a spoon, stir in any remaining flour, white baking bar, and semisweet chocolate.

3 Divide dough in half. Shape each half into a 9-inch-long log. Place logs about 4 inches apart on prepared cookie sheet. Flatten logs slightly until about 2 inches wide.

4 Bake logs in a 375° oven for 20 to 25 minutes or until a wooden toothpick inserted near the centers comes out clean. Cool on the cookie sheet set on a wire rack for 1 hour. Using a serrated knife, cut each log diagonally into ½-inch-thick slices. Lay slices, cut sides down, on ungreased cookie sheets.

5 Bake slices in a 325° oven for 8 minutes. Turn slices over. Bake for 7 to 9 minutes more or until slices are dry and crisp. *(Do not overbake.)* Transfer to wire racks and let cool. Store in an airtight container at room temperature for up to 1 week. Makes about 32 biscotti.

To make ahead: Place cooled biscotti in a freezer container and freeze for up to 3 months. Thaw at room temperature before serving.

♥ *Nutrition facts per biscotti: 87 calories, 4 g total fat (2 g saturated fat), 19 mg cholesterol, 49 mg sodium, 11 g carbohydrate, 0 g fiber, 2 g protein.*

Memorable Main Dishes

Boursin-Stuffed Chicken

1986

The "Be an Outstanding Cook!" article in our February 1986 issue shared with readers the secret to making chicken bundles: It's all in how you pound the chicken. Using the flat side of a meat mallet, pound each chicken breast from the center to the edges until it is an even thickness.

4 medium skinless, boneless chicken breast halves (about 1 pound total)
1 5.2-ounce package Boursin cheese with garlic and herbs, softened
1 tablespoon all-purpose flour

¼ cup shredded carrot
¼ cup coarsely chopped walnuts
¼ cup snipped parsley
¼ cup fine dry bread crumbs
2 tablespoons grated Parmesan cheese
1 tablespoon milk

1 Rinse the chicken; pat dry with paper towels. Place each chicken breast half between 2 pieces of heavy plastic wrap. Working from center to the edges, pound lightly with the flat side of a meat mallet to ¼ to ⅛ inch thickness. Remove plastic wrap.

2 In a small mixing bowl stir together the Boursin cheese and flour until smooth. Stir in the carrot, walnuts, and *2 tablespoons* of the snipped parsley. Place one-fourth of the cheese mixture on each pounded chicken breast half.

3 To roll up the chicken, fold in 2 opposite sides, then roll up. Press edges to seal. Repeat to make 4 bundles.

4 For coating, in a small mixing bowl stir together the remaining parsley, the fine dry bread crumbs, and Parmesan cheese. Brush the chicken bundles with the milk. Roll bundles in the crumb mixture to coat. Place chicken bundles, seam sides down, on a wire rack in an 8×8×2-inch baking pan. Sprinkle with any remaining crumb mixture.

5 Bake in a 350° oven for 40 to 45 minutes or until the chicken juices run clear and coating mixture is golden brown. Makes 4 servings.

♥*Nutrition facts per serving: 287 calories, 15 g total fat (6 g saturated fat), 65 mg cholesterol, 278 mg sodium, 11 g carbohydrate, 1 g fiber, 28 g protein.*

Chicken Vegetable Bake

2½ pounds meaty chicken
    pieces (breasts, thighs,
    and drumsticks)
½ cup all-purpose flour
1 tablespoon paprika
½ teaspoon salt
¼ teaspoon pepper
2 tablespoons cooking oil
1 cup sliced fresh
    mushrooms

1 tablespoon brown sugar
¼ teaspoon ground ginger
    Dash salt
¾ cup water
⅓ cup frozen orange juice
    concentrate, thawed
1½ cups coarsely chopped
    carrot
1 cup frozen small whole
    onions

1 Skin the chicken; rinse chicken and pat dry with paper towels. Place the flour, paprika, the ½ teaspoon salt, and the pepper in a plastic bag. Add chicken, a few pieces at a time, and shake to coat. Set aside 2 tablespoons of the flour mixture.

2 In a 12-inch skillet heat oil over medium heat. Add chicken and cook, uncovered, for 10 minutes, turning to brown evenly. Remove chicken from skillet, reserving 2 tablespoons drippings. Place chicken in a 3-quart rectangular baking dish. Set aside.

3 Add mushrooms to drippings in skillet. Cook and stir, scraping up browned bits, until mushrooms are tender. Stir in the reserved flour mixture, the brown sugar, ginger, and the dash salt. Add the water and orange juice concentrate all at once. Cook and stir until thickened and bubbly. Stir in carrot and onions. Pour sauce over chicken in baking dish.

4 Cover and bake in a 350° oven about 1 hour or until chicken is no longer pink and vegetables are tender. Makes 6 servings.

♥ *Nutrition facts per serving: 265 calories, 10 g total fat (2 g saturated fat), 60 mg cholesterol, 285 mg sodium, 22 g carbohydrate, 2 g fiber, 22 g protein.*

Marge Canfield writes us from St. Augustine, Florida: "In 1965, we lived in Vestal, New York, and had a houseful of growing children. Chicken Vegetable Bake became an immediate 'keeper' the first time we tried it. Now, in our retired years here in Florida, we still use this recipe. I keep an extra copy in my recipe box in our motor home so when we are traveling, I share it with new friends. We think it's a real gem."

1985

Coq au Vin Rosettes

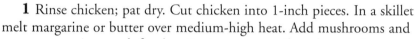

A favorite for extra-special dinner parties, this elegant entrée features rings of lasagna noodles fashioned into rosettes. The reader who sent it in to us, Rosemarie Godfrey of Sussex, New Jersey, says she makes the dish for Christmas Eve dinner.

8 medium skinless, boneless chicken breast halves
2 tablespoons margarine or butter
3 cups sliced fresh mushrooms (8 ounces)
½ cup chopped onion
¾ cup dry white wine
½ teaspoon dried tarragon, crushed
½ teaspoon white pepper
8 lasagna noodles

1 8-ounce package cream cheese, cut up
½ cup dairy sour cream
2 tablespoons all-purpose flour
½ cup half-and-half, light cream, or milk
1 cup shredded Gruyère cheese (4 ounces)
1 cup shredded Muenster cheese (4 ounces)
Slivered almonds, toasted (optional)

1 Rinse chicken; pat dry. Cut chicken into 1-inch pieces. In a skillet melt margarine or butter over medium-high heat. Add mushrooms and onion; cook for 4 to 5 minutes or until tender, stirring occasionally. Add chicken, wine, tarragon, white pepper, and ⅛ teaspoon *salt*. Bring just to boiling; reduce heat. Simmer, covered, for 5 minutes, stirring once. Remove from heat.

2 Meanwhile, cook lasagna noodles according to package directions. Halve each noodle lengthwise. Curl each noodle half into a 2½-inch-diameter ring and place, cut side down, in a 3-quart rectangular baking dish. Using a slotted spoon, spoon chicken mixture into center of lasagna rings, reserving the liquid in skillet. Add the cream cheese to reserved liquid; heat and stir just until cream cheese is melted.

3 In a small bowl stir together sour cream and flour; stir in half-and-half, cream, or milk. Add to the mixture in skillet along with cheeses. Cook and stir over medium heat until thickened and bubbly. Spoon cream cheese mixture over rings. If desired, sprinkle with slivered almonds.

4 Bake, covered, in a 325° oven for 35 minutes or until heated through. Makes 8 servings.

For a lower-fat version: Use reduced-fat cream cheese, light dairy sour cream, and milk in place of regular cream cheese, regular dairy sour cream, and half-and-half.

Nutrition facts per serving: 515 calories, 30 g total fat (16 g saturated fat), 132 mg cholesterol, 358 mg sodium, 21 g carbohydrate, 1 g fiber, 36 g protein.
Lower-fat version: 466 calories, 23 g total fat (12 g saturated fat), 114 mg cholesterol, 397 mg sodium, 23 g carbohydrate, 1 g fiber, 36 g protein.

French Farmhouse Garlic Chicken

1996

4 small boneless, skinless
chicken breast halves
(about 12 ounces total)
¼ teaspoon salt
¼ teaspoon pepper
1 tablespoon cooking oil
40 small cloves unpeeled
garlic*
½ cup dry white wine or
chicken broth

½ cup chicken broth
1 tablespoon lemon juice
1 teaspoon dried basil,
crushed
½ teaspoon dried oregano,
crushed
4 teaspoons all-purpose flour
2 tablespoons dry white wine
or chicken broth
Mashed potatoes or rice
(optional)

From the story "Kitchen Comforts" in February 1996 comes this version of a French favorite. Don't be alarmed by the large amount of garlic in this recipe. Cooking garlic makes it sweet and delicious. Garlic once was believed to have the magical ability to repel evil spirits and keep vampires at bay. Ancient Greek and Egyptian writings touted garlic as a tonic for many ailments. Today, garlic is still said to have numerous curative attributes—from combating heart disease to lowering blood pressure.

1 Rinse chicken; pat dry with paper towels. Season with salt and pepper. In a 10-inch skillet heat oil over medium-high heat. Add chicken and garlic cloves. Cook chicken for 2 to 3 minutes on each side or just until brown, turning once. Slowly add the ½ cup wine or broth, the ½ cup broth, the lemon juice, basil, and oregano. Cover and simmer for 6 to 8 minutes or until chicken is tender and no longer pink.

2 Using a slotted spoon, transfer chicken and garlic to a warm serving platter; keep warm.

3 In a small bowl stir together the flour and the 2 tablespoons wine or broth. Stir into pan juices. Bring to boiling. Cook and stir for 1 minute more. Spoon over chicken. If desired, serve with mashed potatoes or rice. Makes 4 servings.

*Note: If you prefer, peel the garlic before cooking (use the flat side of a large knife to mash them slightly, then peel off the skins). Or, as you eat the cooked cloves, simply slip the skins off with the tip of your dinner knife.

♥*Nutrition facts per serving: 327 calories, 7 g total fat (2 g saturated fat), 48 mg cholesterol, 755 mg sodium, 40 g carbohydrate, 2 g fiber, 22 g protein.*

Peanut-Ginger Chicken with California Salsa

1992

12 chicken thighs (about
  3 pounds total), skinned
½ cup hot water
½ cup creamy peanut butter
¼ cup chili sauce
¼ cup soy sauce
2 tablespoons cooking oil
2 tablespoons vinegar
4 cloves garlic, minced
2 teaspoons grated
  gingerroot or ½ teaspoon
  ground ginger
¼ teaspoon ground red
  pepper

1 cup chopped fresh fruit
  (such as peeled peaches,
  nectarines, pears, or
  plums)
1 cup chopped, seeded
  cucumber
2 tablespoons thinly sliced
  green onion
2 tablespoons snipped
  parsley or fresh cilantro
1 tablespoon sugar
1 tablespoon cooking oil
1 tablespoon vinegar
  Ti leaves (optional)
  Hot cooked rice (optional)

Our 1992 Great American Barbecue Contest prompted Leisla Sansom from Alexandria, Virginia, to enter this sophisticated dish—and win top prize. "Cooking is an escape for me," admits Leisla. "The fruity cucumber sauce and gingery chicken remind me of the delicious spice combinations used on faraway tropical islands."

1 Rinse chicken; pat dry with paper towels. Place chicken in a large plastic bag set in a large, deep bowl.

2 For marinade, in a small mixing bowl gradually stir hot water into peanut butter. (The mixture will stiffen at first.) Stir in the chili sauce, soy sauce, the 2 tablespoons oil, the 2 tablespoons vinegar, the garlic, gingerroot or ground ginger, and ground red pepper.

3 Pour marinade over chicken. Seal the bag and turn to coat chicken thighs with marinade. Marinate in the refrigerator for 12 to 24 hours, turning the bag occasionally.

4 For salsa, in a medium mixing bowl combine the chopped fruit, cucumber, green onion, parsley or cilantro, sugar, the 1 tablespoon oil, and the 1 tablespoon vinegar. Cover and refrigerate for 1 to 2 hours.

5 In a covered grill arrange medium-hot coals around a drip pan. Test for medium heat above the pan. Remove chicken from marinade; discard marinade. Place chicken on the grill rack over the drip pan but not over the coals. Lower the grill hood. Grill chicken for 35 to 45 minutes or until chicken is tender and no longer pink.

6 If desired, serve chicken on ti leaves. Spoon some of the salsa over chicken; pass the remaining salsa. If desired, serve with hot cooked rice. Makes 6 servings.

Nutrition facts per serving: 308 calories, 17 g total fat (4 g saturated fat), 98 mg cholesterol, 324 mg sodium, 8 g carbohydrate, 1 g fiber, 29 g protein.

Cumin Chicken with Hot-Citrus Salsa

1993

Recipe contests help us keep in touch with our readers and learn what they are cooking in their own kitchens. The recipes sent in by readers reflect what they like, how they cook, and how they've incorporated new or somewhat unfamiliar products into their cooking. This prizewinning chicken dish shows how international ingredients have influenced the way we cook today—ginger, cilantro, cumin, and jalapeño peppers have become mainstream ingredients for many cooks.

4 **dried tomato halves (not oil-packed)**
½ **cup boiling water**
1 **medium orange**
2 **teaspoons snipped fresh cilantro, fresh basil, or parsley**
1 **teaspoon grated gingerroot**
½ **teaspoon finely chopped jalapeño pepper***

2 **medium skinless, boneless chicken breast halves (about ½ pound total)**
¾ **teaspoon ground cumin**
⅛ **teaspoon salt**
⅛ **teaspoon black pepper**
1 **tablespoon cooking oil**
Hot cooked rice

1 For salsa, in a small mixing bowl combine the tomatoes and boiling water. Let stand 10 minutes. Drain; chop tomatoes. Peel and chop the orange, reserving about 2 teaspoons of the juice. In a medium mixing bowl combine tomatoes, chopped orange, reserved orange juice, cilantro, gingerroot, and jalapeño pepper. Set aside.

2 Rinse chicken; pat dry with paper towels. Place each breast half between 2 pieces of heavy plastic wrap. Working from center to edges, pound lightly with the flat side of a meat mallet to ¼ inch thickness. Remove plastic wrap. In a small mixing bowl combine cumin, salt, and black pepper; rub on both sides of chicken.

3 In a 10-inch skillet cook chicken in hot oil over medium heat about 3 minutes per side or until chicken is no longer pink. To serve, spoon salsa over chicken. Serve with hot cooked rice. Makes 2 servings.

***Note:** Protect your hands when working with hot peppers by wearing plastic or rubber gloves or working with plastic bags on your hands. If your bare hands touch the peppers, wash your hands and nails thoroughly with soap and water. Avoid rubbing your eyes or face when working with hot peppers.

♥ *Nutrition facts per serving: 427 calories, 10 g total fat (1 g saturated fat), 63 mg cholesterol, 285 mg sodium, 54 g carbohydrate, 3 g fiber, 28 g protein.*

Chicken Rosemary

1963

⅓ cup Sauterne or other
   sweet white wine
1 teaspoon dried rosemary,
   crushed
2 to 2½ pounds meaty
   chicken pieces (breasts,
   thighs, and drumsticks),
   skinned

Salt and pepper
2 cups sliced fresh
   mushrooms or one
   3-ounce can sliced
   mushrooms, drained
2 tablespoons cooking oil

Retired home economics teacher Catherine Kitchens of Decatur, Georgia, has been using Better Homes and Gardens recipes for 50-plus years. She says Chicken Rosemary from our September 1963 issue is one of her family's favorites.

1 In a small bowl combine Sauterne and rosemary; let stand at room temperature for 2 hours. Rinse chicken; pat dry with paper towels. Sprinkle chicken with salt and pepper.

2 In a large skillet cook fresh mushrooms (if using) in hot oil until tender. Add chicken pieces and brown on all sides. Carefully add Sauterne mixture; cover and simmer 30 to 35 minutes or until chicken is tender and no longer pink. Spoon canned mushrooms (if using) over chicken; heat through. Remove chicken to hot platter. Serve cooking liquid and mushrooms over chicken. Makes 4 servings.

♥ *Nutrition facts per serving: 294 calories, 14 g total fat (3 g saturated fat), 92 mg cholesterol, 119 mg sodium, 4 g carbohydrate, 0 g fiber, 30 g protein.*

Vintage Views
1930

Portable Picnics

Today, portable grills for picnicking near a lake or stream are commonplace. But in 1930, portable grills weren't available. The stove pictured here was supposed to make camp cooking more convenient—and as clean as cooking in your own home.

A July story said, "If you prefer a complete electric stove for your summer camp, here is a small one that is light enough in weight to be packed into your car and taken to camp with you."

(Just make sure you have an outlet nearby!)

Chicken with Garden Salsa

1990

Backyard barbecuing was sizzling in the 1950s. But the model-T Ford mogul, Henry Ford, gets credit for inventing charcoal briquettes as early as the '30s. Wood waste from the auto plants was charred, ground, mixed with cornstarch, and compressed into briquettes. By 1935, a Ford Charcoal Picnic Kit became available in all Ford showrooms. By 1951, the business became Kingsford Chemical Company, named for the village where the briquettes were made.

2½ **pounds chicken quarters or meaty chicken pieces (breasts, thighs, and drumsticks)***
Salt and pepper
1 **cup bottled salsa**
1 **tablespoon lime juice**

½ **cup finely chopped, seeded cucumber**
¼ **cup chopped green sweet pepper**
1 **tablespoon snipped fresh cilantro**

1 Rinse chicken; pat dry with paper towels. Sprinkle chicken lightly with salt and pepper.

2 In a covered grill arrange medium-hot coals around a drip pan. Test for medium heat above the pan.

3 Place chicken, skin side up, on the grill rack over the drip pan but not over the coals. Lower grill hood. Grill chicken for 50 to 60 minutes or until tender and no longer pink, adding more coals as needed.

4 Meanwhile, combine salsa and lime juice. Set aside ½ cup of the mixture. Brush chicken occasionally with the remaining salsa mixture during the last 10 to 15 minutes of grilling.

5 For sauce, in a small saucepan combine the reserved salsa mixture, the cucumber, green sweet pepper, and cilantro. Bring just to boiling. Remove from heat. Serve the cucumber mixture with chicken. Makes 4 servings.

***Note:** If you make this recipe with chicken quarters, break the wing, hip, and drumstick joints so the quarters will lie flat on the grill. Also, twist the wing tips under the backs.

Nutrition facts per serving: 348 calories, 17 g total fat (4 g saturated fat), 130 mg cholesterol, 370 mg sodium, 6 g carbohydrate, 0 g fiber, 43 g protein.

India Chicken Curry

1932

Curry, long an Eastern Indian specialty, became especially popular during World War II when G.I.s stationed in India learned to like chicken curry "hot hot." The dish gets its pungency from curry powder, a blend of spices typically including turmeric, cumin, coriander, fenugreek, and red pepper. To get the most flavor from the curry powder, heat it in margarine or butter before adding the liquid ingredients.

½ cup finely chopped onion
½ cup finely chopped celery
¼ cup margarine or butter
⅓ cup all-purpose flour
1 tablespoon curry powder
2 cups chicken broth
1 cup tomato juice
1 teaspoon Worcestershire sauce

Pepper
3 cups cubed, cooked chicken or turkey (1 pound)
Hot cooked rice
Condiments (such as chutney, golden raisins, chopped peanuts, and flaked coconut)

1 In a medium saucepan cook the onion and celery in margarine or butter until tender. Stir in the flour and curry powder. Add chicken broth, tomato juice, and Worcestershire sauce. Cook and stir over medium heat until thickened and bubbly. Season to taste with pepper.

2 Stir in chicken or turkey; heat through. Serve over hot cooked rice. Pass condiments. Makes 6 servings.

Nutrition facts per serving with ½ cup cooked rice and 1 tablespoon of each condiment: 525 calories, 21 g total fat (6 g saturated fat), 62 mg cholesterol, 704 mg sodium, 58 g carbohydrate, 3 g fiber, 28 g protein.

Mixed Grill, Indian Style

1995

1½ pounds desired meat
and/or chicken pieces
(such as boneless pork
chops or beef sirloin
steak, cut ¾ inch thick,
or chicken drumsticks,
thighs, or breast halves)

½ cup bottled barbecue sauce
¼ cup peanut butter
½ teaspoon finely shredded
orange peel
1 to 2 tablespoons orange
juice

What used to be called foreign food in America is now everyday fare. Cooks have embraced all types of cuisines, from German to South American and Eastern Indian. This recipe takes a '90s approach to Indian cooking by using a convenience product, bottled barbecue sauce, and other ingredients people usually have on hand, such as peanut butter and orange juice.

1 Rinse chicken (if using); pat dry with paper towels. Grill desired meat and/or chicken on an uncovered grill directly over medium-hot coals until pork is slightly pink in center and juices run clear, until desired doneness for beef, or until chicken is tender and no longer pink; turn once. (Allow 12 to 14 minutes for pork chops, 12 to 14 minutes for medium steak, and 35 to 45 minutes for chicken pieces.)

2 Meanwhile, for sauce, in a small bowl combine barbecue sauce, peanut butter, orange peel, and enough of the orange juice to make sauce of desired consistency. Brush onto meat and/or chicken the last few minutes of grilling.

3 Place any remaining sauce in a saucepan and heat until boiling. Serve with the grilled meat and/or chicken. Makes 6 servings.

Nutrition facts per serving with beef: 292 calories, 16 g total fat (5 g saturated fat), 76 mg cholesterol, 367 mg sodium, 8 g carbohydrate, 1 g fiber, 29 g protein.

Checking the Coals

To create great-tasting grilled foods, the temperature of the coals must be just right. To judge the temperature, hold your hand, palm down, in the same location you plan to cook the food. Begin counting the seconds as "one thousand one, one thousand two," etc., for as long as you can hold your hand there. Two seconds means the coals are hot, three is medium-hot, four is medium, five is medium-slow, and six is slow.

Deep-Dish Chicken Pie

1989

1 recipe Pastry Topper
2 tablespoons margarine or
   butter
3 medium leeks or 1 large
   onion, chopped
1 cup sliced fresh
   mushrooms
¾ cup sliced celery
½ cup chopped red sweet
   pepper
⅓ cup all-purpose flour

1 teaspoon poultry seasoning
¼ teaspoon salt
¼ teaspoon black pepper
1½ cups chicken broth
1 cup half-and-half, light
   cream, or milk
2½ cups chopped, cooked
   chicken
1 cup frozen peas
1 beaten egg

Grandmother's home cooking was the focus of our April 1989 food story. One of the recipes we suggested for duplicating her magic was this mouthwatering casserole. To save time with the same delicious results, you can easily substitute 1 folded refrigerated unbaked piecrust for the Pastry Topper. Just put the chicken mixture in a 2-quart round casserole and top with the piecrust. Flute, brush, and bake as directed in the recipe.

1 On a lightly floured surface, roll Pastry Topper into a rectangle ⅛ inch thick. Trim to a rectangle 1 inch larger than a 2-quart rectangular baking dish. Using a sharp knife or small cookie cutter, cut some shapes out of center of pastry. Set aside.

2 In a large saucepan melt margarine or butter over medium heat. Add the leeks or onion, mushrooms, celery, and red sweet pepper; cook for 4 to 5 minutes or until tender. Stir in the flour, poultry seasoning, salt, and black pepper. Add the broth and half-and-half, light cream, or milk all at once. Cook and stir until thickened and bubbly. Stir in the cooked chicken and peas. Pour into the baking dish.

3 Place pastry over the hot chicken mixture in dish; turn edges of pastry under and flute to top edges of dish. Brush with the egg. Place reserved pastry shapes on top of pastry. Brush again with egg.

4 Bake in a 400° oven for 30 to 35 minutes or until the crust is golden brown. Cool about 20 minutes before serving. Makes 6 servings.

Pastry Topper: In a medium mixing bowl stir together 1¼ cups *all-purpose flour* and ¼ teaspoon *salt*. Using a pastry blender, cut in ⅓ cup *shortening* until pieces are the size of small peas. Sprinkle 1 tablespoon *cold water* over part of the mixture; gently toss with fork. Push moistened dough to side of bowl. Repeat with 3 to 4 tablespoons *cold water*, using 1 tablespoon at a time, until all dough is moistened. Form into a ball.

Nutrition facts per serving: 484 calories, 26 g total fat (8 g saturated fat), 107 mg cholesterol, 538 mg sodium, 35 g carbohydrate, 4 g fiber, 27 g protein.

Make-Ahead Chimichangas

1993

This Mexican-style top prizewinner from our March 1993 Prize Tested Recipes contest takes the worry out of making dinner because you can prepare this dish ahead. The beauty of these delicious chimichangas is that they're frozen so you can heat them one serving at a time.

1 pound cooked chicken, beef, or pork
1 16-ounce jar salsa
1 16-ounce can refried beans
1 4½-ounce can diced green chili peppers
1 1½-ounce envelope burrito or taco seasoning mix
16 8-inch flour tortillas
16 ounces Monterey Jack or cheddar cheese, cut into sixteen 5×½-inch sticks
Cooking oil (optional)
Salsa (optional)
Dairy sour cream (optional)

1 Using two forks, shred cooked chicken or meat (should have about 3 cups). In a large skillet combine shredded chicken or meat, the 16 ounces salsa, beans, *undrained* chili peppers, and seasoning mix. Cook and stir over medium heat until heated through.

2 In another skillet heat tortillas, *one* at a time, over medium-low heat about 30 seconds per side. To assemble, place ⅓ cup meat mixture onto each tortilla, near one edge. Top each with a cheese stick. Fold in the sides; roll up, starting from edge with the cheese. Place in freezer containers. Seal, label, and freeze for up to 6 months.

3 To prepare, wrap each frozen chimichanga in foil. Bake in a 350° oven about 50 minutes or until heated through.* (Or, wrap each frozen chimichanga in foil. Thaw chimichangas in the refrigerator overnight. Do not remove foil. Bake about 30 minutes.) Remove foil. Bake 10 minutes more or until tortillas are crisp and brown. If desired, serve with additional salsa and dairy sour cream. Makes 16 servings.

*Note: If you want to fry rather than bake the chimichangas, heat about ¼ inch of oil in a skillet. Cook desired number of frozen chimichangas, uncovered, in hot oil about 25 minutes (about 18 minutes, if thawed) over medium-low heat until golden brown, turning often.

♥ *Nutrition facts per serving: 329 calories, 15 g total fat (6 g saturated fat), 51 mg cholesterol, 903 mg sodium, 29 g carbohydrate, 1 g fiber, 21 g protein.*

Chicken Tetrazzini

1933

9 ounces packaged dried
    spaghetti
¼ cup margarine or butter
1½ cups sliced fresh
    mushrooms
3 tablespoons all-purpose
    flour
½ teaspoon salt
¼ teaspoon paprika
⅛ teaspoon pepper
2 cups milk

1 cup half-and-half, light
    cream, or milk
2 slightly beaten egg yolks
3 cups cubed, cooked
    chicken (1 pound)
2 tablespoons dry sherry
2 tablespoons sliced almonds,
    toasted
Grated Parmesan cheese
    (optional)
Snipped parsley (optional)

Chefs have a tradition of paying tribute to an artist by creating a special dish and naming it after them. Madame Luisa Tetrazzini, a famous Italian soprano, was thus honored with Chicken Tetrazzini. This excellent spaghetti dish with its creamy chicken sauce has become more well known than the diva for whom it's named. Although the original ingredients remain intact, we dressed up the dish with toasted almonds and sherry.

1 Cook spaghetti according to package directions. Meanwhile, in a medium saucepan melt the margarine or butter over medium heat. Add the mushrooms and cook until just tender. Stir in the flour, salt, paprika, and pepper. Add the 2 cups milk and the 1 cup half-and-half, light cream, or milk all at once. Cook and stir until slightly thickened and bubbly. Cook and stir 1 minute more.

2 Gradually stir about half of the hot mixture into egg yolks. Add egg mixture to milk mixture in saucepan. Bring to a gentle boil; reduce heat. Cook and stir for 2 minutes more. Stir in cooked chicken and dry sherry. Heat through.

3 Drain spaghetti. Serve chicken mixture over pasta. Sprinkle with almonds, Parmesan cheese, and parsley. Makes 6 servings.

Nutrition facts per serving: 530 calories, 23 g total fat (8 g saturated fat), 159 mg cholesterol, 393 mg sodium, 44 g carbohydrate, 1 g fiber, 34 g protein.

Maryland Fried Chicken

1992

We scoured the country in May 1992 to find and publish the best chicken recipes from coast to coast. This old-fashioned recipe is Maryland's succulent contribution. What sets it apart from the typical recipe is that milk is added after partially cooking the chicken so the pieces simmer rather than fry.

1 **beaten egg**
3 **tablespoons milk**
1 **cup finely crushed saltine crackers (28 crackers)**
1 **teaspoon dried thyme, crushed**
½ **teaspoon paprika**
⅛ **teaspoon pepper**
2½ **to 3 pounds meaty chicken pieces (breasts, thighs, and drumsticks)**

2 **to 3 tablespoons cooking oil**
1 **cup milk**
1 **recipe Cream Gravy**
  Hot mashed potatoes (optional)
  Fresh thyme sprigs (optional)

1 In a small mixing bowl combine the egg and the 3 tablespoons milk. In a shallow bowl combine the crushed crackers, dried thyme, paprika, and pepper. Set aside.

2 Rinse chicken; pat dry with paper towels. Dip chicken pieces, 1 at a time, in egg mixture, then roll in cracker mixture.

3 In a large skillet heat oil over medium heat. Add chicken and cook, uncovered, for 10 to 15 minutes, turning occasionally to brown evenly. Drain well.

4 Add the 1 cup milk to skillet. Reduce heat to medium-low; cover tightly. Cook for 35 minutes. Uncover; cook for 10 minutes more or until chicken is tender and no longer pink. Transfer chicken to a serving platter; cover and keep warm. Prepare Cream Gravy. If desired, serve with mashed potatoes. If desired, garnish with fresh thyme. Makes 6 servings.

Cream Gravy: Skim fat from drippings. Reserve 3 tablespoons of the drippings in skillet. In a screw-top jar combine ¾ cup *milk*, 3 tablespoons *all-purpose flour*, ¼ teaspoon *salt*, and ⅛ teaspoon *pepper*; cover and shake until well mixed. Add to skillet. Stir in ¾ cup additional *milk*. Cook over medium heat, stirring constantly, until thickened and bubbly. Cook and stir 1 minute more. (If desired, thin with additional milk.) Makes about 1½ cups.

Nutrition facts per serving: 367 calories, 17 g total fat (5 g saturated fat), 126 mg cholesterol, 428 mg sodium, 19 g carbohydrate, 1 g fiber, 32 g protein.

★
1994

Spicy Garlic Chicken Pizza

This pizza is bursting with Oriental seasonings. Carol Holt of Bakersfield, California, sent it in with a trio of good things to say. "I love it," she proclaims, "because it's quick, easy, and I know my family will eat it."

12 ounces skinless, boneless chicken breasts
½ cup sliced green onions
2 cloves garlic, minced
2 tablespoons rice vinegar or white vinegar
2 tablespoons reduced-sodium soy sauce
1 tablespoon olive oil or cooking oil
½ teaspoon crushed red pepper or ¼ teaspoon ground red pepper

¼ teaspoon black pepper
1 tablespoon olive oil or cooking oil
1 tablespoon cornstarch
1 16-ounce Italian bread shell (Boboli)
½ cup shredded Monterey Jack cheese
½ cup shredded mozzarella cheese
2 tablespoons pine nuts or sliced almonds

1 Rinse chicken; pat dry with paper towels. Cut chicken into ½-inch pieces. In a large mixing bowl combine *half* of the green onions, the minced garlic, vinegar, soy sauce, 1 tablespoon oil, the red pepper, and black pepper. Add the chicken pieces; stir to coat. Let stand at room temperature for 30 minutes. Drain, reserving liquid.

2 In a large skillet heat the 1 tablespoon oil; add chicken pieces. Cook and stir about 3 minutes or until chicken is no longer pink. Stir cornstarch into reserved liquid. Add to skillet. Cook and stir until thickened and bubbly.

3 Spoon evenly over bread shell on baking sheet. Sprinkle with Monterey Jack cheese and mozzarella cheese. Bake, uncovered, in a 400° oven for 12 minutes. Top with remaining green onions and the nuts. Return to oven for 2 minutes more. Makes 6 servings.

Nutrition facts per serving: 406 calories, 18 g total fat (4 g saturated fat), 48 mg cholesterol, 714 mg sodium, 37 g carbohydrate, 2 g fiber, 27 g protein.

Arroz con Pollo

1 8-ounce package brown-
and-serve sausage links
3 tablespoons all-purpose
flour
½ teaspoon salt
¼ teaspoon pepper
2 pounds meaty chicken
pieces (breasts, thighs,
and drumsticks), skinned
1 tablespoon cooking oil

2 cups water
1 cup chopped onion
½ cup chopped celery
1 cup long grain rice
1 7½-ounce can tomatoes,
cut up
1 cup frozen peas
¼ cup sliced pitted ripe olives
or pimiento-stuffed green
olives

Chicken was a luxury—a food reserved for Sunday or for company—in the late '20s and throughout the Depression. In fact, Herbert Hoover used the slogan "a chicken in every pot" during his 1928 presidential campaign as a promise of prosperity. Despite its scarcity, our magazine published numerous ways to prepare this precious commodity. Here's one of our best chicken recipes from the '30s.

1 Cut the sausages into ½-inch pieces; brown sausages in a kettle. Remove sausages. Set aside.

2 Place the flour, salt, and pepper in a plastic bag. Add chicken, a few pieces at a time, and shake to coat.

3 In the kettle heat oil over medium heat. Add chicken and cook, uncovered, for 10 minutes, turning to brown evenly. Add the water, onion, and celery to chicken in kettle. Simmer, covered, for 20 minutes. Add *uncooked* rice, *undrained* tomatoes, and sausages. Simmer, covered, about 20 minutes more or until rice is tender. Add peas and olives; cook and stir until heated through. Makes 6 servings.

Nutrition facts per serving: 503 calories, 24 g total fat (7 g saturated fat), 95 mg cholesterol, 1,003 mg sodium, 35 g carbohydrate, 2 g fiber, 35 g protein.

1994

Mediterranean-Style Chicken

This tomato- and cinnamon-spiced chicken served over couscous gets top votes from several readers for an all-time best Better Homes and Gardens *magazine recipe.*

2½ **to 3 pounds meaty chicken pieces (breasts, thighs, and drumsticks), skinned**

2 **tablespoons cooking oil**

1 **14½-ounce can tomatoes, cut up**

¼ **cup dry white wine or chicken broth**

3 **tablespoons regular onion soup mix**

1 **9-ounce package frozen artichoke hearts**

½ **cup pitted ripe olives, halved**

⅛ **teaspoon ground cinnamon**

1 **tablespoon cold water**

2 **teaspoons cornstarch**
   Hot cooked couscous or hot cooked rice

1 Rinse chicken; pat dry with paper towels. In a 12-inch skillet heat oil over medium heat. Add chicken and cook, uncovered, for 10 minutes, turning to brown evenly. Drain well.

2 Stir together the *undrained* tomatoes, wine or broth, and soup mix. Add to chicken in skillet. Bring to boiling; reduce heat. Simmer, covered, for 30 minutes. Stir in artichoke hearts, olives, and cinnamon. Simmer, covered, 8 to 10 minutes more or until chicken is tender and no longer pink and artichoke hearts are tender. Use a slotted spoon to transfer chicken and solids to a serving platter.

3 Skim fat from broth. Combine the cold water and cornstarch; add to broth in skillet. Cook and stir until thickened and bubbly; cook 2 minutes more. Spoon over chicken. Serve with couscous or rice. Makes 6 servings.

♥*Nutrition facts per serving: 363 calories, 12 g total fat (2 g saturated fat), 78 mg cholesterol, 513 mg sodium, 31 g carbohydrate, 5 g fiber, 31 g protein.*

*P*ollo Relleno

6 medium skinless, boneless
chicken breast halves
(about 1½ pounds total)
½ cup cornmeal
½ of a 1¼-ounce package
(2 tablespoons) taco
seasoning mix
1 beaten egg
1 4½-ounce can whole green
chili peppers, rinsed,
seeded, and cut in half
lengthwise (6 pieces
total)

2 ounces Monterey Jack
cheese, cut into six
2×½-inch strips
2 tablespoons snipped fresh
cilantro or parsley
¼ teaspoon black pepper
1 8-ounce bottle green or red
taco sauce
2 ounces cheddar or
Monterey Jack cheese,
shredded (½ cup)
(optional)
Chopped tomato (optional)
Fresh cilantro sprigs
(optional)

These chicken breast rolls with cheese-stuffed peppers tucked inside won a prize for Lynne Waldron from Campbell, California, in our January 1993 Prize Tested Recipes contest for Tex-Mex entrées.

1 Rinse chicken; pat dry with paper towels. Place each breast half between 2 pieces of heavy plastic wrap. Working from center to the edges, pound lightly with the flat side of a meat mallet to ⅛ inch thickness. Remove plastic wrap.

2 In a shallow bowl combine cornmeal and seasoning mix. Place egg in another shallow bowl. For each roll, place *one* chili pepper on a chicken piece. Place *one* cheese strip on top of chili pepper near 1 edge. Sprinkle with some of the 2 tablespoons snipped cilantro and the black pepper. To roll up the chicken, fold in 2 opposite sides, then roll up, starting from edge with the cheese. Repeat to make 6 rolls. Dip rolls into egg, then into cornmeal mixture. Place, seam sides down, in a shallow baking pan.

3 Bake, uncovered, in a 375° oven for 25 to 30 minutes or until chicken is tender and no longer pink.

4 In a small saucepan heat taco sauce. If desired, sprinkle chicken with shredded cheese. Serve with taco sauce. If desired, garnish with chopped tomato and cilantro sprigs. Makes 6 servings.

♥ *Nutrition facts per serving: 278 calories, 10 g total fat (5 g saturated fat), 115 mg cholesterol, 927 mg sodium, 16 g carbohydrate, 2 g fiber, 31 g protein.*

1993

Susan Fisher of Kingston, Tennessee, tells us her husband declared these cheese-filled meat loaves from our November 1993 issue one of her "five-star" recipes.

Chili Turkey Loaves

2 4½-ounce cans whole green chili peppers, drained
8 ounces sharp cheddar
2 eggs
¼ cup tomato sauce
½ cup fine dry bread crumbs
½ cup finely chopped onion

1 teaspoon dried oregano, crushed
1 teaspoon chili powder
1 clove garlic, minced
2 pounds ground raw turkey
1 7- or 8¾-ounce can whole kernel corn, drained
Bottled salsa

1 Cut chili peppers into 8 portions; remove seeds. Cut *4 ounces* of the cheese into eight 3×½×½-inch sticks; shred remaining cheese.

2 In a bowl beat eggs; stir in tomato sauce, bread crumbs, onion, oregano, chili powder, ½ teaspoon *salt,* and garlic. Add ground turkey; mix well. Divide into 8 portions; form each portion into a 6×4-inch rectangle. In center of each, place some of the corn, 1 chili pepper portion, and 1 cheese stick. Roll up, starting from a short side; seal.

3 Place loaves, seam down, in a baking pan. Bake, uncovered, in a 350° oven for 30 minutes or until no pink remains. Drain fat. Top with shredded cheese. Bake 2 to 3 minutes more. Top with salsa. Serves 8.

Nutrition facts per serving: 330 calories, 20 g total fat (9 g saturated fat), 125 mg cholesterol, 644 mg sodium, 12 g carbohydrate, 1 g fiber, 26 g protein.

Vintage Views
1926

Yesteryear Meat Loaf

Meat loaf is as American as apple pie, and there are more versions of it than one can imagine. In the October 1926 issue, a recipe called "The Dignified Meat Loaf" was given this praise:

"The meat loaf embodies the round steak in its most pretentious (and some folks think most delicious) style. Often it acts as a dignified substitute for the Sunday roast itself. A nice thing about it, aside from its tastiness, is that it is easily and quickly prepared."

Turkey Enchiladas

1992

½ cup chopped onion
Nonstick spray coating
½ of an 8-ounce package
reduced-fat cream cheese
(Neufchâtel), softened
1 tablespoon water
1 teaspoon ground cumin
¼ teaspoon black pepper
⅛ teaspoon salt
4 cups chopped, cooked
turkey or chicken
¼ cup chopped pecans,
toasted
12 7- to 8-inch flour tortillas

1 10¾-ounce can reduced-fat
and reduced-sodium
condensed cream of
chicken soup
1 8-ounce carton light dairy
sour cream
1 cup skim milk
2 to 4 tablespoons finely
chopped pickled jalapeño
peppers
½ cup shredded reduced-fat
sharp cheddar cheese
(2 ounces)
Snipped fresh cilantro or
parsley (optional)
Chopped tomato (optional)

One of our longtime devoted readers, Kelly Thacker, from Utah, submitted several of her favorite recipes from the magazine. She told us these turkey enchiladas are "now regular fare for dinner" at her household. They were originally sent in by a reader for a makeover because they were so high in fat. They now have a reasonable 10 grams of fat per enchildada.

1 In a small covered saucepan cook onion in a small amount of *boiling water* over medium heat until tender; drain. For enchiladas, spray a 3-quart rectangular baking dish with nonstick coating. In a medium mixing bowl stir together the cream cheese, water, cumin, black pepper, and salt. Stir in cooked onion, turkey, and toasted pecans.

2 Meanwhile, wrap tortillas in foil. Heat in a 350° oven for 10 to 15 minutes or until softened.* Spoon about ¼ cup of the turkey mixture onto each tortilla; roll up. Place, seam sides down, in the baking dish.

3 For sauce, in a medium mixing bowl combine the condensed soup, sour cream, milk, and jalapeño peppers; pour over enchiladas. Bake the enchiladas, covered, in a 350° oven about 40 minutes or until heated through. Sprinkle the enchiladas with the cheddar cheese. Bake, uncovered, for 4 to 5 minutes more or until cheese is melted. If desired, top with snipped cilantro or parsley and tomato. Makes 12 enchiladas.

*Note: To heat the tortillas in a microwave oven, wrap them in a microwave-safe paper towel. Cook on high for 30 to 60 seconds or until softened.

♥*Nutrition facts per enchilada: 256 calories, 10 g total fat (2 g saturated fat), 44 mg cholesterol, 271 mg sodium, 21 g carbohydrate, 1 g fiber, 21 g protein.*

Tropical Fiesta Steak

1992

The first time Gloria Piantek of Nashville, Tennessee, created this summery steak, she served it for her son's surprise birthday party. It turned out to be as big a hit with our tasters in 1992 as it was with her guests. The grilled sirloin steak and fruit relish combination garnered her a prize in our June 1992 Great American Barbecue Contest.

⅓ cup frozen orange juice concentrate, thawed
3 tablespoons cooking oil
3 tablespoons honey
1 tablespoon sliced green onion
2 teaspoons spicy brown or Dijon-style mustard
1 teaspoon snipped fresh mint or ¼ teaspoon dried mint, crushed
Few drops bottled hot pepper sauce

1 1½-pound boneless beef sirloin steak, cut 1 to 1½ inches thick
½ cup chopped red sweet pepper
½ cup chopped red apple
½ cup chopped pear
½ cup chopped peeled peach
¼ cup chopped celery
2 tablespoons sliced green onion
2 teaspoons lemon juice
1 recipe Pineapple-Mustard Sauce (optional)
Salt and pepper

1 For marinade, in a small mixing bowl stir together the orange juice concentrate, oil, honey, the 1 tablespoon green onion, the mustard, mint, and hot pepper sauce. Remove ¼ cup of the mixture to make the relish; cover and refrigerate until needed.

2 Place the steak in a large plastic bag set in a shallow bowl. Pour remaining marinade over meat. Seal bag; turn to coat meat with the marinade. Marinate meat in the refrigerator for 12 to 24 hours, turning the bag occasionally.

3 For the fruit relish, in a medium mixing bowl combine the reserved marinade, the sweet pepper, apple, pear, peach, celery, the 2 tablespoons green onion, and the lemon juice. Cover and refrigerate until serving time, up to 24 hours. If desired, make Pineapple-Mustard Sauce and refrigerate until serving time, up to 24 hours.

4 Remove steak from bag, reserving marinade. Grill steak, uncovered, directly over medium-hot coals until desired doneness. (Allow 12 to 15 minutes for medium doneness on a 1-inch-thick steak or 18 to 22 minutes for medium doneness on a 1½-inch-thick steak.) During cooking, turn once and brush occasionally with marinade. Season to taste with salt and pepper.

5 To serve, slice steak into thin strips; serve with the fruit relish. If desired, pass the Pineapple-Mustard Sauce. Makes 6 servings.

Pineapple-Mustard Sauce: In a small mixing bowl stir together one 8-ounce carton *pineapple yogurt*, 2 tablespoons *milk*, and 1 teaspoon *spicy brown mustard* or *Dijon-style mustard*.

Nutrition facts per serving: 344 calories, 17 total fat (5 g saturated fat), 76 mg cholesterol, 107 mg sodium, 21 g carbohydrate, 1 g fiber, 27 g protein.

Vintage Views
1930
Stopping Time by Freezing

*T*hrough the eyes of an editor writing in the May 1930 issue, we experience the cool wonder of freezing and the first taste of a fresh summer berry grown the summer before.

"In a grocery store in Springfield, Massachusetts, not long ago I saw Springfield homemakers buying fruits, vegetables, meats, and sea foods that had been frozen by the newest of the refrigeration methods which twentieth-century science has been able to pull from its bag of tricks. ... Time had been made to stand still. ... It is strange to think that human invention could have accomplished this astounding thing.

"For several decades refrigeration engineers have been trying to find a satisfactory way to slow Time down with respect to food. But the results have never been quite satisfactory. But now comes something new and revolutionary."

While shopping "a clerk opened a box of berries for my inspection. There they lay; and the only thing to indicate to the eye that they were not fresh from the bush was a slight film of frost over each perfect berry. When that vanished in the heat of the room, the illusion was complete—till you picked up a berry, felt it between your fingers, hard as a pretty red marble, and crunched it between your teeth like a bit of ice. Then, as it melted in your mouth, you understood that here indeed was a miracle. For it had the authentic taste of a perfectly fresh berry."

Flank Steak Bordelaise

1981

When we first published this recipe in 1981, flank steak was an inexpensive, little-used cut of meat. Since then, the popularity of fajitas has turned flank steak into a culinary star. It's important to slice the meat as thin as you can for serving. Use a very sharp knife to cut the meat.

1 **pound beef flank steak**
⅓ **cup red wine vinegar**
¼ **cup chopped onion**
2 **tablespoons cooking oil**
1 **tablespoon Worcestershire sauce**
2 **cloves garlic, minced**
¼ **teaspoon dry mustard**
¼ **cup chopped green onions**
4 **tablespoons margarine or butter**
1 **tablespoon all-purpose flour**

½ **teaspoon dried thyme, crushed**
1 **14½-ounce can beef broth**
¼ **cup dry red wine**
2½ **cups coarsely shredded zucchini**
1 **cup coarsely shredded carrot**
1 **clove garlic, minced**
⅓ **cup coarsely chopped walnuts**
Salt and pepper
Fresh thyme sprigs (optional)

1 Score meat in a diamond pattern on both sides, cutting about ¼ inch deep. Place meat in a large plastic bag set in a shallow dish. In a small mixing bowl combine wine vinegar, onion, oil, Worcestershire sauce, the 2 cloves garlic, and the dry mustard. Pour over meat. Seal the bag; turn to coat. Marinate in the refrigerator for 6 to 24 hours, turning the bag occasionally.

2 For sauce, in a medium saucepan cook the green onions in *2 tablespoons* of the margarine or butter until tender. Stir in the flour and dried thyme. Stir in broth and wine. Bring to a boil, stirring occasionally; reduce heat. Boil gently, uncovered, for 15 to 20 minutes or until reduced to 1 cup. Keep warm.

3 Meanwhile, remove steak from marinade; pat dry with paper towels. Place steak on unheated rack of a broiler pan. Discard marinade. Broil steak 3 to 4 inches from the heat for 13 to 15 minutes (for medium-rare), turning steak halfway through cooking time. Slice flank steak thinly across the grain.

4 Meanwhile, combine zucchini, carrot, and the 1 clove garlic; place in a steamer basket over *boiling water*. Steam for 3 to 4 minutes or just until tender. Stir in the remaining margarine or butter and the walnuts. Season to taste with salt and pepper.

5 To serve, spoon some of the sauce over meat slices; pass remaining sauce. Serve the zucchini and carrot mixture with the meat. If desired, garnish with fresh thyme. Makes 4 to 6 servings.

Nutrition facts per serving: 394 calories, 28 g total fat (7 g saturated fat), 53 mg cholesterol, 602 mg sodium, 9 g carbohydrate, 2 g fiber, 25 g protein.

1965

Round Steak Sauerbraten

Round Steak Sauerbraten has played an important part in the life of one of our St. Louis readers, Sue Anderson. She explains, "I tried this recipe for the first time the evening before our youngest daughter was born in 1965. It became a family favorite through the years. Now, she is married. Last year when her first child was born, I traveled to Chicago to be there for her first night home, and her request for dinner was Round Steak Sauerbraten!"

1½ **pounds boneless beef round steak, cut ½ inch thick**
1 **tablespoon cooking oil**
1 **1.2-ounce envelope brown gravy mix**
1 **tablespoon dried minced onion**

2 **tablespoons brown sugar**
2 **tablespoons white wine vinegar or cider vinegar**
1 **teaspoon Worcestershire sauce**
½ **teaspoon ground ginger**
1 **bay leaf**
  Hot cooked noodles

1 Cut meat into 1-inch pieces. In a large skillet brown meat, half at a time, in hot oil. Remove meat from skillet. Stir gravy mix into skillet; carefully stir in ½ cup *water*. Heat to boiling, stirring constantly.

2 Stir in onion, brown sugar, vinegar, Worcestershire sauce, ginger, bay leaf, and ¼ teaspoon *pepper*. Return meat to skillet. Simmer, covered, for 1¼ hours or until meat is tender, stirring occasionally. Discard bay leaf. Serve over hot cooked noodles. Makes 5 servings.

♥ *Nutrition facts per serving with ½ cup noodles: 367 calories, 10 total fat (3 g saturated fat), 111 mg cholesterol, 357 mg sodium, 29 g carbohydrate, 2 g fiber, 36 g protein.*

Vintage Views
1926

The Original Meat Loaf

The recipe for Beef Loaf (the probable forerunner of today's meat loaf) typifies how our magazine wrote recipes in the early years. "Mix together with the hand about two and one-half pounds of the ground meat—including a bit of salt pork or suet to keep the steak from being too solid—one-half a cupful of fine bread crumbs, one egg, two teaspoonfuls of salt and one saltspoonful of pepper, one teaspoonful of sage, if you like it—I do—and moisten with about half a cupful of tomato juice or water; press into a well-greased bread pan or mold and bake about an hour in a hot oven. Serve hot with tomato sauce poured around it."

15-Minute Beef Stroganoff

1959

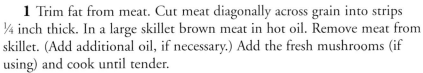

12 ounces boneless beef
    round steak
1 tablespoon cooking oil
2 cups sliced fresh
    mushrooms or one
    2½-ounce can sliced
    mushrooms, drained
¾ cup water

1 envelope regular onion
    soup mix
1 8-ounce carton dairy sour
    cream
2 tablespoons all-purpose
    flour
    Hot cooked fine noodles or
    hot cooked rice

1 Trim fat from meat. Cut meat diagonally across grain into strips ¼ inch thick. In a large skillet brown meat in hot oil. Remove meat from skillet. (Add additional oil, if necessary.) Add the fresh mushrooms (if using) and cook until tender.

2 Return meat to skillet. Add the water and canned mushrooms (if using). Stir in the soup mix. Heat to boiling. In a small mixing bowl stir together the sour cream and flour. Stir into mixture in skillet. Cook and stir until mixture is thickened and bubbly. Cook and stir for 1 minute more. Serve over hot cooked noodles or rice. Makes 5 servings.

For a lower-fat version: Use light dairy sour cream.

Nutrition facts per serving with ½ cup noodles: 361 calories, 17 g total fat (8 g saturated fat), 89 mg cholesterol, 757 mg sodium, 28 g carbohydrate, 3 g fiber, 23 g protein.

♥ *Lower-fat version: 322 calories, 10 g total fat (3 g saturated fat), 74 mg cholesterol, 784 mg sodium, 32 g carbohydrate, 3 g fiber, 25 g protein.*

Ever since she started subscribing to the magazine in 1950, June Robinson of Seattle, has been trying out Better Homes and Gardens *recipes. She remembers: "I tried many new recipes on my new husband who declared each one a 'tosser' or a 'keeper'." One of June's favorite "keepers" is this easy round steak recipe because it's quick and tasty.*

*V*intage Views
1923
Planning a Perfect Menu

*I*n September 1923, there were rules for planning a menu. Some still seem sound today, but others may not have kept up with the times. Here, the editor, a professor in home economics, shares guidelines she believes to be essential for a successful meal:

1. Not over two starchy dishes.
2. One meat or some such dish as omelet or macaroni and cheese or cheese loaf.
3. One fresh or leafy green vegetable or fruit.
4. A balance of dry and of creamed foods.
5. One acid and one sweet dish.
6. No two foods cooked the same way, as fried, creamed, etc.
7. Don't over-clog the system with sugar and fat.
8. Don't serve meat and dishes containing such things as beans, cheese or eggs in the same meal.

Indonesian Saté with Peanut Sauce

1982

- 1 pound boneless beef round steak or sirloin steak, cut into 1-inch cubes
- 1 pound boneless lamb, cut into 1-inch cubes
- 1 pound chicken breasts, boned, skinned, and cut into 1-inch cubes
- 1 cup unsweetened coconut milk
- ⅓ cup finely chopped onion
- 2 teaspoons dry mustard
- 1½ teaspoons ground coriander
- ½ teaspoon salt
- ½ teaspoon ground turmeric
- ½ teaspoon ground cumin
- 1 clove garlic, minced
- 2 tablespoons sliced green onion
- 1 clove garlic
- 1 teaspoon cooking oil
- ¼ cup peanut butter
- ½ cup chicken broth or beef broth
- 1 tablespoon soy sauce
- ½ teaspoon finely shredded lemon peel
- 1 tablespoon lemon juice
- 1 teaspoon chili powder
- ½ teaspoon brown sugar
- ¼ teaspoon ground ginger
  Cherry tomatoes (optional)

This recipe appeared in our June 1982 issue as part of an outdoor dinner party menu. It's as terrific for entertaining today as it was then. You can marinate the meat, prepare the peanut sauce, and thread the skewers ahead of time. Just grill the kabobs when guests arrive. If fresh coconuts aren't available for the unsweetened coconut milk, look for canned coconut milk in the Oriental section of the supermarket or at an Asian food market.

1 Place the meat cubes and chicken cubes in a shallow nonmetal bowl. In a small mixing bowl stir together the coconut milk, onion, dry mustard, coriander, salt, turmeric, cumin, and 1 clove garlic. Pour over meat, tossing to coat. Cover and marinate in the refrigerator for several hours or overnight. Drain, reserving marinade.

2 On long metal skewers thread meat and chicken, leaving ¼ inch between pieces. Grill on rack of uncovered grill directly over medium coals for 12 to 14 minutes or until tender and no longer pink, turning kabobs once and brushing with reserved marinade.

3 Meanwhile, for peanut dipping sauce, in a small saucepan cook the green onion and the 1 clove garlic in hot oil until tender. Stir in peanut butter. Gradually stir in broth until smooth. Stir in the soy sauce, lemon peel, lemon juice, chili powder, brown sugar, and ginger. Bring just to boiling; reduce heat. Simmer, uncovered, for 5 to 8 minutes or until thickened.

4 If desired, add a cherry tomato to the end of each skewer. Serve the kabobs with the peanut dipping sauce. Makes 8 servings.

Nutrition facts per serving: 339 calories, 18 g total fat (9 g saturated fat), 98 mg cholesterol, 450 mg sodium, 5 g carbohydrate, 1 g fiber, 39 g protein.

Steak Roll-Ups with Noodles

1952

Entered by Margaret Morrisroe of Golden's Bridge, New York, this company-special beef roll won first prize in our 1952 one-dish-meal contest. Back then, we suggested serving it with a crisp, tossed salad and buttered French bread. That combination still sounds tantalizing.

1½ pounds boneless beef round steak

1½ teaspoons snipped fresh thyme or ½ teaspoon dried thyme, crushed

1 teaspoon snipped fresh sage or ¼ teaspoon dried sage, crushed

1 teaspoon snipped fresh basil or ¼ teaspoon dried basil, crushed

2 tablespoons cooking oil

2 14½-ounce cans tomatoes, cut up

1 6-ounce can tomato paste

1 cup chopped onion

1 clove garlic, minced

1½ teaspoons chili powder

½ teaspoon salt

¼ teaspoon pepper

12 ounces packaged dried wide noodles

¼ cup snipped parsley Fresh thyme sprigs (optional)

1 Place the steak between 2 pieces of plastic wrap. Using the flat side of a meat mallet, pound steak to a 12×8-inch rectangle. Sprinkle the steak with the 1½ teaspoons fresh or ½ teaspoon dried thyme, the sage, and basil. Roll up, jelly-roll style, starting from a long side. Tie meat roll with string.

2 In a 12-inch skillet brown the meat roll on all sides in hot oil. Drain well. In a medium mixing bowl stir together the *undrained* tomatoes, tomato paste, onion, garlic, chili powder, salt, and pepper. Pour over meat. Bring mixture to boiling; reduce heat. Simmer, covered, for 1¼ to 1½ hours or until meat is tender.

3 Meanwhile, cook the noodles according to package directions. Drain noodles and toss with *2 tablespoons* of the parsley. Remove meat roll from skillet. Remove string and cut meat into 18 slices. Serve meat slices with the noodles. Serve tomato mixture over noodles and meat. Sprinkle with the remaining parsley. If desired, garnish with the fresh thyme sprigs. Makes 6 servings.

♥ *Nutrition facts per serving: 441 calories, 12 g total fat (3 g saturated fat), 106 mg cholesterol, 697 mg sodium, 48 g carbohydrate, 5 g fiber, 35 g protein.*

Sweet-Sour Stew

This hearty beef, onion, and carrot stew with its tangy catsup gravy has special memories for Betsy Papp of Woodstock, Illinois. She told us she and her husband enjoyed it regularly when they were newlyweds.

¼ cup all-purpose flour
1 teaspoon salt
  Dash pepper
1½ pounds beef stew meat, cut into 1-inch pieces
2 tablespoons cooking oil
1 cup water
½ cup catsup

¼ cup packed brown sugar
¼ cup vinegar
1 tablespoon Worcestershire sauce
1 cup chopped onion
6 medium carrots, cut into ¾-inch pieces

1 In a plastic bag combine flour, salt, and pepper; add meat pieces, a few at a time, shaking to coat. In a large skillet brown meat, half at a time, in hot oil, adding additional oil, if necessary. Drain well. Return all the meat to the skillet.

2 Combine water, catsup, brown sugar, vinegar, and Worcestershire sauce. Stir into meat in skillet; stir in the onion. Bring to boiling; reduce heat. Simmer, covered, for 1 hour. Add carrots and simmer about 30 minutes more or until meat and carrots are tender. Makes 4 servings.

Nutrition facts per serving: 462 calories, 19 g total fat (5 g saturated fat), 105 mg cholesterol, 1,289 mg sodium, 39 g carbohydrate, 4 g fiber, 35 g protein.

Hearty Hodgepodge

A Tuscaloosa, Alabama, reader, Imogene Gibson, has loved this soup since it appeared in December 1969. She raves: "I think it is the best soup that I have ever eaten. The men in my family compliment me on this soup. I have made copies for my nephews and other young men who love to cook. I also have granddaughters in three different states, and you can bet that Hearty Hodgepodge is in their recipe files!"

1½ pounds lean ground beef
1½ cups chopped celery
¾ cup chopped onion
1 clove garlic, minced
3 10½-ounce cans condensed minestrone soup

1 31-ounce can pork and beans in tomato sauce
3 cups water
1 tablespoon Worcestershire sauce
½ teaspoon dried oregano, crushed

1 In a kettle cook ground beef, celery, onion, and garlic for 5 to 7 minutes or until beef is brown and vegetables are tender. Drain well. Stir in the condensed soup, pork and beans, water, Worcestershire sauce, and oregano. Bring to boiling; reduce heat. Simmer, covered, for 20 minutes. Makes 10 to 12 servings.

♥ *Nutrition facts per serving: 276 calories, 10 g total fat (4 g saturated fat), 49 mg cholesterol, 1,135 mg sodium, 27 g carbohydrate, 5 g fiber, 21 g protein.*

*V*intage Views
1930

When the Man Of the House Cooks

*I*n 1930, it was a well-known fact that women cooked and men ate. Period. So a cooking contest for men was big news. Although more such cooking contests for men followed in the years ahead, the first contest for males was published in February 1930. Accompanying the winning recipes was a delightful story about men in the kitchen. In "When the Man of the House Cooks," Orville Sprague wrote:

"… [W]hen I get behind a very large, and at times, a very white apron, and start fussing with food, I have a very stupendous time. By the way, those aprons are worthy of discussion. There's nothing sissy about them; they're the kind chefs use, and they're mine; nobody else uses them.

… My wife is firmly convinced that it's good to eat food that she herself does not prepare, even tho I develop a terrific mess in the kitchen. And I think the food I cook is mighty good, because I cook it.

… The way to a man's heart is via his stomach. The esophagus lies close to the right ventricle, or whatever it is that makes the works go. And so, it may be inferred, a man knows good cookery when he tastes it."

Yankee Doodle Stew With Vegetables

1941

¼ cup all-purpose flour
2 pounds boneless beef chuck, cut into 1-inch pieces
3 tablespoons cooking oil
4 cups water
½ cup chopped onion
1 clove garlic, minced
2 bay leaves
1 teaspoon sugar
1 teaspoon lemon juice
1 teaspoon Worcestershire sauce

½ teaspoon salt
½ teaspoon pepper
½ teaspoon paprika
Dash ground allspice
6 tiny new potatoes, halved
6 medium carrots, quartered
1 pound boiling onions*
1 tablespoon all-purpose flour
2 tablespoons cold water
¼ cup dry sherry (optional)
Snipped parsley (optional)

Cooking preferences have changed a lot in the last half century. When this beef stew was originally published in 1941, the meat was browned in suet, the recipe used 1½ teaspoons of salt, and the mixture cooked for 2½ hours. As we updated it for the '90s, we switched from suet to cooking oil and decreased the amount of salt substantially. We also cut the cooking time to keep the vegetables a bit firmer.

1 Place the ¼ cup flour in a plastic bag. Add the meat pieces, a few at a time, shaking to coat. In a kettle brown meat, one-third at a time, in hot oil. Drain well. Return all the meat to the kettle. Add the 4 cups water, the chopped onion, garlic, and bay leaves to meat. Stir in the sugar, lemon juice, Worcestershire sauce, salt, pepper, paprika, and allspice. Bring to boiling; reduce heat. Simmer, covered, about 1½ hours or until meat is nearly tender.

2 Add the potatoes, carrots, and the boiling onions. Return to boiling; reduce heat. Simmer, covered, for 20 to 30 minutes more or until vegetables are tender. Discard bay leaves. Remove meat and vegetables to a serving dish. Cover and keep warm.

3 For gravy, in a small mixing bowl stir the 1 tablespoon flour into the 2 tablespoons cold water until smooth. Stir into the mixture in kettle. Cook and stir until thickened and bubbly. Cook and stir for 1 minute more. If desired, stir in sherry. Pour gravy over meat and vegetables. If desired, sprinkle with snipped parsley. Makes 6 to 8 servings.

***Note:** To make peeling the boiling onions easier, place them in boiling water for 3 minutes; drain. Trim off root ends and gently press the onions to slip the skins off.

Nutrition facts per serving: 558 calories, 34 g total fat (11 g saturated fat), 103 mg cholesterol, 278 mg sodium, 31 g carbohydrate, 4 g fiber, 32 g protein.

Grilled Basil Burgers

1990

In August 1990, we featured "Great Food for Family Reunions." This basil-accented burger was one of our enticing suggestions. It's especially versatile because you can double the recipe to make 16 servings, or make two separate double batches for 32 servings, depending on the size of your family.

1 **slightly beaten egg**
⅔ **cup chopped onion**
½ **cup grated Parmesan cheese**
¼ **cup snipped fresh basil or 1 tablespoon dried basil, crushed**
¼ **cup catsup**
2 **cloves garlic, minced**
¼ **teaspoon salt**
¼ **teaspoon pepper**
1 **pound lean ground beef**
1 **pound ground raw turkey**
8 **hamburger buns, split and toasted**
8 **lettuce leaves**
8 **tomato slices**

1 In a large mixing bowl combine egg, onion, Parmesan cheese, basil, catsup, garlic, salt, and pepper. Add ground beef and turkey; mix well.

2 Shape meat mixture into eight ¾-inch-thick patties. (If you want to tote the burgers, wrap patties individually in plastic wrap; pack the patties with ice in a cooler for up to 4 hours.)

3 Grill patties on rack of uncovered grill directly over medium coals for 15 to 18 minutes or until juices run clear, turning once. (Meat patties will appear pink when done because of catsup added to mixture.) Serve patties on buns with lettuce and tomato. Makes 8 servings.

To make ahead: Prepare and shape meat mixture as directed above. Wrap uncooked patties individually in freezer wrap; freeze for up to 3 months. The night before grilling, thaw wrapped patties in refrigerator.

Nutrition facts per serving: 383 calories, 17 g total fat (6 g saturated fat), 113 mg cholesterol, 603 mg sodium, 27 g carbohydrate, 2 g fiber, 30 g protein.

Beef Bunburgers

1½ pounds lean ground beef
½ cup chopped onion
⅓ cup chopped green sweet
    pepper
1 10¾-ounce can condensed
    tomato soup
1½ teaspoons vinegar

1 teaspoon dry mustard
1 teaspoon poultry seasoning
½ teaspoon dried thyme,
    crushed
¼ teaspoon salt
6 to 8 hamburger buns, split
    and toasted

1 In a large skillet cook ground beef, onion, and green pepper until beef is brown and onion is tender. Drain well. Stir in the soup, vinegar, dry mustard, poultry seasoning, thyme, and salt. Bring to boiling; reduce heat. Simmer, uncovered, about 15 minutes or until desired consistency. Serve on toasted hamburger buns. Makes 6 to 8 servings.

Nutrition facts per serving: 373 calories, 16 g total fat (5 g saturated fat), 71 mg cholesterol, 756 mg sodium, 31 g carbohydrate, 2 g fiber, 26 g protein.

According to Ann Torkar of Menor, Ohio, this home-style recipe is a lifesaver. She says: "We were building a summer cottage in 1953. This recipe was a perfect make-ahead and served a working group well, both children and adults. Over the many years, the tasty and nutritional burgers have traveled to family outings and picnics. (I keep the filling hot in a crockery cooker.) It's an often requested 'bring along' dish."

Hot Tamale Pie

1½ pounds lean ground beef
1 cup chopped onion
1 10¾-ounce can condensed
    tomato soup
¾ cup frozen whole kernel
    corn
½ cup chopped ripe olives
3 tablespoons chili powder

½ teaspoon pepper
¾ cup cornmeal
½ cup all-purpose flour
1 teaspoon baking powder
½ teaspoon baking soda
1 cup buttermilk
1 beaten egg
2 tablespoons cooking oil

1 In a skillet cook beef and onion until beef is brown and onion is tender. Drain. Stir in soup, corn, olives, chili powder, and pepper. Bring to boiling over medium heat. Pour into a 2-quart square baking dish.

2 In a medium mixing bowl stir together the cornmeal, flour, baking powder, baking soda, and ½ teaspoon *salt*. In a small mixing bowl combine buttermilk, egg, and oil; add to flour mixture and stir just until batter is smooth. Pour over hot meat mixture, spreading evenly. Bake in a 425° oven about 25 minutes or until golden brown. Makes 8 servings.

♥*Nutrition facts per serving: 327 calories, 15 g total fat (4 g saturated fat), 81 mg cholesterol, 663 mg sodium, 28 g carbohydrate, 3 g fiber, 21 g protein.*

Our casserole topped with corn bread goes back a long way in Ann Reinyheimer's family. The St. Louis reader tells us, "When my Aunt Gladys went into a retirement home 14 years ago, she gave me all her recipes, including two three-ring binders full of Cook's Round Table recipes. Her personal favorite was the Hot Tamale Pie from November 1941. She copied and gave the recipe to all she knew. I still serve it today. Oh, by the way, my Aunt Gladys is 104—it must have been all those good Better Homes and Gardens recipes."

1965

Skillet Spaghetti

Voting for Skillet Spaghetti as one of our more outstanding recipes, Ellen Spaulding of Derby, Kansas, says, "This is a wonderfully simple and quick recipe. Good, too!"

1 pound lean ground beef
1 cup chopped onion
2 cloves garlic, minced
2 cups tomato juice
1½ cups water
1 8-ounce can tomato sauce
1 6-ounce can tomato paste
2 to 3 teaspoons chili powder

1 teaspoon sugar
1 teaspoon dried oregano, crushed
½ teaspoon salt
Dash pepper
8 ounces packaged dried spaghetti
¼ cup grated Parmesan cheese

1 In a 12-inch skillet cook ground beef, onion, and garlic until the beef is brown and the onion is tender. Drain well. Stir in tomato juice, water, tomato sauce, tomato paste, chili powder, sugar, oregano, salt, and pepper.

2 Bring to boiling; reduce heat. Simmer, covered, for 30 minutes, stirring occasionally. Add the *uncooked* spaghetti; stir to separate strands. Simmer, covered, about 30 minutes more or until spaghetti is tender, stirring frequently. Sprinkle with Parmesan cheese. Makes 4 to 6 servings.

Nutrition facts per serving: 548 calories, 16 g total fat (6 g saturated fat), 76 mg cholesterol, 1,735 mg sodium, 67 g carbohydrate, 7 g fiber, 35 g protein.

Spaghetti Pie

1974

6 ounces packaged dried
   spaghetti
2 tablespoons margarine or
   butter
⅓ cup grated Parmesan
   cheese
2 well-beaten eggs
1 pound lean ground beef or
   bulk pork sausage
½ cup chopped onion
¼ cup chopped green
   sweet pepper

1 7½-ounce can (1 cup)
   tomatoes, cut up
1 6-ounce can tomato paste
1 teaspoon sugar
1 teaspoon dried oregano,
   crushed
½ teaspoon garlic salt
1 cup cream-style cottage
   cheese
½ cup shredded mozzarella
   cheese (2 ounces)

Do you have this problem? Lynn Edwards of Decatur, Illinois, says she has a bad habit of making too much spaghetti when she makes spaghetti and meatballs. Her creative solution to her problem is to freeze the leftover spaghetti to make this can't-miss casserole.

1 Cook the spaghetti according to package directions; drain (should have about 3¼ cups cooked spaghetti). Stir margarine or butter into hot spaghetti. Stir in Parmesan cheese and eggs. Form spaghetti mixture into a "crust" in a buttered 10-inch pie plate.

2 In a large skillet cook the ground beef or pork sausage, onion, and sweet pepper until meat is brown and vegetables are tender. Drain well. Stir in the *undrained* tomatoes, tomato paste, sugar, oregano, and garlic salt. Heat through.

3 Spread cottage cheese over spaghetti mixture in pie plate. Top with the meat mixture. Bake, uncovered, in a 350° oven for 20 minutes. Sprinkle the mozzarella cheese over the top. Bake about 5 minutes more or until mozzarella cheese melts. Makes 6 servings.

Nutrition facts per serving: 414 calories, 18 total fat (7 g saturated fat), 62 mg cholesterol, 821 mg sodium, 33 g carbohydrate, 3 g fiber, 30 g protein.

Tostada Pizza

1975

This Mexican-style pizza captured second prize in our 1975 Budget Recipe Contest for Tedd Shinn of Grand Junction, Colorado. The biscuit mix crust layered with refried beans, taco-seasoned ground meat, and American cheese is just right for families. The zesty flavor proves that cooking on a budget doesn't have to be boring.

1 **pound lean ground beef**
¾ **cup water**
1 **4½-ounce can diced green chili peppers, drained**
½ **of a 1½-ounce envelope taco seasoning mix (about 2 tablespoons)**
1 **teaspoon chili powder**
2 **tablespoons cornmeal**
2 **cups packaged biscuit mix**
½ **cup cold water**
1 **15-ounce can refried beans**
1 **cup shredded sharp American cheese or cheddar cheese (4 ounces)**
1 **cup shredded lettuce**
1 **medium tomato, chopped**
½ **cup thinly sliced green onions**
Taco sauce (optional)

1 In a large skillet cook ground beef until brown. Drain well. Stir in the ¾ cup water, the chili peppers, taco seasoning mix, and chili powder. Simmer, uncovered, about 15 minutes or until thick.

2 Meanwhile, generously grease a 12- to 14-inch pizza pan. Sprinkle with the cornmeal. In a medium mixing bowl stir together the biscuit mix and the ½ cup cold water with a fork until dough follows fork around the bowl. With floured fingers, pat dough into bottom and up edge of prepared pan. Spread refried beans over dough. Spoon meat mixture over refried beans.

3 Bake, uncovered, in a 450° oven for 18 to 20 minutes or until crust is golden brown. Sprinkle with the cheese. Bake for 3 to 5 minutes more or until cheese is melted. Top with lettuce, tomato, and green onions. If desired, serve with taco sauce. Makes 6 servings.

Nutrition facts per serving: 486 calories, 21 total fat (8 g saturated fat), 65 mg cholesterol, 1,480 mg sodium, 46 g carbohydrate, 6 g fiber, 27 g protein.

Hamburger Pie

1945

A prizewinning family casserole from the '40s, this perennial Better Homes and Gardens favorite was one of our earliest convenience recipes because it used canned green beans and tomato soup. If you use the instant mashed potato option and preshredded cheddar cheese, it goes together even more quickly these days.

1 **pound lean ground beef**
½ **cup chopped onion**
1 **14½-ounce can cut green beans, drained, or 2 cups frozen cut green beans, cooked and drained**
1 **10¾-ounce can condensed tomato soup**

⅛ **teaspoon pepper**
5 **medium potatoes, cooked***
½ **cup warmed milk**
1 **beaten egg**
½ **cup shredded American or cheddar cheese (2 ounces)**

1 In a large skillet cook the beef and onion until beef is lightly brown and onion is tender. Drain well. Stir in the beans, tomato soup, and pepper; pour into a 1½-quart casserole.

2 Mash potatoes while hot; add milk and egg. Season to taste with *salt* and additional *pepper*. Spoon in mounds over casserole. Bake in a 350° oven about 25 minutes or until heated through. Sprinkle with cheese and bake 4 to 5 minutes more or until cheese is melted. Makes 4 to 6 servings.

***Note:** Or, prepare 4 servings packaged instant mashed potatoes according to package directions, except reserve the milk. Add egg and season to taste with salt and pepper. Add just enough of the reserved milk so potatoes are stiff enough to form a mound. (Or, use frozen mashed potatoes and decrease milk used in preparation to ⅓ cup. After heating, add just enough of the ⅓ cup milk so potatoes are stiff enough to form a mound.)

Nutrition facts per serving: 504 calories, 20 g total fat (9 g saturated fat), 139 mg cholesterol, 1,003 mg sodium, 50 g carbohydrate, 4 g fiber, 32 g protein.

Mexican-Style Meat Loaf

1940

1 beaten egg
½ cup cornmeal
½ cup chopped onion
¼ cup chopped green sweet
pepper or one 4½-ounce
can diced green chili
peppers, drained
1 7½-ounce can whole
tomatoes, cut up

1 to 2 teaspoons chili powder
½ teaspoon salt
½ teaspoon ground sage
¼ teaspoon black pepper
1 pound ground pork
1 pound lean ground beef
Hot-style catsup or salsa
catsup (optional)

Sometimes it seems that everything but the kitchen sink has been an ingredient in meat loaf. Take, for example, a 1945 recipe that used ground bologna (a cheap meat back then) in place of some of the ground beef. Or, a 1991 version made with ground turkey and stuffed with spinach. This spiced-up meat loaf from 1940 is close to our hearts—and tummies.

1 In a large mixing bowl combine the egg, cornmeal, onion, sweet pepper or chili peppers, *undrained* tomatoes, chili powder, salt, sage, and black pepper. Add pork and beef; mix thoroughly. Shape into a 9×5-inch loaf in a shallow baking pan.

2 Bake meat loaf in a 350° oven about 1¼ hours or until juices run clear. If desired, serve with hot-style or salsa catsup. Makes 10 servings.

♥ *Nutrition facts per serving: 220 calories, 12 g total fat (5 g saturated fat), 84 mg cholesterol, 194 mg sodium, 7 g carbohydrate, 1 g fiber, 19 g protein.*

Vintage Views
1924

Pork Pointers

An article on pork informed the novice cook how to serve it and enlightened readers about the healthful way to include it in meals. The editors offered a chart comparing the cost of various cuts along with this tip on how not to prepare it—which rings a bell, considering today's health standards:

"Possibly in the desert or on a long-drawn-out camping trip thru the woods it may be necessary to live on a diet consisting chiefly of fried smoked pork, but in our state of civilization such a diet is to be avoided."

Puffy Tortilla Bake

1960

During the '60s, the travel bug bit most Americans. They vacationed all over the world and enjoyed many new dishes. Back home, the memory of these new foods lingered, and cooks began trying to make them. In response, our magazine offered more and more internationally inspired recipes, such as these zippy south-of-the-border enchiladas. Note: The "puffy" tortillas don't live up to their name—they don't really puff.

¾ cup chopped onion
1 tablespoon cooking oil
1 14½-ounce can tomatoes, cut up
1 8-ounce can tomato sauce
1 clove garlic, minced
1 4½-ounce can diced green chili peppers
2 teaspoons chili powder
1 teaspoon sugar
12 ounces lean ground beef
1 clove garlic, minced
½ cup sliced green onions

3 tablespoons chopped pitted ripe olives
1 tablespoon chili powder
¼ teaspoon salt
1 recipe Puffy Tortillas or 12 purchased corn tortillas
1½ cups shredded sharp American cheese, cheddar cheese, or Monterey Jack cheese with jalapeños (6 ounces)

1 Grease a 3-quart rectangular baking dish. Set aside.

2 In a large skillet cook chopped onion in hot oil until tender. Stir in the *undrained* tomatoes, tomato sauce, 1 clove garlic, chili peppers, the 2 teaspoons chili powder, and the sugar. Simmer, uncovered, 20 minutes or until reduced to 3 cups. Set aside.

3 In a medium skillet cook beef and the 1 clove garlic until beef is brown. Drain well. Stir in green onions, chopped olives, the 1 tablespoon chili powder, and salt. With browned side down, fill each Puffy Tortilla or purchased tortilla with about 2 tablespoons meat mixture and *1 tablespoon* cheese; roll up. Arrange in the prepared baking dish. Pour the tomato mixture over.

4 Bake, covered, in a 350° oven for 20 minutes. Uncover; sprinkle with remaining cheese and bake, uncovered, about 5 minutes more or until cheese is melted. Makes 6 servings.

Puffy Tortillas: Stir together ¾ cup *all-purpose flour* and ¾ cup *cornmeal*. Add 1¾ cups *water* and 1 beaten *egg*. Beat until smooth. Heat a lightly greased 6-inch skillet. Remove from heat. Spoon in 3 tablespoons of the batter; lift and tilt the skillet to spread batter. Cook 1 to 2 minutes or until browned on bottom and just set on top. Invert pan over paper towels; remove tortilla. Repeat with remaining batter, greasing skillet occasionally. Makes 12.

Nutrition facts per serving: 397 calories, 19 g total fat (8 g saturated fat), 98 mg cholesterol, 971 mg sodium, 34 g carbohydrate, 4 g fiber, 22 g protein.

Spinach Sausage Pie

1989

1 **pound bulk Italian sausage**
1 **10-ounce package frozen chopped spinach, thawed and well drained**
1 **8-ounce can tomato sauce**
1 **4-ounce can sliced mushrooms, drained**
⅓ **cup fine dry bread crumbs**

1 **2-ounce jar sliced pimiento, drained**
1 **16-ounce loaf frozen whole wheat or white bread dough, thawed**
1 **tablespoon margarine or butter, melted**

In 1989, we recommended this pie with Eastern Indian seasonings as an effortless yet distinctive entrée for the holidays. We still think it makes a spectacular meal. To make the best use of your precious holiday time, you may want to follow the handy make-ahead directions.

1 Grease a 9-inch springform pan. Set aside.

2 For filling, in a large skillet cook sausage until brown. Drain well. Add the spinach, tomato sauce, mushrooms, bread crumbs, and pimiento. Mix thoroughly and set aside.

3 For crust, on a lightly floured surface roll *two-thirds* of the bread dough into an 11-inch circle. Carefully place in the prepared pan, patting dough 1 inch up the side. Spoon filling into crust.

4 On a lightly floured surface, roll remaining bread dough into a 10-inch circle. Cut dough circle into 10 to 12 wedges. Arrange wedges on top of the filling, sealing edges to bottom crust along edge of pan. Brush top with melted margarine or butter.

5 Bake in a 375° oven for 30 to 35 minutes or until filling is hot. If necessary, cover top with foil the last 10 minutes of baking to prevent overbrowning. Cool on a wire rack for 10 minutes. Remove side of pan. Serve warm. Makes 8 servings.

To make ahead: Prepare and bake pie as directed above. Cool pie nearly to room temperature, then cover with foil. Refrigerate for up to 24 hours. Reheat, covered, in a 325° oven for 30 to 35 minutes or until heated through, removing foil after 20 minutes.

♥ *Nutrition facts per serving: 298 calories, 12 g total fat (3 g saturated fat), 23 mg cholesterol, 864 mg sodium, 37 g carbohydrate, 3 g fiber, 14 g protein.*

1970

Sicilian Meat Roll

Four of our readers—from Massachusetts, Colorado, Montana, and California— nominated this recipe as an all-time greatest recipe. All four told us they have served the dish as the star attraction at dinner parties.

2 slightly beaten eggs
¾ cup soft bread crumbs (1 slice)
½ cup tomato juice
2 tablespoons snipped parsley
½ teaspoon dried oregano, crushed
¼ teaspoon salt
¼ teaspoon pepper

1 clove garlic, minced
2 pounds lean ground beef
6 1-ounce thin slices boiled ham
1½ cups shredded mozzarella cheese (6 ounces)
3 slices (4×4 inches each) mozzarella cheese, halved diagonally

1 In a large mixing bowl combine the eggs, bread crumbs, tomato juice, parsley, oregano, salt, pepper, and garlic. Add the ground beef and mix well. On foil, pat meat mixture to a 12×10-inch rectangle. Arrange ham slices on top of the meat, leaving a ¾-inch border around all edges. Sprinkle shredded mozzarella cheese over ham. Starting from a short side, carefully roll up meat, jelly-roll style, using foil to lift; seal edges. Place roll, seam side down, in a 13×9×2-inch baking pan.

2 Bake in a 350° oven for 1¼ hours or until an instant-read thermometer registers 170° and juices run clear. (Center of roll will be pink due to ham.) Place mozzarella cheese wedges over top of roll; return to oven about 5 minutes or until cheese melts. Makes 8 to 10 servings.

Nutrition facts per serving: 323 calories, 19 g total fat (8 g saturated fat), 152 mg cholesterol, 604 mg sodium, 4 g carbohydrate, 0 g fiber, 33 g protein.

Hamburger Cheese Bake

1967

12 ounces lean ground beef
½ cup chopped onion
 1 15-ounce can tomato sauce
 1 teaspoon sugar
¼ teaspoon salt
¼ teaspoon garlic powder
¼ teaspoon black pepper
 4 cups packaged dried
    medium noodles
 1 cup cream-style cottage
    cheese

½ of an 8-ounce package
   cream cheese, softened
¼ cup dairy sour cream
⅓ cup sliced green onions
¼ cup chopped green sweet
   pepper
¼ cup grated or finely
   shredded Parmesan
   cheese

Octogenarian Melva White of Meshappen, Pennsylvania, has been preparing this easy dish since it was first published in 1967. She writes: "I cherish this recipe because it is always good to serve to company, and it can be made a day ahead and baked the next day. Our adult children always say when they visit us now, 'Hope you make your great recipe with the hamburger that's so good.'"

1 In a large skillet cook the ground beef and onion until meat is brown and onion is tender. Drain well. Stir in the tomato sauce, sugar, salt, garlic powder, and black pepper. Remove from heat.

2 Meanwhile, cook the noodles according to package directions; drain. Stir together the cottage cheese, cream cheese, sour cream, green onions, and sweet pepper.

3 Spread half of the noodles in a 2-quart rectangular baking dish. Top with about half of the meat mixture. Top with the cottage cheese mixture. Top with remaining noodles and remaining meat mixture. Sprinkle with Parmesan cheese. Bake in 350° oven about 30 minutes or until heated through. Makes 6 to 8 servings.

To make ahead: Prepare casserole as above; cover unbaked casserole with plastic wrap. Refrigerate for up to 24 hours. Remove plastic wrap and cover loosely with foil. Bake in a 350° oven for 30 minutes. Uncover and bake about 15 minutes more or until heated through.

Nutrition facts per serving: 358 calories, 19 g total fat (10 g saturated fat), 90 mg cholesterol, 845 mg sodium, 25 g carbohydrate, 2 g fiber, 23 g protein.

Marvelous Mustard Ribs

1992

he choice of several on our staff, this recipe from Carolyn Funk of Mount Pleasant, Pennsylvania, won second place in our July 1992 Prize Tested Recipes contest for barbecued ribs. The spice rub makes the ribs taste and look marvelous.

⅓ cup granulated sugar
1 teaspoon pepper
2 teaspoons paprika
1 teaspoon curry powder
½ teaspoon salt
3½ to 4 pounds pork country-style ribs
1 cup packed brown sugar

⅔ cup white vinegar or cider vinegar
½ cup chopped onion
⅓ cup spicy brown mustard or Dijon-style mustard
2 cloves garlic, minced
2 tablespoons honey
2 teaspoons liquid smoke
¼ teaspoon celery seed

1 In a small mixing bowl combine the granulated sugar, pepper, paprika, curry powder, and salt. Rub over ribs, coating well. Place ribs in a shallow pan. Cover and refrigerate for 2 to 6 hours.

2 In a covered grill arrange medium coals around a drip pan. Test for medium-low heat above pan. Place ribs, fat side up, on grill rack over drip pan but not over coals. Lower grill hood. Grill about 1¼ hours or until tender, turning once and adding more coals as needed.

3 Meanwhile, for sauce, in a medium saucepan combine the brown sugar, vinegar, onion, mustard, garlic, honey, liquid smoke, and celery seed. Bring to boiling; reduce heat. Cook sauce, uncovered, for 25 to 30 minutes or until slightly thickened, stirring occasionally.

4 Brush sauce over ribs occasionally during the last 10 to 15 minutes of grilling. Heat any remaining sauce until bubbly and pass with ribs. Makes 8 servings.

♥*Nutrition facts per serving: 319 calories, 11 g total fat (3 g saturated fat), 43 mg cholesterol, 317 mg sodium, 38 g carbohydrate, 1 g fiber, 19 g protein.*

Spiced Beef

1960

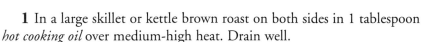

1 2½- to 3-pound beef arm
   or blade pot roast
   (bone in)
1 14½-ounce can tomatoes,
   cut up
¼ cup white wine vinegar

1 clove garlic, minced
¼ teaspoon pepper
6 whole cloves
2 teaspoons pickling spice
2 tablespoons all-purpose
   flour

1 In a large skillet or kettle brown roast on both sides in 1 tablespoon *hot cooking oil* over medium-high heat. Drain well.

2 In a bowl combine *undrained* tomatoes, the vinegar, ¼ cup *water*, garlic, and pepper. Pour over meat. Tie spices in a 6-inch square of 100-percent-cotton cheesecloth. Add to skillet. Bring mixture to boiling; reduce heat. Simmer, covered, for 2 to 2½ hours until meat is tender.

3 Transfer meat to a warm platter. Skim fat from cooking liquid. Discard spice bag. Measure cooking liquid; add water, if necessary, to measure 2 cups liquid. In a bowl stir the flour into ¼ cup *cold water*. Gradually stir into liquid. Cook and stir until thickened and bubbly; cook and stir 1 minute more. Serve with gravy. Makes 6 to 8 servings.

♥*Nutrition facts per serving: 327 calories, 15 g total fat (5 g saturated fat), 124 mg cholesterol, 193 mg sodium, 5 g carbohydrate, 1 g fiber, 41 g protein.*

According to Jennifer McElhaney of Montgomery, Alabama, this tangy pot roast has a long legacy in her family. "We have four sons," she explains, "and they all claim this recipe is their very favorite. My daughters-in-law have told me how their husbands start smiling when they come home and smell this roast cooking."

*V*intage Views
1936

Magic with Meat

"For the envied and much sung 'good cook' is known first and foremost by her ability to cook meat with skill and imagination. It was true when the first cavewoman struggled to make tough reindeer flank taste like filet mignon. It's still true today.

"But don't mistake me. By real artistry in cooking meat, I don't mean the gentle accomplishment of broiling a steak or a chop, delightful as this knowledge is. It's skill in creating magic with plain everyday shanks, humble pot roasts, and not-too-tender shoulder cuts that sends the guests home marveling—and spreads cheer over the food budget!"

Zesty Steak Carbonnade

1994

This recipe won first place in the June 1994 Prize Tested Recipes contest. Carbonnade is a Flemish dish generally made with slices of beef that are cooked with onions and beer. The word comes from the Italian carbonata, which means "charcoal-grilled." Sharon Naylor of New Jersey submitted the recipe and said she spiced up the classic with a few ingredients.

⅔ cup beer
½ cup chopped onion
⅓ cup salsa catsup or catsup
2 tablespoons sugar
1 tablespoon Worcestershire sauce

4 teaspoons lemon juice
½ teaspoon paprika
½ teaspoon chili powder
¼ teaspoon pepper
6 top loin steaks, cut 1 inch thick (about 2 pounds)

1 In a small saucepan combine beer, onion, catsup, sugar, Worcestershire sauce, lemon juice, paprika, chili powder, and pepper. Bring to boiling, reduce heat. Simmer, uncovered, 5 minutes. Cool.

2 Use a sharp knife to score steaks on both sides. Place steaks in a plastic bag set inside a deep bowl. Pour marinade over steaks. Seal bag and turn steaks to coat. Marinate in the refrigerator for at least 1 hour or up to 24 hours.

3 Remove steaks from bag; reserve marinade. Place steaks on the grill rack of an uncovered grill directly over medium-hot coals. Grill steaks, uncovered, for 8 to 12 minutes for rare doneness or 13 to 15 minutes for medium doneness, turning the meat halfway through grilling.

4 Meanwhile, place reserved marinade in a small saucepan; bring to a full boil. Cook and stir for 1 to 2 minutes. Serve with steaks. Makes 6 servings.

♥ *Nutrition facts per serving: 283 calories, 10 g total fat (4 g saturated fat), 101 mg cholesterol, 282 mg sodium, 11 g carbohydrate, 1 g fiber, 35 g protein.*

Peppered Chutney Roast

¾ cup unsweetened pineapple
  juice
½ cup steak sauce
⅓ cup port wine
⅓ cup Worcestershire sauce
¼ cup lemon juice
1 teaspoon seasoned salt
1 teaspoon lemon-pepper
  seasoning
1 teaspoon dry mustard

1 teaspoon ground black
  pepper
1 2½- to 3-pound beef
  tenderloin
1 teaspoon cracked black
  pepper
3 slices bacon, cooked and
  drained
½ cup chutney
  Chutney

This marinated beef tenderloin is a Christmas regular at the Gammill house in Huntsville, Alabama. Barbara Gammill says, "I purchase the tenderloin when it is on sale, prepare it with the marinade, then freeze it until Christmas. Christmas dinner is a feast at my house, but the only work involved on Christmas Day is putting the tenderloin in the oven. All the preparations are done ahead of time so I can enjoy Christmas."

1 For marinade, in a medium mixing bowl stir together the pineapple juice, steak sauce, port wine, Worcestershire sauce, lemon juice, seasoned salt, lemon-pepper seasoning, dry mustard, and the ground pepper. To score the beef tenderloin, make shallow cuts at 1-inch intervals diagonally across top of meat in a diamond pattern. Repeat on other side. Place tenderloin in a large plastic bag; set in a large, deep bowl. Pour marinade over tenderloin; seal bag. Marinate in the refrigerator for 4 to 8 hours, turning bag occasionally. Drain meat, reserving marinade.

2 Rub tenderloin with cracked pepper. Place on a rack in a shallow roasting pan. Insert meat thermometer. Roast, uncovered, in a 425° oven for 30 to 45 minutes or until meat thermometer registers 135°. Baste tenderloin with the reserved marinade twice during roasting.

3 Arrange bacon strips along top of tenderloin. Cut up any large pieces in the ½ cup chutney; spoon evenly over tenderloin. Return to oven for 5 to 10 minutes more or until thermometer registers 140°. Remove tenderloin to serving platter. Let stand, covered, about 15 minutes before slicing. Serve with additional chutney. Makes 12 servings.

♥ *Nutrition facts per serving: 203 calories, 7 g total fat (3 g saturated fat), 55 mg cholesterol, 507 mg sodium, 13 g carbohydrate, 0 g fiber, 19 g protein.*

Beef Tenderloin with Port Sauce

1990

Every year our editors work hard to give our readers new ideas for holiday meals. The task is a delicate one because it involves giving traditional foods a new twist. Take, for example, the following menu from our December 1990 issue.

Beef Tenderloin with
Port Sauce

———

Glazed Vegetables

———

Whole Wheat Brioche

———

Cranberry-Pear Relish

———

Double-Chocolate
Torte

———

Crème de Menthe Coffee

The meal features traditional roast beef spiffed up with puff pastry cutouts and a tawny port sauce. Instead of simple buttered vegetables, we suggest a glazed vegetable combination, and rather than plain dinner rolls, we recommend brioche. We even dressed up the cranberry relish by adding pears.

½ **of a 17¼-ounce package (1 sheet) frozen puff pastry, thawed**
1 **beaten egg white**
1 **3-pound beef tenderloin**
1½ **cups beef broth**
¾ **cup tawny port or dry red wine**
2 **tablespoons finely chopped shallot or onion**
½ **teaspoon dried rosemary, crushed**
1 **bay leaf**
3 **tablespoons margarine or butter, softened**
2 **tablespoons all-purpose flour**

1 Unfold puff pastry. On a lightly floured surface, roll puff pastry to eliminate crease. With a small cookie cutter or hors d'oeuvre cutter, cut 16 small shapes out of the puff pastry. Transfer pastry shapes to an ungreased baking sheet. Brush shapes with egg white. Bake in a 400° oven about 10 minutes or until golden brown and flaky. Cool. If desired, tightly cover and store at room temperature for up to 12 hours.

2 If tenderloin is long and thin, fold narrow ends under and tie. If tenderloin is flat and wide, tie crosswise in 2 or 3 places to form a rounder shape. (The tenderloin should be about 8×4½ inches after tying.) Place on rack in shallow roasting pan. Insert meat thermometer.

3 Roast tenderloin, uncovered, in a 425° oven about 45 minutes or until desired doneness (140° for medium rare). Let stand, covered, about 10 minutes before slicing. (Meat temperature should rise about 5° while standing.)

4 Meanwhile, for port sauce, in a medium saucepan combine the beef broth, tawny port or red wine, shallot or onion, dried rosemary, and bay leaf. Bring to boiling; reduce heat. Simmer, uncovered, for 15 to 20 minutes. (You should have about 1⅓ cups sauce after simmering.) Discard the bay leaf.

5 In a small mixing bowl stir together the margarine or butter and flour. Stir into the wine mixture. Cook and stir until thickened and bubbly. Cook and stir for 1 minute more.

6 To serve, place tenderloin pieces on dinner plates. Spoon 2 to 3 tablespoons of the port sauce over each. Garnish each serving with 2 pastry puffs. Makes 8 servings.

To make sauce ahead: Prepare and simmer sauce as directed above, but do not add margarine-flour mixture. Cool. Transfer to a storage container and refrigerate for up to 2 days. Before serving, return to a medium saucepan and heat through. Continue by stirring together margarine or butter and flour and thickening sauce as directed above.

Nutrition facts per serving: 465 calories, 26 g total fat (6 g saturated fat), 106 mg cholesterol, 424 mg sodium, 14 g carbohydrate, 0 g fiber, 39 g protein.

Marinated Rump Roast

1955

arbecuing has been a feature on the pages of Better Homes and Gardens *for many decades, but it wasn't until the '50s that the grill became a fixture in almost every backyard. This tongue-tingling roast is one of many recipes from the magazine's golden age of barbecue.*

1 **3-pound boneless beef rump roast (rolled and tied)**
2½ **cups water**
2½ **cups vinegar**
2 **medium onions, sliced**
1 **medium lemon, sliced**
2 or 3 **bay leaves**
12 **whole cloves**
6 **whole black peppercorns**
1 **teaspoon salt**

1 Place meat in a large plastic bag; set in a large, deep bowl. For marinade, in a medium mixing bowl combine the water, vinegar, onions, lemon, bay leaves, cloves, peppercorns, and salt. Pour marinade over meat; seal bag. Marinate in the refrigerator for 2 to 3 days, turning bag occasionally. Drain meat, reserving marinade.

2 Center roast on spit of grill* and secure with holding forks. On grill with motorized spit, fit spit in place over medium-low coals. Turn on motorized spit. Grill until desired doneness, brushing occasionally with reserved marinade and adding additional coals as needed. (Allow 2 to 2½ hours for medium doneness—160° on instant-read thermometer.) To serve, remove from spit and slice meat. Makes 12 to 14 servings.

*Note: If you don't have a grill with a motorized spit, in a covered grill arrange medium coals around drip pan. Test for medium-low heat over drip pan. Place the roast on the grill rack over drip pan. Cover and grill roast 1½ to 2 hours or until instant-read thermometer registers 160° (medium), brushing occasionally with reserved marinade and adding additional coals as needed.

♥*Nutrition facts per serving: 147 calories, 5 g total fat (2 g saturated fat), 72 mg cholesterol, 83 mg sodium, 0 g carbohydrate, 0 g fiber, 24 g protein.*

Festive Pork Roast

★
1979

1	5-pound boneless pork loin roast (rolled and tied)
¾	cup dry red wine
⅓	cup packed brown sugar
¼	cup vinegar
¼	cup catsup
¼	cup water

2	tablespoons cooking oil
1	tablespoon soy sauce
1	clove garlic, minced
1	teaspoon curry powder
½	teaspoon ground ginger
¼	teaspoon pepper
2	teaspoons cornstarch

When it comes to holiday meals, Mary Kroodsma of Charlotte, Michigan, relies on this people-pleasing pork roast. The leftovers make terrific sandwiches for a quick meal the next day.

1 Place roast in a large, plastic bag; set in a large, deep bowl. For marinade, in a small mixing bowl combine wine, brown sugar, vinegar, catsup, water, oil, soy sauce, garlic, curry powder, ginger, and pepper. Pour marinade over meat; seal bag. Marinate in refrigerator for 6 to 8 hours or overnight, turning bag several times. Drain meat, reserving 1¼ cups marinade. Pat meat dry with paper towels.

2 Place the meat on a rack in a shallow roasting pan. Insert meat thermometer. Roast in a 325° oven for 2¼ to 2½ hours or until meat thermometer registers 155°.

3 About 25 minutes before the meat is done, make sauce. In a small saucepan stir cornstarch into reserved marinade. Cook and stir until thickened and bubbly. Cook 2 minutes more. Brush roast frequently with sauce during the last 15 minutes of roasting.

4 Let meat stand, covered, about 15 minutes before slicing. (Meat temperature should rise about 5° while standing.) Reheat remaining sauce and pass with meat. Makes 15 servings.

♥ *Nutrition facts per serving: 210 calories, 11 g total fat (4 g saturated fat), 68 mg cholesterol, 134 mg sodium, 4 g carbohydrate, 0 g fiber, 22 g protein.*

Pork Chop Barbecue

We loved this story from Janet Watkins of Harrison, Arkansas: "In the summer of 1953, a young housewife and mother of two served Pork Chop Barbecue to guests out in the 'Oil Patch' of west Texas. Forty-three years later, a retired high school teacher, mother of seven, and grandmother of 14, served the same recipe to a guest on a quarter horse farm in Arkansas. By the way, I am both these women! I have used the recipe all these years because it never fails to elicit compliments. It is a 'prepare ahead and forget' dish that's very well seasoned and always tender."

½ cup water
3 tablespoons vinegar
2 tablespoons sugar
1 tablespoon prepared mustard
¼ teaspoon salt
¼ to ½ teaspoon black pepper
⅛ teaspoon ground red pepper
1 slice lemon

1 medium onion, sliced
½ cup catsup
2 tablespoons Worcestershire sauce
1 to 2 teaspoons liquid smoke
6 pork rib chops, ¾-inch thick
1 to 2 tablespoons cooking oil

1 For sauce, in a small saucepan combine water, vinegar, sugar, mustard, salt, black pepper, and red pepper. Add lemon slice and onion. Bring mixture to boiling; reduce heat. Simmer, uncovered, for 20 minutes. Stir in catsup, Worcestershire sauce, and liquid smoke. Return to boiling. Remove from heat; discard lemon slice.

2 In a large skillet brown pork chops, half at a time, in hot oil over medium-high heat. Place pork chops in a 3-quart rectangular baking dish; pour sauce over top.

3 Bake chops, uncovered, in a 350° oven for 25 to 30 minutes or until pork chops are slightly pink in the center and juices run clear, turning chops once. Remove chops to a serving platter. Pour sauce over all. Makes 6 servings.

♥*Nutrition facts per serving: 253 calories, 15 g total fat (4 g saturated fat), 52 mg cholesterol, 481 mg sodium, 13 g carbohydrate, 1 g fiber, 16 g protein.*

Meatballs Stroganoff

¼ cup finely crushed saltine
    crackers (7)
1 egg
¼ cup milk
¼ teaspoon salt
    Dash dried thyme, crushed
    Dash dried oregano,
      crushed
    Dash pepper
½ pound ground pork
½ pound ground beef
1 tablespoon cooking oil

½ cup water
1 teaspoon instant beef
    bouillon granules
2 tablespoons all-purpose
    flour
1 8-ounce carton dairy sour
    cream
¾ cup water
1 4.5-ounce can sliced
    mushrooms, drained
¼ teaspoon salt
    Hot cooked noodles or rice

Stroganoff, a classic Russian dish, has been known in Europe since the 18th century. Named after the wealthy Stroganov family, the dish is generally made with strips of beef and served over rice. Here we've teamed it with noodles and used meatballs instead of beef strips.

1 Combine crackers, egg, milk, ¼ teaspoon salt, thyme, oregano, and pepper. Add ground meats; mix well. Form meat mixture into 40 meatballs, about 1½-inch balls. In a 12-inch skillet brown the meatballs in hot oil, turning carefully to brown all sides. Stir together the ½ cup water and bouillon; add to skillet. Bring to boiling; reduce heat. Cover and simmer 20 minutes or until juices are no longer pink. Remove meatballs from skillet; skim fat from drippings.

2 Meanwhile, combine the flour and sour cream. Stir in the ¾ cup water, mushrooms, and the ¼ teaspoon salt. Stir into skillet or large saucepan, scraping up any browned bits. Cook and stir over medium heat until thickened and bubbly. Cook and stir 1 minute more. Add the meatballs. Heat through. Serve over hot cooked noodles. Makes 4 to 6 servings.

For a lower-fat version: Substitute light dairy sour cream for regular sour cream.

Nutrition facts per serving with ¹/₂ cup noodles: 551 calories, 33 g total fat (14 g saturated fat), 184 mg cholesterol, 763 mg sodium, 31 g carbohydrate, 2 g fiber, 31 g protein.
Lower-fat version: 490 calories, 21 g total fat (7 g saturated fat), 158 mg cholesterol, 778 mg sodium, 39 g carbohydrate, 2 g fiber, 33 g protein.

Oven-Barbecued Ribs

This recipe has turned into a year-round favorite for Sandra Remde and her family in Plymouth, Minnesota. Sandra writes: "This is the recipe that my husband and three sons request for their birthday dinners. We think the sauce for the ribs is extra special. When the weather allows, we enjoy the ribs done on the outdoor grill."

4 **pounds pork loin back ribs or meaty spareribs, cut into serving-size pieces**
1 **clove garlic, minced**
1 **tablespoon margarine or butter**
½ **cup catsup**
⅓ **cup chili sauce**
2 **tablespoons brown sugar**

2 **tablespoons chopped onion**
1 **tablespoon prepared mustard**
1 **tablespoon Worcestershire sauce**
¾ **teaspoon celery seed**
¼ **teaspoon salt**
  Dash bottled hot pepper sauce

1 Place ribs in a kettle; add enough water to cover ribs. Bring to boiling; reduce heat. Simmer, covered, for 1 hour.

2 Meanwhile, for sauce, in a small saucepan cook the garlic in hot margarine or butter for 1 minute. Stir in catsup, chili sauce, brown sugar, onion, mustard, Worcestershire sauce, celery seed, salt, and hot pepper sauce. Bring to boiling, stirring to dissolve the sugar. Remove from heat; set aside.

3 Drain ribs; place in a shallow baking pan. Pour sauce over ribs. Bake, covered, in a 350° oven about 20 minutes or until heated through. Makes 4 servings.

Nutrition facts per serving: 493 calories, 19 g total fat (6 g saturated fat), 142 mg cholesterol, 1,032 mg sodium, 20 g carbohydrate, 1 g fiber, 59 g protein.

Cranberry-Burgundy Glazed Ham

1969

1 10- to 14-pound bone-in cooked ham Whole cloves	½ cup brown sugar ½ cup burgundy or other dry red wine
1 16-ounce can whole cranberry sauce	1 tablespoon prepared mustard

Twenty-eight years ago, Allene Neitzke of Whittier, California, entered this full-flavored berry-glazed ham in our Prize Tested Recipes contest. In sending us this time-honored recipe as her all-time favorite, she says, "I still remember the thrill of receiving $50 and having my recipe published."

1 Place the ham, fat side up, on rack in a shallow roasting pan. Score fat in diamond pattern; stud with whole cloves. Insert meat thermometer into thickest portion of ham without touching bone. Bake in 325° oven about 3 hours or until thermometer registers 140°.

2 Meanwhile, in a medium saucepan stir together the cranberry sauce, brown sugar, wine, and mustard. Bring to boiling; reduce heat. Simmer, uncovered, for 5 minutes. Spoon half of the sauce over ham during the last 30 minutes of roasting. Reheat remaining sauce and pass with ham. Makes 32 servings.

♥*Nutrition facts per serving: 187 calories, 5 g total fat (2 g saturated fat), 54 mg cholesterol, 1,306 mg sodium, 8 g carbohydrate, 0 g fiber, 24 g protein.*

Heavenly Ham

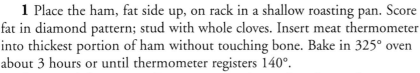

The wonderful flavor of ham has been a part of America's culinary heritage ever since the earliest settlers. Its savory flavor comes from the salt used to cure it and the wood used to smoke it. Through the years, the equipment and specific techniques used to make ham have changed a great deal, but the basic process is much the same. First, ham is cured with salt, then it's suspended over a hardwood fire that cooks the meat and gives it a smoky flavor. For most hams, the processing ends here, but a few specialty hams, such as Westphalian and prosciutto, are aged to intensify their flavor. At the supermarket, you'll find everything from country-style ham, which is dry-cured but uncooked, to cooked ham that comes already glazed. You also can choose between bone-in ham, semi-boneless ham, boneless ham, and canned ham. What's more, today ham comes in lower-fat and lower-sodium versions.

Roast Pork Tangerine

1965

1 4- to 5-pound pork loin
center rib roast,
backbone loosened
1 teaspoon dry mustard
1 teaspoon dried marjoram,
crushed
½ teaspoon salt
2 teaspoons finely shredded
tangerine or orange peel
½ cup tangerine or orange
juice
1 tablespoon brown sugar

Chicken broth or beef
broth
⅔ cup chicken broth or
beef broth
3 tablespoons all-purpose
flour
⅛ teaspoon dry mustard
⅛ teaspoon dried marjoram,
crushed
3 tangerines or 2 oranges,
peeled, sectioned,
and seeded

When this recipe first appeared in the magazine in the '60s, most center-cut pork rib roasts would have included bone. Today, boneless roasts are becoming more popular because the roasts are easier to serve and have less waste. If you prefer a boneless roast, purchase a 3- to 4-pound boneless pork loin center rib roast and be sure to cook it until a meat thermometer inserted in the center of the roast registers 155°.

1 Place pork, rib side down, in a shallow roasting pan. In a small bowl combine the 1 teaspoon dry mustard, the 1 teaspoon marjoram, and the salt; rub over meat. Insert a meat thermometer in center of meat without touching bone. Roast, uncovered, in a 325° oven for 1¾ hours.

2 In a small mixing bowl stir together the peel, juice, and brown sugar; spoon over the meat. Roast about 30 minutes more or until thermometer registers 155°, spooning pan juices over meat once or twice. Transfer meat to platter. Let stand, covered, about 10 minutes before slicing. (Meat temperature should rise about 5° while standing.)

3 Meanwhile, strain pan juices. Skim off fat. Measure juices; add enough broth to juices to equal ¾ cup liquid. Place the liquid in a medium saucepan. In a screw-top jar combine the ⅔ cup broth and the flour; shake well. Add to saucepan along with the ⅛ teaspoon dry mustard and the ⅛ teaspoon marjoram. Cook and stir until thickened and bubbly; cook and stir for 1 minute more. Season to taste with *salt* and *pepper*. Stir in the tangerines or oranges; heat through. Serve with pork. Makes 10 servings.

♥ *Nutrition facts per serving: 266 calories, 14 g total fat (5 g saturated fat), 87 mg cholesterol, 246 mg sodium, 7 g carbohydrate, 1 g fiber, 26 g protein.*

Pork Medaillons with Brandy Cream

1990

Treat your friends and family to this sophisticated entrée from the October 1990 issue. It was the headliner for the following elegant harvest menu.

Pork Medaillons with Brandy Cream

Wild Rice and Cranberry Pilaf

Sourdough or French bread

Steamed baby pattypan squash

Fume Blanc or Chardonnay wine

Amaretto Compote

Coffee or Tea

---

1 2- to 2½-pound boneless pork loin roast
  Pepper
  Salt
½ cup chicken broth
2 tablespoons chopped shallot or green onion
⅓ cup whipping cream

3 tablespoons brandy or cognac
¾ cup unsalted butter, cut into small pieces and softened
4 teaspoons lemon juice
¼ teaspoon white pepper
  Fresh chives (optional)

1 Rub pork roast with pepper. Lightly sprinkle with salt. Place on a rack in a shallow baking pan. Insert a meat thermometer in center of meat. Roast in a 325° oven for 1 to 1½ hours or until thermometer registers 155°. Let stand, covered, about 10 minutes before slicing. (The meat temperature should rise about 5° while standing.)

2 Meanwhile, for sauce, in a medium saucepan combine chicken broth and shallot or green onion. Bring to boiling; reduce heat. Simmer, covered, for 2 minutes. Stir in whipping cream and brandy or cognac. Simmer, uncovered, over medium heat for 12 to 14 minutes or until sauce is reduced to ½ cup. Remove from heat. Strain sauce; return sauce to pan.

3 Add butter to sauce, *one* piece at a time, stirring constantly with a wire whisk. Stir in lemon juice and white pepper.

4 To serve, slice meat across the grain into thin slices. Place 2 or 3 slices on each dinner plate; spoon sauce over meat. If desired, garnish with chives. Makes 10 servings.

Nutrition facts per serving: 298 calories, 23 total fat (13 g saturated fat), 102 mg cholesterol, 151 mg sodium, 1 g carbohydrate, 0 g fiber, 19 g protein.

*V*intage Views
1936

Shall We Join the Ladies?

*I*n the October 1936 issue of *Better Homes and Gardens* magazine, an editor raised the question, "Shall we join the Ladies?" He continued:

"One by one the barriers have been crashed. All territories formerly sacred to me have been invaded by women. Even the barrooms, barbershops, and smoking cars on commuting trains—the last three male strongholds—have capitulated.

… If women are to muscle in on the erstwhile masculine rackets, men are privileged to take a whirl at those activities which in the past were thought exclusively feminine. Take a thing like cooking. … Despite the fact that the great epicures, from Brillat-Savarin to Julian Street, have all been men, women have continued to hold prior rights to the kitchen. The idea of a man coming off well in a bout with pots and pans is, to most women, comical, something to be accepted with amused tolerance.

… Men run, box, swim, test their endurance in all sorts of ways. Surely they're tough enough to stand 'bending over a hot stove.' If you haven't been taught how to cook there's not much gain in blistering yourself. The thing which prevents the uninitiated boy from cooking isn't fear of the flame. It's the fact that he can't produce anything edible. In other words, it's not the heat; it's the futility."

Five-Spice Pork Sandwiches

1995

mericans were introduced to five-spice powder when the popularity of Oriental food soared in the '70s. Over the years, cooks experimented with the seasoning in all types of dishes. By 1995, our magazine was even using it in home-style recipes, such as this shredded pork sandwich.

1 2½- to 3-pound boneless pork shoulder roast
1 cup apple juice
2 tablespoons soy sauce
2 tablespoons hoisin sauce

1½ teaspoons Homemade Five-Spice Powder or purchased five-spice powder
6 to 8 kaiser rolls, split and toasted
1½ to 2 cups shredded Chinese cabbage

1 Trim excess fat from roast. If necessary, cut roast to fit into a 3½- or 4-quart electric crockery cooker. Place roast in cooker. For sauce, in a small mixing bowl combine the apple juice, soy sauce, hoisin sauce, and Homemade Five-Spice Powder or purchased five-spice powder. Pour over roast. Cover and cook on low-heat setting for 10 to 12 hours or on high-heat setting for 5 to 6 hours.

2 Remove the roast from the cooker. Remove meat from bone; discard bone and fat. Using 2 forks, shred meat. Skim fat from cooking juices. Divide juices among 6 to 8 small bowls. Serve meat on toasted rolls with shredded cabbage. Serve with juices. Makes 6 to 8 sandwiches.

Homemade Five-Spice Powder: In a blender container combine 3 tablespoons *ground cinnamon,* 6 *star anise* or 2 teaspoons *aniseed,* 1½ teaspoons *fennel seed,* 1½ teaspoons *whole Szechwan pepper* or *whole black pepper,* and ¾ teaspoon *ground cloves.* Cover and blend to a fine powder. Store in a tightly covered container. Makes ⅓ cup.

Nutrition facts per sandwich: 477 calories, 20 g total fat (6 g saturated fat), 112 mg cholesterol, 861 mg sodium, 36 g carbohydrate, 0 g fiber, 36 g protein.

Pork Pie with Sweet Potato Biscuits

1936

1½ pounds lean ground pork
½ cup chopped onion
½ cup chopped celery
3 tablespoons all-purpose flour
1½ teaspoons dried savory, crushed
1 teaspoon paprika
1 teaspoon instant chicken bouillon granules

½ teaspoon salt
⅛ teaspoon pepper
1¼ cups water
1 tablespoon brown sugar
3 tart medium cooking apples, peeled, cored, and sliced
1 recipe Sweet Potato Biscuits

Although they were a far cry from today's hybrids, sweet potatoes were growing in North America long before Europeans settled here. These flavorful tubers were good enough to tide the first settlers over during those lean years. At Better Homes and Gardens magazine, these sweet, golden root vegetables have been popular with our readers through many decades as evidenced by this hearty 1930s stew with a sweet potato topper.

1 In a large skillet cook pork, onion, and celery until meat is brown and vegetables are tender. Drain well. Stir flour, savory, paprika, chicken bouillon granules, salt, and pepper into meat mixture. Stir in water. Cook and stir until thickened and bubbly. In a mixing bowl sprinkle brown sugar over apples; stir to coat.

2 In a 2-quart casserole combine apples and meat. Cover; bake at 425° for 20 minutes. Top with Sweet Potato Biscuits. Bake, uncovered, about 20 minutes more or until wooden toothpicks inserted into biscuits come out clean. Makes 6 servings.

Sweet Potato Biscuits: In a medium mixing bowl stir together 1 cup *all-purpose flour,* 1 tablespoon *baking powder,* and ¼ teaspoon *salt.* Cut in ¼ cup *shortening* until the mixture is the size of small peas. Add one 8-ounce can *sweet potatoes,* drained and mashed (⅔ cup), and ½ cup *milk;* stir just until combined. Drop in 6 mounds onto hot stew.

Nutrition facts per serving: 501 calories, 26 g total fat (9 g saturated fat), 77 mg cholesterol, 761 mg sodium, 41 g carbohydrate, 3 g fiber, 25 g protein.

Rack of Lamb

1983

1 1½- to 2-pound rack of lamb (9-rib rack)
2 cups dry white wine
½ cup chopped onion
4 shallots or green onions, chopped
1 teaspoon olive oil or cooking oil
½ teaspoon cracked black pepper
½ teaspoon dried basil, crushed
¼ teaspoon dried rosemary, crushed
1 bay leaf
1 recipe Rich Brown Sauce*
2 tablespoons brandy
2 tablespoons margarine or butter
¼ teaspoon dried thyme or basil, crushed

In our November 1983 issue, we featured "Holiday Favorites from Country Inns." This lamb roast is marinated and served with a flavorful brown sauce. The dish is served at the posh Mount View Hotel nestled in Calistoga, California, a small town in the Napa Valley.

1 Trim fat from meat. Place meat in a large plastic bag; set in a large, deep bowl. For marinade, in a medium mixing bowl combine the wine, onion, shallots or green onions, oil, pepper, the ½ teaspoon basil, the rosemary, and bay leaf. Pour marinade over meat; seal bag. Marinate in refrigerator about 8 hours or overnight, turning the bag several times.

2 Drain meat, reserving marinade. Pat meat dry with paper towels. Place the meat, rib side down, in a shallow roasting pan. Roast in a 450° oven for 15 minutes. Reduce oven temperature to 400°; roast meat 20 minutes for medium-rare or 25 minutes for medium. Transfer meat to a platter; cover and keep warm.

3 Meanwhile, in a saucepan bring reserved marinade to boiling. Boil gently, uncovered, 20 minutes or until reduced to about ¾ cup. Strain, discarding solids (should have ¼ cup liquid; if not, boil to reduce).

4 For sauce, skim fat from drippings in roasting pan. Add drippings to pan with the ¼ cup reduced marinade. Add the Rich Brown Sauce, brandy, margarine or butter, and the ¼ teaspoon thyme or basil. Bring to boiling; reduce heat. Simmer, uncovered, for 10 minutes. To serve, spoon some of the sauce over each serving of meat. Makes 3 or 4 servings.

Rich Brown Sauce: In a saucepan cook ½ cup chopped *onion* and ½ cup sliced *carrot* in 2 tablespoons *margarine* or *butter* over medium heat until tender. Stir in 2 teaspoons *sugar.* Cook and stir 5 minutes. Stir in 4 teaspoons *all-purpose flour.* Cook and stir 6 to 8 minutes or until flour is brown. Add 1½ cups *beef broth;* 2 tablespoons *tomato paste;* ½ teaspoon *dried thyme,* crushed; 1 *bay leaf;* and ⅛ teaspoon *pepper.* Bring to boiling; reduce heat. Simmer, uncovered, 10 minutes or until reduced to 1⅓ cups. Strain. Makes about 1 cup sauce.

*Note: You can substitute a purchased package of demi-glacé sauce mix for homemade sauce. Prepare sauce according to package directions.

Nutrition facts per serving: 441 calories, 20 g total fat (6 g saturated fat), 90 mg cholesterol, 463 mg sodium, 11 g carbohydrate, 1 g fiber, 30 g protein.

Plum-Sauced Roast Lamb

1933

This dish was served at a popular dining spot of the '30s and was shared with the magazine's readers. Serving the roast lamb with plum sauce rather than the traditional mint jelly made it novel for the times.

1 4- to 5-pound leg of lamb
1 clove garlic, halved
1 tablespoon snipped parsley
½ teaspoon celery salt
½ teaspoon pepper
¼ teaspoon paprika
2 tablespoons margarine or butter
¼ cup finely chopped carrot
1 tablespoon finely chopped onion
⅛ teaspoon ground bay leaf (optional)
¾ cup soft bread crumbs (1 slice)
1 recipe Plum Jelly Sauce

1 Rub leg of lamb all over with cut sides of garlic. In a small bowl combine parsley, celery salt, pepper, and paprika; rub into lamb. Place the lamb, fat side up, on rack in a shallow roasting pan. Insert meat thermometer in the center of the meat without touching bone. Roast, uncovered, in a 325° oven for 1¼ hours.

2 Meanwhile, in a small saucepan melt margarine; add carrot, onion, and ground bay leaf (if using). Cook until vegetables are tender; stir in bread crumbs. Pat crumb mixture over top of lamb. Continue roasting 45 to 60 minutes or until desired doneness (140° to 145° for medium-rare or 155° for medium). Let stand, covered, for 10 minutes before slicing. (Meat temperature should rise about 5° while standing.) Serve with warm or cool Plum Jelly Sauce. Makes 8 to 10 servings.

Plum Jelly Sauce: In a medium saucepan combine ¾ cup *plum jelly,* ¼ cup *unsweetened pineapple juice,* 1 tablespoon *orange juice,* 1 teaspoon *all-purpose flour,* ¼ teaspoon *dry mustard,* and dash *ground mace.* Cook and stir until thickened and bubbly. Cook and stir 2 minutes more. Makes about 1 cup.

♥ *Nutrition facts per serving: 314 calories, 10 g total fat (3 g saturated fat), 94 mg cholesterol, 231 mg sodium, 24 g carbohydrate, 1 g fiber, 31 g protein.*

Oxtail Stew with Parsley Dumplings

1945

⅓ cup all-purpose flour
½ teaspoon salt
   Dash pepper
2½ to 3 pounds oxtails, cut in
      1½-inch lengths, or
      1½ pounds beef stew
      meat, cut into 1-inch
      cubes
2 tablespoons cooking oil
3 cups water
1 14½-ounce can tomatoes,
   cut up
1 medium onion, sliced

1 tablespoon lemon juice
1½ teaspoons celery salt
1 teaspoon sugar
1 teaspoon Worcestershire
   sauce
1 clove garlic, halved
2 bay leaves
4 whole cloves
12 small whole onions
2 cups sliced carrots
1 cup diced peeled potato
1 recipe Parsley Dumplings

The World War II song "Praise the Lord and Pass the Ammunition" was also the affectionate way some families referred to the popular but presumably leaden dumplings moms served. With recipes such as this one, however, light, fluffy dumplings are a snap. If you like, you can make dumplings from a purchased biscuit mix. Simply follow the directions for dumplings on the box and stir in the snipped parsley.

1 In a shallow dish combine the flour, salt, and pepper. Coat the oxtails with the seasoned flour.

2 In a kettle brown the oxtails in the hot oil; drain well. Add the water, *undrained* tomatoes, sliced onion, lemon juice, celery salt, sugar, Worcestershire sauce, garlic, bay leaves, and cloves. Bring to boiling; reduce heat. Simmer, covered, until meat is tender. (Allow 2½ to 3 hours for oxtails or 1 to 1¼ hours for beef stew meat.) Add small whole onions, carrots, and potato; return mixture to boiling. Cover and cook for 15 minutes more or until vegetables are almost tender. Discard bay leaf and whole cloves.

3 Drop the Parsley Dumplings in 8 large mounds onto the bubbling stew. Cover (do not lift cover) and simmer over low heat for 12 to 15 minutes or until a toothpick inserted into a dumpling comes out clean. Makes 8 servings.

Parsley Dumplings: In a medium mixing bowl stir together 2 cups *all-purpose flour,* 4 teaspoons *baking powder,* and ½ teaspoon *salt.* Combine 1 cup *milk,* ½ cup snipped *parsley,* and ¼ cup *cooking oil;* pour into flour mixture. Stir with a fork just until combined.

Nutrition facts per serving: 462 calories, 19 total fat (4 g saturated fat), 61 mg cholesterol, 992 mg sodium, 51 g carbohydrate, 4 g fiber, 24 g protein.

Pepper Shrimp in Peanut Sauce

1995

To save yourself some work, check at your local fish market to see if raw, peeled shrimp with the tails left on are available. If you peel the shrimp yourself, open the shell of each shrimp lengthwise down the body. Starting at the head and working toward the tail, gently peel back the shell. Be sure to leave the tail intact. Devein each shrimp by making a shallow slit with a sharp knife along the back from head to tail. Locate the black vein. Rinse away the vein by holding the shrimp under cold running water. Or, remove it using the tip of a knife, then rinse the shrimp.

1 pound fresh or frozen shrimp in shells
6 ounces packaged dried bow-tie pasta or linguini
½ cup water
¼ cup orange marmalade
2 tablespoons soy sauce
2 tablespoons peanut butter
2 teaspoons cornstarch

¼ teaspoon crushed red pepper
1 tablespoon cooking oil
6 green onions, bias-sliced into 1-inch pieces
2 medium red, yellow, and/or green sweet peppers, cut into thin strips
Chopped peanuts (optional)

1 Thaw shrimp, if frozen. Peel and devein the shrimp, leaving tails intact. Rinse the shrimp and pat dry with paper towels. Set aside. Cook the pasta according to package directions.

2 Meanwhile, for sauce, in a small mixing bowl stir together the water, marmalade, soy sauce, peanut butter, cornstarch, and crushed red pepper. Set aside.

3 Pour cooking oil into a wok or large skillet. (Add more oil as necessary during cooking.) Preheat over medium-high heat. Stir-fry green onions and sweet pepper strips for 1 to 2 minutes or until crisp-tender. Remove from wok and keep warm. Add shrimp to wok or skillet. Stir-fry for 2 to 3 minutes or until shrimp turn pink; remove and keep warm.

4 Stir sauce; add to center of wok or skillet. Cook and stir until thickened and bubbly. Cook and stir for 2 minutes more. Remove from heat. Drain pasta and return to hot saucepan; add cooked vegetables, shrimp, and thickened sauce. Toss to combine. If desired, sprinkle chopped peanuts over the top. Makes 4 servings.

♥ *Nutrition facts per serving: 385 calories, 9 g total fat (1 g saturated fat), 135 mg cholesterol, 722 mg sodium, 54 g carbohydrate, 3 g fiber, 23 g protein.*

1993

Blackened Shrimp Stroganoff

With her vote for these Cajun-style shrimp as her favorite recipe, Pamela Ann DeFord described the first time she served them: "I just had had our second child, Madelyn, and wanted something elegant to have for a surprise dinner for my husband when he came home from work. My husband loves Cajun food, so I gave this recipe a try. I set a candle-lit table with Caesar salad, bread, white wine, and the shrimp. … It was a surprise for me, too, because it was like ordering a restaurant special and enjoying it."

1 pound fresh or frozen shrimp in shells
1 tablespoon olive oil or cooking oil
1 to 2 tablespoons blackened seasoning
3 cups sliced fresh mushrooms (8 ounces)
1 tablespoon chopped shallot
1 tablespoon margarine or butter
⅔ cup vermouth, white wine, shrimp broth,* or chicken broth

½ cup dairy sour cream
1 tablespoon cornstarch
1 cup shrimp broth* or chicken broth
1 7-ounce jar roasted red sweet peppers, drained and cut into thin strips
1 tablespoon drained capers (optional)
6 ounces packaged dried fettuccine, cooked and drained, or 2 cups hot cooked rice

1 Peel and devein shrimp.* In a small mixing bowl combine shrimp and oil. Add blackened seasoning, stirring to coat shrimp. Set aside.

2 In a 10-inch skillet cook mushrooms and shallot in hot margarine or butter until tender. Remove from skillet. In same skillet cook and stir shrimp over medium-high heat for 2 to 3 minutes or until shrimp turn pink. Remove from skillet. Add the ⅔ cup vermouth, wine, or shrimp or chicken broth to skillet. Bring to boiling. Cook, uncovered, until reduced to ¼ cup (2 to 3 minutes).

3 Stir together the sour cream and cornstarch; stir in the 1 cup shrimp or chicken broth. Add to skillet. Cook and stir until thickened and bubbly. Cook 1 minute more. Stir in the shrimp, mushroom mixture, roasted peppers, and capers (if using). Heat through. Season to taste with *salt*. Serve over fettuccine or rice. Makes 4 servings.

For a lower-fat version: Use light dairy sour cream.

***Note:** To make shrimp broth, reserve shrimp shells. In a medium saucepan combine the shrimp shells and 2 cups water. Bring to boiling; reduce heat. Simmer, covered, for 10 minutes. Strain; discard shells.

♥*Nutrition facts per serving: 435 calories, 15 g total fat (5 g saturated fat), 156 mg cholesterol, 640 mg sodium, 43 g carbohydrate, 2 g fiber, 23 g protein.*
♥*Lower-fat version: 409 calories, 10 g total fat (2 g saturated fat), 135 mg cholesterol, 363 mg sodium, 47 g carbohydrate, 2 g fiber, 23 g protein.*

Salmon Croquettes with Creamed Pea Sauce

1933

3 medium potatoes
1 14¾-ounce can salmon
1 beaten egg
3 tablespoons milk
½ teaspoon salt
½ teaspoon dried dillweed
⅛ teaspoon black pepper
¾ cup plain or seasoned fine dry bread crumbs
2 tablespoons margarine or butter, melted

1 beaten egg
2 tablespoons water
1 10-ounce package frozen peas
2 tablespoons margarine or butter
4 teaspoons all-purpose flour
¼ teaspoon salt
Dash white pepper
1½ cups milk

During the '30s, plentiful canned salmon was a mealtime standby from coast to coast. Good cooks creamed it, sauced it, used it in soufflés, and formed it into crusty croquettes like these. To make the croquettes easier and more healthful, we modified the original method. We suggest you bake the cones rather than fry them.

1 Grease a 13×9×2-inch baking pan. Set aside.

2 For croquettes, wash and peel potatoes; cut into quarters. In a covered medium saucepan cook potatoes in a small amount of *boiling water* for 20 to 25 minutes or until tender. Drain potatoes and mash. Measure 1⅔ cups of mashed potato. Drain the salmon; remove the bones and skin.

3 In a large mixing bowl mash salmon well with a fork. Stir in the mashed potatoes, 1 beaten egg, the 3 tablespoons milk, the ½ teaspoon salt, dillweed, and black pepper. Refrigerate mixture about 45 minutes or until it can be easily shaped with hands. Form into 12 cones (each approximately 2¾ inches high and 1¾ inches in bottom diameter).

4 In a shallow dish toss bread crumbs with 2 tablespoons melted margarine or butter until moistened. In another shallow dish combine the 1 beaten egg and the 2 tablespoons water. Roll salmon cones in bread crumb mixture, then in egg mixture. Roll again in crumbs. Place in the prepared baking pan. Bake in a 450° oven for 20 to 25 minutes or until hot in center and golden brown.

5 Meanwhile, for sauce, cook frozen peas according to package directions; drain well. In a small saucepan melt the 2 tablespoons margarine or butter. Stir in the flour, the ¼ teaspoon salt, and white pepper. Add the 1½ cups milk. Cook and stir until thickened and bubbly. Cook 1 minute more. Stir in cooked peas; heat through. Serve with the croquettes. Makes 6 servings.

Nutrition facts per serving: 375 calories, 16 g total fat (4 g saturated fat), 114 mg cholesterol, 929 mg sodium, 35 g carbohydrate, 3 g fiber, 23 g protein.

Thai Shrimp & Noodles

1995

1 pound fresh or frozen
   shrimp in shells
8 ounces packaged dried
   spaghetti, broken
5 cups broccoli flowerets
   (about 1½ pounds)
⅓ cup creamy peanut butter
¼ to ⅓ cup soy sauce
3 tablespoons rice vinegar

2 tablespoons sesame oil
1 tablespoon chili oil*
1 tablespoon grated
   gingerroot
3 cloves garlic, minced
4 green onions, chopped
⅓ cup cashews or chopped
   almonds

This 30-minute meal earned Sharon Green from Decatur, Georgia, first-place honors in the April 1995 Prize Tested Recipes contest. One of the reasons it's so quick is the pasta, vegetables, and shrimp all cook in one pot.

1 Thaw shrimp, if frozen. Peel and devein the shrimp, leaving tails intact. Rinse the shrimp and pat dry with paper towels.

2 In a kettle bring a large amount of *water* to boiling. Add spaghetti; cook 4 minutes. Add broccoli; cook 2 minutes. Add shrimp; cook 2 to 3 minutes more or until shrimp turn pink.

3 Meanwhile, in a small mixing bowl combine the peanut butter and soy sauce. Stir in the vinegar, sesame oil, chili oil, gingerroot, and garlic. Drain spaghetti mixture. Return to kettle. Add peanut butter mixture, green onions, and nuts. Toss gently to coat. Makes 6 servings.

*Note: If you can't find chili oil at your supermarket or local Asian food store, substitute 1 tablespoon cooking oil plus a dash of bottled hot pepper sauce for the 1 tablespoon chili oil.

Nutrition facts per serving: 417 calories, 19 g total fat (3 g saturated fat), 87 mg cholesterol, 849 mg sodium, 41 g carbohydrate, 5 g fiber, 23 g protein.

Spicy Red Snapper with Mango Salsa

1994

Cool, juicy tropical fruits help quench the heat of the peppery spices rubbed onto the fish fillets in this Caribbean dish. Red snapper is the traditional fish of choice, but you can use other firm-fleshed whitefish, such as orange roughy, redfish, or haddock, if you like.

1 **pound fresh or frozen red snapper fillets**
1 **tablespoon lime juice**
1 **tablespoon water**
1 **teaspoon paprika**
½ **teaspoon salt**
¼ **teaspoon ground ginger**
¼ **teaspoon ground allspice**
¼ **teaspoon black pepper**
1 **recipe Mango Salsa**
1 **medium lime, cut into wedges (optional)**
Fresh cilantro or parsley sprigs (optional)

1 Thaw fish, if frozen. Rinse and pat dry with paper towels. Cut into 4 serving-size pieces. Measure thickness of fish. In a small bowl combine lime juice and water; brush onto fish. In another small bowl combine paprika, salt, ginger, allspice, and black pepper; rub onto fish.

2 Arrange the fish in a shallow baking pan. Bake, uncovered, in a 450° oven until fish flakes easily when tested with a fork. (Allow 4 to 6 minutes for each ½ inch of thickness.)

3 To serve, brush the fish with pan juices. Serve with Mango Salsa. If desired, garnish with lime wedges and cilantro or parsley sprigs. Makes 4 servings.

Mango Salsa: In a medium mixing bowl combine 1 *mango,* peeled, seeded, and chopped (about 1½ cups); 1 medium *red sweet pepper,* seeded and finely chopped; ¼ cup thinly sliced *green onions;* 1 *Scotch bonnet* or *hot green chili pepper,* seeded and finely chopped; 3 tablespoons *olive oil;* ½ teaspoon finely shredded *lime peel;* 2 tablespoons *lime juice;* 1 tablespoon *vinegar;* ¼ teaspoon *salt;* and ¼ teaspoon *black pepper.* Makes about 2 cups.

♥*Nutrition facts per serving: 222 calories, 11 g total fat (2 g saturated fat), 28 mg cholesterol, 437 mg sodium, 15 g carbohydrate, 3 g fiber, 17 g protein.*

Sizzling Vegetable Sandwiches

1996

Over the past several years, professional and home cooks alike have been experimenting with new ingredient and flavor combinations. The editors for our magazine are right in the swing of things with this '90s-style grilled vegetable sandwich that's spruced up with an intriguing cumin-flavored mayonnaise.

1 small eggplant, cut lengthwise into ½-inch-thick slices
1 medium zucchini, cut lengthwise into ¼-inch-thick slices
1 medium yellow summer squash, cut lengthwise into ¼-inch-thick slices
1 medium red sweet pepper, seeded and cut into ½-inch-wide strips
1 small onion, cut into ½-inch-thick slices
⅓ cup olive oil
4 Kaiser rolls, split
¼ cup Cumin Mayo

1 Brush eggplant, zucchini, yellow squash, sweet pepper, and onion with some of the olive oil. Place onion slices on a long metal skewer. Grill onions on rack of uncovered grill directly over medium coals for 5 minutes.* Arrange remaining vegetables on grill rack; grill for 12 to 15 minutes more or until vegetables are tender, turning once. (If some vegetables cook more quickly than others, remove and keep warm.)

2 Meanwhile, brush the split sides of the rolls with remaining olive oil; grill rolls, split sides down, about 1 minute or until toasted.

3 Layer roasted vegetables on the bottom halves of the rolls. Spread top layer of each sandwich with *1 tablespoon* of the Cumin Mayo. Cover sandwiches with tops of rolls. Makes 4 servings.

*Note: To use the broiler instead of the grill, brush vegetables with some of the oil. Place half of the vegetables on the unheated rack of a broiler pan. Broil 3 to 4 inches from the heat for 12 to 15 minutes or until vegetables are tender, turning once. Remove and cover broiled vegetables to keep warm. Repeat with remaining vegetables. Toast rolls under broiler about 1 minute.

Cumin Mayo: In a small mixing bowl stir together 1 cup *light mayonnaise dressing;* 2 tablespoons *lime juice;* 1 clove *garlic,* minced; and 1 teaspoon *cumin seed,* crushed. Makes about 1 cup.

Nutrition facts per serving with 1 tablespoon Cumin Mayo: 417 calories, 26 g total fat (4 g saturated fat), 0 mg cholesterol, 424 mg sodium, 41 g carbohydrate, 3 g fiber, 7 g protein.

California Pizzas

1993

1 16-ounce loaf frozen whole wheat or white bread dough
2 tablespoons cornmeal
3 tablespoons olive oil or cooking oil
⅛ teaspoon ground red pepper
1½ cups shredded mozzarella cheese (6 ounces)
3 medium red, yellow, and/or green sweet peppers, roasted* and cut into 1-inch-wide strips, or one 12-ounce jar roasted red sweet peppers, drained and cut into 1-inch-wide strips

1 large tomato, chopped
1 medium red onion, cut into very thin wedges and separated into strips
6 ounces semisoft goat cheese (chèvre) or feta cheese, cut up or crumbled (1½ cups)
10 pitted black olives (such as kalamata or ripe olives), quartered lengthwise
3 to 4 tablespoons fresh oregano leaves or snipped fresh basil**

In April 1993, we dubbed this tantalizing pizza one of "The New American Classics" because it takes its inspiration from the nouvelle California cuisine made famous by such chefs as Wolfgang Puck.

1 Thaw the bread dough. On a lightly floured surface, divide dough into 8 pieces. Cover; let dough rest for 10 minutes. Roll each piece of dough into a 6-inch circle. Grease 2 extra-large baking sheets; sprinkle with the cornmeal. Transfer dough circles to baking sheets. Bake in a 450° over for 5 minutes. Place baking sheets on wire racks to cool.

2 Meanwhile, in a small bowl stir together the olive oil or cooking oil and ground red pepper; brush onto crusts. Sprinkle with the mozzarella cheese. Top with the roasted peppers, tomato, onion, goat cheese or feta cheese, and olives.

3 Bake in a 450° oven for 5 to 7 minutes more or until crusts are crisp. Before serving, sprinkle with oregano or basil. Makes 8 servings.

*Note: To roast the sweet peppers, halve peppers; remove stems, membranes, and seeds. Place peppers, cut sides down, on a foil-lined baking sheet. Bake in a 425° oven for 20 to 25 minutes or until skins are bubbly and brown. Place in a clean paper bag; close bag and let stand for 20 to 30 minutes or until peppers are cool enough to handle. Pull off skins gently using a paring knife.

**Note: You can substitute 1 tablespoon dried oregano or dried basil, crushed, for the fresh herb. Instead of sprinkling it over the pizzas, stir the dried herb into the olive oil mixture before brushing the crusts.

Nutrition facts per serving: 356 calories, 18 g total fat (7 g saturated fat), 28 mg cholesterol, 522 mg sodium, 34 g carbohydrate, 5 g fiber, 18 g protein.

★
1979

Vegetarian Chili

Carol Jo Waters of Mercer, Pennsylvania, has been a vegetarian for more than 10 years, and she swears by this flavorful chili. "In 1984, I personally changed to a nonmeat regime," she says. "My husband still does eat meat, but loves this chili recipe as much as I do. It is one of the best recipes to cook on a Friday, so it can be served on the weekend while you're working on a project and don't want to stop and cook."

2 tablespoons olive oil or cooking oil
1½ cups chopped celery
1½ cups chopped green sweet pepper
1 cup chopped onion
3 cloves garlic, minced
2 28-ounce cans tomatoes, cut up
3 15- to 16-ounce cans beans (such as kidney, black, northern, pinto, and/or garbanzo beans), rinsed and drained
½ cup raisins
¼ cup red wine vinegar
3 to 4 teaspoons chili powder

1 tablespoon snipped parsley
1 teaspoon sugar
1½ teaspoons dried basil, crushed
1½ teaspoons dried oregano, crushed
1½ teaspoons ground cumin
1 teaspoon ground allspice
½ teaspoon salt
¼ teaspoon black pepper
¼ teaspoon bottled hot pepper sauce
1 bay leaf
1 12-ounce can beer
¾ cup cashew nuts
1 cup shredded Swiss, mozzarella, or cheddar cheese (4 ounces)

1 In a 4- to 6-quart pot heat oil. Add celery, sweet pepper, onion, and garlic. Cover and cook over medium heat about 10 minutes or until vegetables are tender, stirring occasionally.

2 Stir in *undrained* tomatoes, drained beans, raisins, vinegar, chili powder, parsley, sugar, basil, oregano, cumin, allspice, salt, black pepper, hot pepper sauce, and bay leaf. Bring to boiling; reduce heat. Simmer, covered, for 1½ hours. Stir in the beer. Return to boiling. Simmer, uncovered, for 30 minutes more or until desired consistency. Discard bay leaf. Stir in cashews. Sprinkle cheese over each serving. Makes 6 servings.

Note: If you're concerned about sodium, use low-sodium whole tomatoes, reduced-sodium canned beans, and unsalted cashew nuts.

Nutrition facts per serving: 515 calories, 19 g total fat (6 g saturated fat), 17 mg cholesterol, 1,329 mg sodium, 70 g carbohydrate, 15 g fiber, 26 g protein.

Green Beans in Yellow Pepper Butter

1 tablespoon margarine or
    butter
1 medium yellow sweet
    pepper, coarsely
    shredded
6 tablespoons margarine or
    butter, softened

¼ cup pine nuts
1 tablespoon lemon juice
¼ teaspoon salt
⅛ teaspoon black pepper
1½ pounds green beans,
    trimmed
1 large yellow sweet pepper,
    cut into thin strips

1994

This recipe was part of one family's Hanukkah menu of foods they shared during their traditional Jewish celebration of the "festival of lights." The family's story was recounted in the December issue of Better Homes and Gardens *in 1994.*

1 In a small saucepan melt the 1 tablespoon margarine or butter. Add the shredded sweet pepper. Cook over medium-high heat for 5 minutes or until crisp-tender. Set aside.

2 In a blender container or food processor bowl, combine the 6 tablespoons softened margarine or butter and the pine nuts. Cover; blend or process until almost smooth. Add cooked sweet pepper, lemon juice, salt, and black pepper. Cover; blend or process until almost smooth. Set aside.

3 In a covered saucepan cook beans in a small amount of boiling water for 12 minutes. Add the sweet pepper strips the last 3 minutes of cooking. Drain the beans and sweet pepper strips.

4 To serve, transfer beans and sweet pepper strips to a serving bowl. Add the blended margarine mixture; toss to coat. Makes 8 servings.

Nutrition facts per serving: 159 calories, 13 g total fat (7 g saturated fat), 27 mg cholesterol, 71 mg sodium, 11 g carbohydrate, 2 g fiber, 3 g protein.

Eggplant Casserole

1954

In the '50s when we first published this zesty crumb-topped side dish, most cooks would have found only one type of eggplant at their grocery stores. Today cooks have more choices. In addition to the traditional pear-shaped eggplant, many supermarkets also carry round eggplant, long and slender Japanese eggplant, and even white eggplant. To use one of the more exotic types in this recipe, purchase slightly more than a pound. This should be enough to give you the 5 to 5½ cups of cubes you'll need.

1 medium eggplant
  (1 pound), peeled
2 tablespoons cooking oil
1½ cups chopped onion
2 cups chopped green sweet
  pepper
1 tablespoon cooking oil
1 tablespoon all-purpose
  flour
¼ teaspoon salt
¼ teaspoon black pepper

½ cup sliced pitted ripe olives
½ cup shredded sharp
  American cheese or
  cheddar cheese
  (2 ounces)
1 8-ounce can tomato sauce
¾ cup soft bread crumbs
  (1 slice)
1 tablespoon margarine or
  butter, melted

1 Cut eggplant into ½-inch cubes. Cook eggplant cubes in the 2 tablespoons oil until tender. Remove from skillet.

2 In the same skillet cook onion and sweet pepper in the 1 tablespoon oil until tender, stirring frequently. Remove from heat. Stir in flour, salt, and black pepper. Add olives.

3 Layer half the eggplant in a 1½-quart casserole. Add half the olive mixture and half the cheese. Repeat layers. Pour tomato sauce over all. Mix crumbs with melted margarine or butter; sprinkle over tomato sauce. Bake, uncovered, in a 375° oven about 30 minutes or until edges are bubbly. Makes 6 to 8 servings.

Nutrition facts per serving: 191 calories, 13 g total fat (3 g saturated fat), 5 mg cholesterol, 469 mg sodium, 17 g carbohydrate, 4 g fiber, 4 g protein.

Orange-Sauced Broccoli & Peppers

1989

3½ cups broccoli flowerets
1 medium red or yellow sweet pepper, cut into 1-inch pieces
2 tablespoons finely chopped onion
1 clove garlic, minced
1 tablespoon margarine or butter
1½ teaspoons cornstarch
⅔ cup orange juice
2 teaspoons Dijon-style mustard

Deck your table in traditional Christmas colors with this combination of red and green vegetables. The side dish accented with citrus and mustard makes a festive addition to any meal.

1 In a medium saucepan cook broccoli and sweet pepper in a small amount of lightly salted boiling water about 8 minutes or until broccoli is crisp-tender. Drain; keep warm.

2 Meanwhile, for sauce, in a small saucepan cook onion and garlic in hot margarine or butter until onion is tender. Stir in cornstarch. Add orange juice and mustard. Cook and stir until mixture is thickened and bubbly. Cook and stir 2 minutes more. Toss sauce with broccoli-pepper mixture. Makes 6 servings.

♥*Nutrition facts per serving: 58 calories, 2 g total fat (0 g saturated fat), 0 mg cholesterol, 82 mg sodium, 8 g carbohydrate, 3 g fiber, 2 g protein.*

Vintage Views 1935

Lament of the Vegetables

The age-old problem of how to get your family to eat vegetables remains today. A June 1935 article observed:

"Have you ever groaned over a dinner served by a woman reputed to be the best cook in three counties? You arrived with a mouth frankly watering and you came away forgetting all the masterpieces, remembering only the sad gray potatoes, the cabbage a mere ghost of its fresh green self, the wan and anemic beets?

Alas, who hasn't? And who hasn't been up against the same bug-bear in her own kitchen? Which lands us neatly astride the question—just what is the miracle that will change a finicky family of vegetable scorners into voracious enthusiasts?" The solution was to not overcook vegetables, so they'd stay vibrant.

Provolone Polenta with Red Pepper Sauce

1995

3 cups water
1½ cups cornmeal
1½ cups cold water
1 teaspoon salt
1½ cups shredded provolone
   cheese (6 ounces)

2 medium red sweet peppers,
   halved and seeded
2 teaspoons sugar
2 teaspoons balsamic vinegar
⅛ teaspoon salt
   Olive oil
   Curly endive

Way back in 1930, a recipe called Italian Polenta won the Cook's Round Table. It contained processed American cheese and was topped with a sauce of ground beef and tomato. This modern version of the now-trendy dish stars roasted sweet peppers, a '90s favorite, in the sauce.

1 For polenta, in a 3-quart saucepan bring the 3 cups water to boiling. In a medium mixing bowl combine cornmeal, the 1½ cups cold water, and the 1 teaspoon salt. Slowly add cornmeal mixture to the boiling water, stirring constantly. Cook and stir until mixture returns to boiling. Reduce heat to very low. Cover and simmer for 15 minutes, stirring occasionally. Stir ¾ *cup* of the shredded cheese into the hot polenta. Turn the mixture into an ungreased 13×9×2-inch pan. Cool slightly. Cover and refrigerate for several hours or until firm.

2 Meanwhile, for sauce, place sweet pepper halves, cut sides down, on a foil-lined baking sheet. Bake in a 425° oven for 20 to 25 minutes or until skin is brown. Immediately place hot peppers in a clean paper bag; seal. Let stand for 10 minutes.

3 When peppers are cool enough to handle, peel off skins, using a sharp knife. In a blender container combine peppers, sugar, vinegar, and the ⅛ teaspoon salt. Cover and blend until smooth. Transfer to a small saucepan; heat through.

4 Cut chilled polenta into 18 triangles.* Arrange triangles on a lightly greased baking sheet. Brush with olive oil. Broil 4 to 5 inches from heat for 4 minutes. Turn over triangles. Brush with additional oil. Broil for 4 minutes more or until golden brown. Sprinkle remaining cheese over polenta. Let stand 2 minutes or until cheese melts.

5 To serve, line individual small plates with endive. Arrange polenta triangles on plates and spoon warm sauce over. Makes 9 servings.

***Note:** To get 18 triangles, cut the chilled polenta crosswise into thirds, then cut lengthwise into thirds. Cut each polenta rectangle in half diagonally.

Nutrition facts per serving: 173 calories, 7 g total fat (3 g saturated fat), 13 mg cholesterol, 436 mg sodium, 21 g carbohydrate, 1 g fiber, 7 g protein.

Oriental Cashew Asparagus

1996

Oriental seasonings have become so widely accepted that cooks now are using them for all types of dishes. Take for example, this April 1996 winner of the spring vegetable side-dish category of our Prize Tested Recipes contest. The teriyaki sauce spices up tender stalks of asparagus and fresh mushrooms.

1 pound fresh asparagus, trimmed and bias-sliced into 1-inch pieces
1½ cups quartered fresh mushrooms
1 medium onion, cut into thin wedges
¼ cup chopped red sweet pepper

2 tablespoons margarine or butter
1 teaspoon cornstarch
⅛ to ¼ teaspoon black pepper
1 tablespoon teriyaki sauce
1 tablespoon dry sherry
2 teaspoons water
2 tablespoons cashew halves

1 Place asparagus in a steamer basket over, but not touching, *gently boiling water.* Cover; reduce heat. Steam for 2 minutes. Add mushrooms, onion, and sweet pepper. Cover; steam for 2 to 5 minutes more or until crisp-tender. Remove basket; discard liquid.

2 In the same saucepan melt margarine or butter; stir in cornstarch and black pepper. Add the teriyaki sauce, sherry, and the 2 teaspoons water. Cook and stir until thickened and bubbly. Return vegetables to saucepan; toss gently to coat. Heat through. Top with cashews. Makes 4 servings.

Nutrition facts per serving: 121 calories, 8 g total fat (2 g saturated fat), 0 mg cholesterol, 269 mg sodium, 10 g carbohydrate, 2 g fiber, 4 g protein.

Zucchini & Feta Cheese Soufflés

2 cups shredded zucchini
1 teaspoon salt
3 tablespoons margarine or butter
¼ cup all-purpose flour
¼ teaspoon dry mustard

1 cup milk
½ cup crumbled feta cheese
1 tablespoon grated Parmesan cheese
4 egg yolks
4 egg whites

Every year at harvesttime, our readers who have backyard gardens are eager to learn new ways to help them use up their crops. We're only too happy to oblige by featuring garden vegetable recipes, such as this zucchini soufflé, first published in the August 1993 issue.

1 Grease six 6-ounce soufflé dishes or custard cups. Place shredded zucchini in a colander; sprinkle with salt and toss lightly. Let stand 30 minutes. Rinse and drain. Squeeze out excess liquid. Set aside.

2 In a medium saucepan melt the margarine or butter. Stir in flour and dry mustard. Add milk. Cook and stir until thickened and bubbly. Remove from heat. Stir in the zucchini, feta cheese, and Parmesan cheese. In a large mixing bowl beat egg yolks with a fork. Gradually stir in zucchini mixture.

3 In a mixing bowl beat egg whites with an electric mixer on high speed until stiff peaks form (tips stand straight). Fold half of the beaten egg whites into the zucchini mixture. Gently fold remaining whites into zucchini mixture. Spoon into prepared soufflé dishes or custard cups.

4 Bake in a 375° oven for 20 to 25 minutes or until a knife inserted near the center of each comes out clean. Serve immediately. Serves 6.

Nutrition facts per serving: 174 calories, 12 g total fat (4 g saturated fat), 154 mg cholesterol, 276 mg sodium, 8 g carbohydrate, 1 g fiber, 8 g protein.

Risotto Primavera

1995

Risotto usually takes an inordinate amount of patience to prepare, due to all the stirring, stirring, stirring at the stove. Our Test Kitchen modified this recipe so it's easier to make. For cooks who want a more classic risotto, we've included the traditional method of adding a little broth at a time while stirring constantly.

¼ cup thinly sliced celery
¼ cup thinly sliced shallots or green onions
2 cloves garlic, minced
⅛ teaspoon pepper
1 tablespoon margarine or butter
1 cup Arborio or long grain rice
1 14½-ounce can reduced-sodium chicken broth

1¾ cups water
½ cup fresh or frozen peas, thawed
½ cup coarsely chopped yellow summer squash and/or zucchini
½ teaspoon finely shredded lemon peel
Fresh herb sprigs (optional)

1 In a 3-quart saucepan cook celery, shallots or green onions, garlic, and pepper in hot margarine until tender. Add *uncooked* rice. Cook and stir for 2 minutes more.

2 Carefully stir in broth and water. Bring to boiling; reduce heat. Simmer, covered, for 25 minutes. (Do not lift cover.) Remove from heat.

3 Stir in peas, squash or zucchini, and lemon peel. Cover and let stand 5 minutes. Serve immediately. If desired, garnish with fresh herb sprigs. Makes 6 servings.

Traditional method: Cook celery mixture as directed above; add *uncooked* rice. Cook and stir for 2 minutes more. In a 1-quart saucepan bring broth and water to boiling. Add broth mixture, ¾ cup at a time, to rice mixture, stirring constantly until rice is almost tender but firm to the bite. (It should have a creamy consistency.) This should take about 20 minutes. During cooking, adjust the heat as necessary to keep the broth at a gentle simmer. Stir in peas, squash or zucchini, and lemon peel. Cover and let stand for 5 minutes. Serve immediately.

♥ *Nutrition facts per serving: 156 calories, 3 g total fat (0 g saturated fat), 0 mg cholesterol, 227 mg sodium, 29 g carbohydrate, 1 g fiber, 4 g protein.*

Sage & Onion Mashed Potatoes

1995

Today's cooks are eager to re-create the old family favorites their grandmothers and mothers used to make, but they want to do it '90s style. Being inventive with golden oldies as we were with these mashed potatoes is the answer. Slow roasting the potatoes with onion and fresh sage gives them a remarkable herb flavor and mashing them with buttermilk adds a delightful old-fashioned tang.

1 **pound baking potatoes (such as russet), peeled and cut into eighths**
1 **medium onion, cut into thin wedges**
3 **tablespoons olive oil or cooking oil**

1 **tablespoon snipped fresh sage or ½ teaspoon ground sage**
⅛ **to ¼ teaspoon pepper**
2 **to 4 tablespoons buttermilk, plain yogurt, dairy sour cream, or milk**

1 In a greased 2-quart casserole combine potatoes and onion. In a 1-cup measure combine ¼ cup *water,* oil, sage, ½ teaspoon *salt,* and pepper; drizzle over potatoes and onion.

2 Bake, uncovered, in a 450° oven for 40 to 50 minutes or until the vegetables are tender, stirring twice.

3 Transfer to a medium mixing bowl. Mash with a potato masher or beat with an electric mixer on low speed. Gradually beat in enough buttermilk to make light and fluffy potatoes. Makes 5 servings.

Nutrition facts per serving: 170 calories, 8 g total fat (1 g saturated fat), 0 mg cholesterol, 227 mg sodium, 22 g carbohydrate, 1 g fiber, 3 g protein.

Vintage Views
1935

Do the Mashed Potato

Making great mashed potatoes as explained in the June 1935 issue is an art as fine as any dance: "If mashed or riced potatoes—billows of fluffy whiteness—are the goal, still perfectly cooked, completely tender potatoes form the starting point. The simplest way to reduce every lump is to put the potatoes thru a ricer heated by running boiling water thru it.

"Or if they're to be mashed, ... work them until all lumps are broken, then add butter and scalded milk or cream. Beat the whole mass enthusiastically, with a strong fork or masher and a powerful arm (it's grand exercise!), until snowy white and fluffy. Heap it lightly into a hot serving dish and garnish with a dash of paprika or pepper and square of butter. ... [G]ravy is a delectable accompaniment, but perfect mashed potatoes never require it."

Creamy Potluck Potatoes

1992

5 large potatoes
(2½ pounds), peeled and
chopped (7½ cups)
1 10¾-ounce can reduced-
sodium condensed cream
of chicken soup
½ cup light dairy sour cream
½ of an 8-ounce package
reduced-fat cream cheese
(Neufchâtel), softened

½ of a ½-ounce package
(about 1 tablespoon)
butter-flavored
seasoning mix
¾ cup shredded reduced-fat
sharp cheddar cheese
(3 ounces)
¼ cup sliced green onions
¼ cup skim milk
1 tablespoon dried parsley
flakes
¼ teaspoon garlic salt
¼ teaspoon pepper

*For the March food story in
1992, readers sent in their most
cherished "naughty" recipes for a
healthy makeover. We shaped up
the potatoes in this entry so they
have only 7 grams of fat per
serving. We kept the deceivingly
rich flavor so you can feel as if
you're indulging.*

1 In a large saucepan cook potatoes in boiling water for 10 to
12 minutes or until tender. Drain. Rinse with cold water. Drain again.

2 In a large mixing bowl stir together the soup, sour cream, cream
cheese, and the dry butter-flavored mix. Stir in *¼ cup* of the shredded
cheese, *3 tablespoons* of the green onions, the skim milk, parsley, garlic
salt, and pepper. Stir in the cooked potatoes. Transfer the mixture to a
2-quart rectangular baking dish.

3 Bake, uncovered, in a 350° oven for 30 to 35 minutes or until
heated through. Sprinkle with remaining shredded cheese. Bake
5 minutes more or until cheese melts. Sprinkle with remaining green
onions. Makes 10 servings.

*Nutrition facts per serving: 202 calories, 7 g total fat (3 g saturated fat),
18 mg cholesterol, 28 g carbohydrate, 315 mg sodium, 2 g fiber, 7 g protein.*

1986

Dolores Altamurao of Tunersville, New Jersey, wrote us in praise of this December 1986 winner of our Prize Tested Recipes contest. She said: "It's a great recipe. I make it quite often and get so many compliments and requests for the recipe. The most frequent comment is, 'I've never tasted anything so different and delicious.'"

Cranberry-Apple Sweet Potatoes

5 or 6 medium sweet potatoes, peeled and sliced (about 2 pounds), or two 18-ounce cans sweet potatoes, drained and sliced

1 21-ounce can apple pie filling

½ of a 16-ounce can (¾ cup) whole cranberry sauce

2 tablespoons apricot preserves

2 tablespoons orange marmalade

1 In a large covered saucepan cook fresh sweet potatoes (if using) in enough *boiling salted water* to cover about 15 minutes or until tender. Drain and set aside.

2 Spread pie filling in a 2-quart square baking dish; arrange sweet potatoes on top of pie filling. In a small mixing bowl stir together the cranberry sauce, apricot preserves, and orange marmalade; spoon over sweet potatoes. Bake, covered, in a 350° oven for 20 to 25 minutes or until heated through. Makes 6 to 8 servings.

♥ *Nutrition facts per serving: 313 calories, 0 g total fat, 0 mg cholesterol, 67 mg sodium, 79 g carbohydrate, 6 g fiber, 2 g protein.*

Vintage Views
1923

Just Make a List

In 1923, an editor offered this solution for when you get tired of cooking the same foods day in and day out:

"When your meals are uninteresting, and you know it, take an hour off, make a list of every meat dish you ever heard of, and invent a few new ones. Then list all the vegetables available. Never mind if one of your family objects to parsnips or squash; put these on the list. Perhaps some vegetables suggest salads, and often meals lack the acid, crispness, and color that vegetable salads give a meal. Since in every meal we must have an acid food to bring out flavors, if we have not used a salad for this purpose, we can serve sour pickles or a tart jelly."

Barbecued Limas

1939

2 cups dry lima beans
4 slices bacon, cut in ½-inch
   pieces
½ cup chopped onion
1 clove garlic, minced
1 10¾-ounce can condensed
   tomato soup

2 tablespoons vinegar
1 tablespoon brown sugar
2 teaspoons prepared
   mustard
2 teaspoons Worcestershire
   sauce
½ teaspoon chili powder

This 1939 side dish was published as part of our Cook's Round Table, a countrywide reader recipe exchange you may know as our Prize Tested Recipes contest. In rejuvenating this flavorful lima variation of baked beans, we discovered that when we used large limas (rather than baby limas), they weren't quite done, so we lengthened the cooking time. Be sure to follow the time noted in the recipe for the size of lima bean you use.

1 Rinse lima beans. In a large saucepan combine beans and 5 cups *water*. Bring to boiling; reduce heat. Simmer for 2 minutes. Remove from heat. Cover and let stand for 1 hour. (Or, place beans in water in a large saucepan. Cover and let stand in a cool place for 6 to 8 hours or overnight.) Drain beans in a colander and rinse. Return beans to saucepan. Add 4 cups fresh *water*.

2 In skillet fry the bacon over medium heat until crisp. Remove bacon from skillet, reserving 1 tablespoon drippings. Add bacon to beans. Bring to boiling; reduce heat. Simmer, covered, until beans are tender, adding more water (if necessary) and stirring occasionally. (Allow 45 to 60 minutes for baby limas or 1 to 1¼ hours for large limas.)

3 Drain, reserving 1 cup liquid. In reserved drippings cook onion and garlic until onion is tender. Stir in reserved bean liquid, tomato soup, vinegar, brown sugar, mustard, Worcestershire sauce, and chili powder. Bring to boiling; simmer 5 minutes. Add beans. Transfer to a 2-quart casserole. Bake, uncovered, in a 350° oven for 45 minutes, stirring twice. Makes 8 servings.

♥ *Nutrition facts per serving: 212 calories, 3 g total fat (1 g saturated fat), 3 mg cholesterol, 349 mg sodium, 36 g carbohydrate, 4 g fiber, 12 g protein.*

Mustard Seed Relish

1980

3 cups water	¾ cup finely chopped onion
3 cups finely chopped cabbage	½ cup chopped pimiento
3 cups finely chopped cucumber	⅓ cup pickling salt
1 cup finely chopped green sweet pepper	1⅔ cups vinegar
1 cup finely chopped celery	¾ cup water
	¾ cup sugar
	2 tablespoons mustard seed

Make this zesty relish in late summer when all the vegetables are at their peak. You'll have enough to last the whole year with plenty to share with friends. Our editors think the relish (pictured on page 264 in open jar with spoon and in lower right bowl) is terrific on hot dogs, Polish sausage, and brats.

1 In a large bowl combine the 3 cups water, the cabbage, cucumber, sweet pepper, celery, onion, pimiento, and pickling salt; toss to mix thoroughly. Let stand 3 hours. Drain; rinse well with cold water. Drain again.

2 In a 4-quart kettle combine the vinegar, the ¾ cup water, the sugar, and mustard seed. Bring to boiling; reduce heat. Simmer, uncovered, for 3 minutes. Add drained vegetables. Return to boiling; reduce heat. Cook, uncovered, for 5 minutes more.

3 Ladle hot relish into hot, sterilized half-pint jars, leaving a ½-inch headspace. Wipe jar rims and adjust lids. Process jars in boiling-water canner for 10 minutes (start timing when water covering jars returns to boiling). Remove the jars from canner and cool jars on wire racks. Makes 7 half-pints.

♥ *Nutrition facts per tablespoon: 9 calories, 0 g total fat, 0 mg cholesterol, 198 mg sodium, 2 g carbohydrate, 0 g fiber, 0 g protein.*

Clockwise from jars on shelf:
Best Tomato Catsup, recipe page 267;
Mustard Seed Relish, recipe this page;
Sweet Peppers and Pickles, recipe page 268;
Gingered Holiday Chutney, recipe page 266

Gingered Holiday Chutney

1985

Do your Christmas shopping right from home and make this winner in the food gifts category of our 1985 Holiday Recipe Contest. For an extra-memorable present, pack a ham along with this bold-flavored pear and sweet pepper relish (pictured on page 264 in bowl on left).

2 cups packed brown sugar
¾ cup vinegar
½ cup water
½ teaspoon salt
¼ teaspoon ground cinnamon
¼ teaspoon ground red pepper
1 large lemon
1 large lime

1 pound fresh Anjou pear, peeled, cored, and coarsely chopped (about 3 cups)
1 cup chopped green sweet pepper
1 cup chopped red sweet pepper
1 cup chopped onion
1 cup golden raisins
1 tablespoon finely chopped crystallized ginger

1 In a 4-quart kettle stir together brown sugar, vinegar, water, salt, cinnamon, and ground red pepper. Bring to boiling; reduce heat to medium-low. Simmer, uncovered, for 10 minutes. Meanwhile, finely shred peel from lemon and lime (about 2 tablespoons peel total); squeeze juice from lemon and lime (about ⅓ cup juice total).

2 Add peels, juices, pear, sweet peppers, onion, raisins, and ginger to hot syrup mixture. Return to boiling; reduce heat to medium-low. Simmer, uncovered, about 25 minutes or until thick, stirring occasionally (should have about 3¾ cups).

3 Ladle chutney at once into hot, sterilized half-pint jars, leaving a ¼-inch headspace. Wipe jar rims and adjust lids. Process in boiling-water canner for 10 minutes (start timing when water covering jars returns to boiling). Remove the jars from the canner; cool jars on wire racks. Serve as accompaniment to ham, poultry, or other meat. Makes 4 half-pints.

♥ *Nutrition facts per tablespoon: 38 calories, 0 g total fat, 0 mg cholesterol, 20 mg sodium, 10 g carbohydrate, 0 g fiber, 0 g protein.*

Best Tomato Catsup

1 cup white vinegar	1 medium onion, chopped
1½ inches stick cinnamon, broken	¼ teaspoon ground red pepper
1½ teaspoons whole cloves	1 cup sugar
1 teaspoon celery seed	¼ cup lemon juice
8 pounds tomatoes	2 teaspoons salt

1 In a small saucepan combine the vinegar, cinnamon, cloves, and celery seed. Bring to boiling. Remove from heat; cover and let stand. Wash, core, and quarter tomatoes; drain in colander, discarding liquid.

2 Place tomatoes in a large pot or kettle. Stir in onion and red pepper. Bring to boiling. Cook, uncovered, for 15 minutes, stirring occasionally. Put tomato mixture through food mill or coarse sieve. Discard seeds and skins. Stir sugar into tomato mixture. Bring to boiling; reduce heat. Simmer briskly, uncovered, for 1½ to 2 hours or until mixture is reduced to half (measure the depth with a wooden ruler at the beginning and the end of cooking).

3 Strain vinegar mixture into tomato mixture; discard spices. Stir in lemon juice and salt. Simmer about 30 minutes or until desired consistency, stirring often.

4 Ladle hot catsup into hot, clean half-pint jars, leaving a ½-inch headspace. Wipe jar rims and adjust lids. Process in a boiling-water canner for 15 minutes (start timing when water covering jars returns to boiling). Remove the jars from the canner; cool the jars on wire racks. Makes 4 half-pints.

♥ *Nutrition facts per tablespoon: 29 calories, 0 g total fat, 0 mg cholesterol, 82 mg sodium, 7 g carbohydrate, 1 g fiber, 1 g protein.*

Our wartime advice in the '40s was, "Play up those gold-plated garden vegetables." That advice for nutritious, refreshing meals still rings true today. There's nothing better than grilled burgers topped with catsup made from garden fresh tomatoes (pictured on page 264 in jars on shelf).

Sweet Peppers & Pickles

1942

A Cook's Round Table contest searching for pickle recipes required lots of cucumbers for testing. This tidbit from the July 1942 issue shares the solution (food pictured on page 264 in bowl in front): "Cucumbers were even grown to specifications for next month's Cook's Round Table! Contest recipes have to be tested the first week in March, but the recipe contest—and pickles—are August items. Thru a local fruit company, orders were given to grow a bushel of 2-inch cucumbers, a bushel of 4-inch, and a bushel of 6-inch cucumbers for slicing. Must be strictly these sizes. All those diverse BH&G family pickle recipes must be tested. The complete order, right down to the last pickle, was delivered promptly the first week in March."

4 quarts (16 cups) unpeeled
   medium cucumbers, cut
   into ⅛-inch-thick slices
6 cups sliced white onions
1⅔ cups sliced green sweet
   peppers
⅓ cup pickling salt

3 cloves garlic, halved
   Cracked ice
5 cups sugar
3 cups cider vinegar
2 tablespoons mustard seed
1½ teaspoons celery seed
1½ teaspoons ground turmeric

1 In a very large bowl combine cucumbers, onions, sweet peppers, salt, and garlic. Stir in a large amount of cracked ice. Let stand 3 hours; drain well. Remove garlic.

2 In an 8-quart pot or kettle combine sugar, vinegar, mustard seed, celery seed, and turmeric; add drained cucumber mixture. Bring to boiling.

3 Pack cucumber mixture and liquid into hot, sterilized pint jars, leaving a ½-inch headspace. Wipe jar rims and adjust lids. Process in a boiling-water canner for 10 minutes (start timing when water covering jars returns to boiling). Remove jars from canner; cool jars on wire racks. Makes 7 pints (70 servings).

♥ *Nutrition facts per serving: 65 calories, 0 g total fat, 0 mg cholesterol, 275 mg sodium, 17 g carbohydrate, 0 g fiber, 0 g protein.*

Canning in Review

In years gone by, homemakers canned so often they knew just what to do. Today, however, most cooks have to learn or review canning techniques whenever they "put up" relishes, pickles, or other items. To ensure that the foods you preserve at home are the best quality and safe for your family to eat, use the latest in canning techniques. Look for details on using a boiling-water canner in government publications, country extension materials, or information supplied by manufacturers of canning supplies.

Sweet Endings

English Toffee Ice Cream

1934

This easy-to-make ice cream won top honors in one of the magazine's recipe contests in the '30s. The recipe's original contributor wrote, "If there's a better refrigerator-made ice cream than this one, I haven't found it. I'd vote twice for this one any day." We agree. If you're making this frozen treat for kids, you can substitute milk for the coffee.

4   1.4-ounce bars chocolate-covered English toffee
2   cups whipping cream

1   14-ounce can sweetened condensed milk
½   cup strong coffee, cooled
1½ teaspoons vanilla

1 Crush the toffee bars by placing them between 2 pieces of waxed paper and crushing with rolling pin; set aside. Combine the whipping cream, sweetened condensed milk, coffee, and vanilla. Refrigerate until completely chilled.

2 Beat chilled mixture with a rotary beater or an electric mixer on low speed until it's of custardlike consistency. Fold in toffee. Spoon into a 2-quart square baking dish or a 9×5×3-inch loaf pan. Cover; freeze several hours or until firm. Makes 6 cups (twelve ½-cup servings).

Nutrition facts per ½ cup: 315 calories, 21 g total fat (12 g saturated fat), 68 mg cholesterol, 94 mg sodium, 27 g carbohydrate, 0 g fiber, 4 g protein.

Vintage Views
1932

Vanilla Wins!

Vanilla ice cream, an all-time favorite, took top honors in the August 1932 recipe contest. It was a basic recipe but gave seven variations, all simple additions. It was chosen from 7,826 recipes that were tested in six refrigerator freezers, five of which were loaned to the Test Kitchen just for the contest. Everyone was so excited about having a freezer compartment in refrigerators during the '30s that ice cream was the rage.

The Test Kitchen home economists conducted the arduous testing and shared their findings with readers in an article. As for tasting these frozen delights, the cooks confessed: "Some of the judges of the contest ate far more than was good for them, but it was in the interest of scientific research."

Frosty Mocha Wedges

★
1974

1 **cup finely crushed
    chocolate chip cookies
    (10 to 12 cookies)**
2 **tablespoons butter or
    margarine, melted**
½ **cup milk**

1 **to 2 tablespoons instant
    coffee crystals**
1 **pint vanilla ice cream**
1 **4-serving size package
    instant vanilla
    pudding mix**

*laine Sheehan of Palm Coast,
Florida, writes us that Frosty
Mocha Wedges is one of her
family's favorites. Although it
was originally part of an Easter
menu, Elaine's family liked the
rich, frozen dessert so much that
she now serves it year-round.*

1 Line a 9×5×3-inch loaf pan with foil. In a small mixing bowl
combine crushed cookies and melted butter or margarine. Set aside
¼ cup of the crumb mixture. Press the remaining crumb mixture into
bottom of pan.

2 Combine milk and coffee crystals, stirring to dissolve. In a medium
mixing bowl stir ice cream just to soften. Add milk mixture and dry
pudding mix to softened ice cream. Beat with a rotary beater or an
electric mixer on low speed for 2 minutes or until well mixed and slightly
thickened. Pour into the crust-lined pan, spreading evenly. Sprinkle with
the reserved crumbs. Cover and freeze several hours or until firm.

3 To serve, remove from freezer and let stand 10 minutes before
cutting into wedges or slices. Makes 6 to 8 servings.

For a lower-fat version: Use reduced-fat chocolate chip cookies, skim
milk, vanilla frozen yogurt, and fat-free instant vanilla pudding mix.

*Nutrition facts per serving: 321 calories, 16 g total fat (7 g saturated fat),
31 mg cholesterol, 302 mg sodium, 44 g carbohydrate, 1 g fiber, 2 g protein.
Lower-fat version: 283 calories, 11 g total fat (4 g saturated fat), 7 mg cholesterol,
197 mg sodium, 40 g carbohydrate, 0 g fiber, 5 g protein.*

Coffee Éclairs

1 cup water
½ cup butter or margarine
1 cup all-purpose flour
4 eggs
1 quart coffee or vanilla ice cream
1½ cups cold water
3 tablespoons cornstarch

1 tablespoon instant coffee powder
1 cup light-colored corn syrup
2 tablespoons butter or margarine
1 teaspoon vanilla
½ cup chopped pecans (optional)

The French know how to do these luscious pastries right. These gooey confections can't help but be a favorite for anyone of any nationality. The sumptuous, tender shells are filled with ice cream and topped with a smooth coffee-flavored sauce.

1 Grease a large baking sheet. Set aside.

2 In a medium saucepan combine the 1 cup water and the ½ cup butter or margarine; bring to boiling. Add flour all at once, stirring vigorously. Cook and stir until mixture forms a ball that doesn't separate. Remove from heat. Cool 10 minutes.

3 Add eggs, *one* at a time, beating well after each addition until smooth. Spoon dough into a decorating bag fitted with a large plain round tip (about ½-inch opening). Pipe 10 to 12 strips of dough, 3 inches apart, onto prepared baking sheet, making each strip about 4 inches long, 1 inch wide, and ¾ inch high.

4 Bake éclairs in a 400° oven about 40 minutes or until golden brown. Transfer to a wire rack and let cool.

5 Cut éclairs in half lengthwise and remove soft dough from centers. Fill bottom halves with ice cream; replace tops. Cover and freeze until serving time. To serve, remove from the freezer and let stand about 15 minutes to soften.

6 Meanwhile, in a medium saucepan combine the 1½ cups cold water, the cornstarch, and coffee powder. Stir in corn syrup. Cook and stir until thickened and bubbly. Cook and stir for 2 minutes more. Remove from heat. Add the 2 tablespoons butter or margarine and the vanilla; stir until butter melts. (Sauce can be made ahead up to this point. Cover and refrigerate for up to 1 week. Rewarm to serve.) Serve some of the warm sauce over éclairs. If desired, sprinkle with the pecans. (Cover and refrigerate any leftover sauce for up to 1 week. Rewarm sauce and serve with ice cream.) Makes 10 to 12 éclairs.

Nutrition facts per éclair: 385 calories, 19 g total fat (11 g saturated fat), 139 mg cholesterol, 207 mg sodium, 49 g carbohydrate, 0 g fiber, 6 g protein.

Parfait Pie with Coconut Shell

1953

Parfait pies, a trendsetting dessert of the '50s, were developed in the United States as a promotion by a flour miller and a manufacturer of fruit-flavored gelatins. Single-crust concoctions with a fruit, gelatin, and ice-cream filling, parfait pies were especially popular because they were so simple and versatile.

2 cups flaked coconut
3 tablespoons butter or margarine, melted
1 10-ounce package frozen red raspberries, thawed

1 3-ounce package raspberry-flavored gelatin
1 pint vanilla ice cream
Whipped cream (optional)
Toasted coconut (optional)

1 In a medium mixing bowl combine the coconut and melted butter or margarine. Press evenly into the bottom and sides of a 9-inch pie plate. Bake in a 325° oven for 20 minutes. Cool on a wire rack.

2 Drain raspberries, reserving syrup. Set aside. Add enough *water* to syrup to measure 1¼ cups liquid. In a medium saucepan combine the gelatin and the syrup mixture. Heat and stir until gelatin is dissolved. Remove from heat.

3 Add ice cream by spoonfuls; stir until melted. Cover and refrigerate until mixture mounds when spooned. Fold in raspberries. Pour into coconut shell. Refrigerate at least 4 hours or until set. If desired, garnish with whipped cream and toasted coconut. Makes 8 servings.

Nutrition facts per serving: 256 calories, 14 g total fat (10 g saturated fat), 26 mg cholesterol, 95 mg sodium, 35 g carbohydrate, 3 g fiber, 3 g protein.

Vintage Views
1922

The Christmas Dinner

Our magazine's 1922 Christmas menu included three choices for the entrée—Little Roast Pig, Roast Goose with Dressing, or Roast Turkey with Chestnut Dressing. Even in its infancy, the magazine helped cooks with the planning. Time schedules helped novice cooks know when to make the dressing and bake the rolls. Serving suggestions were meant to take the worry out of the meal:

"Serve only small portions of plum pudding, for it is so very rich and may prove distressing after the turkey and its trimmings. Nuts and candies are served at these dinners to fill up the last niches, if there are any such free spaces."

Candy Bar Pie

1992

6 1- to 1½-ounce bars milk
   chocolate with almonds,
   chopped
15 large marshmallows or
    1½ cups tiny
    marshmallows
½ cup milk

1 cup whipping cream
½ teaspoon vanilla
1 recipe Walnut Crust
   Whipped cream (optional)
   Coarsely chopped milk
   chocolate bars with
   almonds (optional)

The history of this pie isn't known other than it was handed down among the family of a magazine staff member, who shared it with readers in the December 1992 issue. Don't try to cut corners by using a pastry crust—the walnut crust is what makes this pie exquisite.

1 For filling, in a medium saucepan combine the 6 chopped chocolate bars, the marshmallows, and milk. Heat and stir over medium-low heat until chocolate is melted. Remove from heat. Let the chocolate mixture stand until cooled to room temperature. Chill a large mixing bowl and beaters.

2 In the chilled mixing bowl beat the 1 cup cream and the vanilla with an electric mixer on medium speed until soft peaks form (tips curl).

3 Fold whipped cream mixture into cooled chocolate mixture. Spoon chocolate mixture into Walnut Crust. Freeze about 5 hours or until firm.

4 To serve, remove from the freezer and let stand about 10 minutes before cutting into wedges.* If desired, garnish with additional whipped cream and chopped chocolate bars. Makes 8 servings.

Walnut Crust: In a medium mixing bowl combine 1½ cups coarsely ground *walnuts* (6 ounces), 3 tablespoons melted *butter* or *margarine* and 2 tablespoons *sugar.* Press onto the bottom and side of a 9-inch pie plate to form a firm, even crust. Bake in a 325° oven about 10 minutes or until edge is golden brown. Cool on a wire rack.

*Note: For easier serving, set the pie on a warm, damp towel for a couple of minutes before cutting the first wedge.

Nutrition facts per serving: 440 calories, 36 g total fat (12 g saturated fat), 46 mg cholesterol, 92 mg sodium, 27 g carbohydrate, 2 g fiber, 6 g protein.

Sour Cream-Apple Pie

1953

Sour Cream-Apple Pie with streusel topping is a specialty of the Pennsylvania Dutch, who prefer it made with Summer Duchess apples just before they turn red. In the '50s, this pie appealed to many people because it combined the latest thing— dairy sour cream—with the old standby apple pie.

1 slightly beaten egg
1 8-ounce carton dairy sour cream
¾ cup granulated sugar
2 tablespoons all-purpose flour
1 teaspoon vanilla
¼ teaspoon salt

4 cups coarsely chopped, peeled tart apple
1 unbaked 9-inch piecrust
½ cup all-purpose flour
⅓ cup packed brown sugar
2 tablespoons butter or margarine

1 In a large mixing bowl stir together the egg, sour cream, granulated sugar, the 2 tablespoons flour, the vanilla, and salt. Stir in chopped apple. Pour mixture into the unbaked piecrust. Cover edge of piecrust with foil. Bake in a 400° oven for 25 minutes.

2 Meanwhile, in a small mixing bowl combine the ½ cup flour and the brown sugar. Cut in butter or margarine until crumbly. Remove foil from pie. Sprinkle brown sugar mixture over pie. Bake 20 minutes more or until top is golden brown. Cool on wire rack. Refrigerate within 2 hours; cover for longer storage. Makes 8 to 10 servings.

For lower-fat version: Use light dairy sour cream.

Nutrition facts per serving: 408 calories, 18 g total fat (7 g saturated fat), 49 mg cholesterol, 189 mg sodium, 57 g carbohydrate, 2 g fiber, 5 g protein. Lower-fat version: 383 calories, 14 g total fat (5 g saturated fat), 38 mg cholesterol, 205 mg sodium, 60 g carbohydrate, 1 g fiber, 5 g protein.

Piecrust on the Double

When cooks in days gone by wanted to make pies, they had no choice but to make pastry from scratch. Today you can make your favorite recipe for piecrust or purchase one of several easy-does-it options. In your supermarket's refrigerated dairy case, look for folded refrigerated piecrust. Each package contains two rounds— enough for two 9-inch single-crust pies or one 9-inch double-crust pie. In the freezer case, you'll find frozen unbaked pie shells. (For the recipes in this book, be sure to choose the deep-dish shells.) In the baking aisle, look for a piecrust mix.

Lemon Meringue Pie

1963

A bit of Better Homes and Gardens folklore says that years ago famous chef James Beard tried without success to get Myrna Johnston (then the food editor) to tell him the magazine's secret to perfect lemon pie. Although she wouldn't share it with James, we will pass it along to you: Preserve the fresh lemon flavor and keep the filling from becoming runny by removing it from the heat before you stir in the lemon juice and margarine or butter.

1½ cups sugar
3 tablespoons cornstarch
3 tablespoons all-purpose flour
1½ cups water
3 slightly beaten egg yolks
2 tablespoons butter or margarine, cut up

½ teaspoon finely shredded lemon peel
⅓ cup lemon juice
1 baked 9-inch piecrust, cooled
1 recipe Meringue

1 In a medium saucepan stir together the sugar, cornstarch, and flour. Gradually add the water, stirring constantly. Cook and stir over medium-high heat until thickened and bubbly. Reduce heat. Cook and stir 2 minutes more.

2 Gradually stir about 1 cup of the hot mixture into the egg yolks. Pour egg yolk mixture into remaining hot filling in saucepan. Bring to a gentle boil. Cook and stir 2 minutes more. Remove from heat.

3 Stir in the butter or margarine and lemon peel. Gently stir in the lemon juice.

4 Pour hot filling into cooled piecrust. Spread the Meringue over the hot lemon pie filling; carefully seal all around the edge of the piecrust to prevent shrinkage. Bake the pie in a 350° oven for 15 minutes. Cool on a wire rack for 1 hour. Refrigerate 3 to 6 hours before serving; cover for longer storage. Makes 8 servings.

Meringue: In a large mixing bowl combine 3 *egg whites,* ½ teaspoon *vanilla,* and ¼ teaspoon *cream of tartar.* Beat with an electric mixer on medium speed until soft peaks form (tips curl). Gradually add 6 tablespoons *sugar,* beating the meringue until stiff and glossy peaks form (tips stand straight) and all the sugar is dissolved.

Nutrition facts per serving: 400 calories, 14 g total fat (5 g saturated fat), 88 mg cholesterol, 122 mg sodium, 67 g carbohydrate, 1 g fiber, 5 g protein.

*T*oday's French Silk Pie

1 cup whipping cream
1 6-ounce package (1 cup)
   semisweet chocolate
   pieces
⅓ cup butter
⅓ cup sugar
2 beaten egg yolks

3 tablespoons crème de cacao
   or whipping cream
1 baked 9-inch piecrust,
   cooled
   Whipped cream
   Chocolate curls (optional)

In 1995, we revamped this rich perennial pie. Why did we tamper with perfection? On the advice of food-safety experts, we reworked the filling so the egg yolks are completely cooked.

1 In a heavy 2-quart saucepan combine the 1 cup whipping cream, the chocolate pieces, butter, and sugar. Cook over low heat, stirring constantly, until chocolate is melted (this should take about 10 minutes). Remove from heat. Gradually stir about half of the hot mixture into beaten egg yolks. Return egg mixture to mixture in saucepan. Cook over medium-low heat, stirring constantly, until mixture is slightly thickened and near bubbly (this should take 3 to 5 minutes). Remove from heat. (Mixture may appear to separate.) Stir in the 3 tablespoons crème de cacao or whipping cream. Place the saucepan in a bowl of ice water; stir occasionally until the mixture stiffens and becomes hard to stir (this should take about 20 minutes). Transfer the chocolate mixture to a medium mixing bowl.

2 Beat cooled chocolate mixture with an electric mixer on medium to high speed for 2 to 3 minutes or until light and fluffy. Spread filling in the baked piecrust. Cover and refrigerate pie for 5 to 24 hours. To serve, top with whipped cream. If desired, garnish with chocolate curls. Makes 10 servings.

Nutrition facts per serving: 379 calories, 28 g total fat (9 g saturated fat), 75 mg cholesterol, 136 mg sodium, 31 g carbohydrate, 0 g fiber, 3 g protein.

1965

Pumpkin Pecan Pie

Filled with lots of crunchy pecans, this company-special dessert was sent in by not one but two of our readers as favorites. Mrs. Edward D. Spellman of Omaha, Nebraska, and Mrs. Elaine Ritterling of Novi, Michigan, both declare it a must at their Thanksgiving celebrations.

3 **slightly beaten eggs**
1 **15-ounce can pumpkin**
¾ **cup sugar**
½ **cup dark-colored corn syrup**

1 **teaspoon vanilla**
¾ **teaspoon ground cinnamon**
1 **unbaked 9-inch piecrust**
1 **cup chopped pecans**
   Whipped cream (optional)

1 In a medium mixing bowl combine the eggs, pumpkin, sugar, corn syrup, vanilla, and cinnamon; mix well. Pour into the piecrust. Sprinkle with the pecans.

2 Bake in 350° oven for 50 to 55 minutes or until knife inserted off center comes out clean. Cool on wire rack. Refrigerate within 2 hours; cover for longer storage. If desired, serve with whipped cream. Serves 8.

Nutrition facts per serving: 412 calories, 20 g total fat (4 g saturated fat), 80 mg cholesterol, 108 mg sodium, 55 g carbohydrate, 3 g fiber, 6 g protein.

Cranberry-Pear Pie

1992

4 medium pears
1 cup sugar
¼ cup all-purpose flour
1 tablespoon finely shredded
  orange peel
1 teaspoon ground cinnamon
2 cups cranberries

Pastry for a double-crust
  pie
1 tablespoon butter or
  margarine, cut up
Glazed Nut Topping
Sweetened whipped cream
  (optional)

Tell the guests you dazzle with this pie that it's worth every last calorie. Mrs. Marilu Locche of New Hartford, Connecticut, ran away with top honors for this lattice-topped pie in the October 1992 Prize Tested Recipes contest. The glazed topping that crowns the pie is a treat in itself.

1 Peel, core, and slice pears (should have 5 cups). In a large mixing bowl combine sugar, flour, orange peel, and cinnamon. Add pears and cranberries; toss to coat. Set aside.

2 For pie shell, prepare double-crust pastry. Roll out half of the pastry; line a 9-inch pie plate with pastry. Fill the pastry-lined pie plate with pear mixture. Dot filling with butter or margarine. Trim bottom pastry to ½ inch beyond edge of plate. Roll out remaining pastry; cut into ½-inch-wide strips. Weave strips on top of filling to make a lattice. Press ends of strips into rim of bottom crust. Fold bottom pastry over strips; seal and crimp edge. Cover edge of pie with foil.

3 Bake in a 375° oven for 25 minutes. Remove foil; bake for 25 to 30 minutes more or until crust is golden. Spoon Glazed Nut Topping evenly over warm pie. Cool pie on wire rack before serving. If desired, serve with sweetened whipped cream. Makes 8 servings.

Glazed Nut Topping: In a saucepan combine ½ cup chopped *walnuts* and 2 tablespoons *butter* or *margarine.* Cook and stir over medium heat until walnuts are lightly browned. Stir in 3 tablespoons *brown sugar.* Heat and stir until sugar is dissolved. Stir in 1 tablespoon *milk.*

Nutrition facts per serving: 529 calories, 27 g total fat (7 g saturated fat), 12 mg cholesterol, 188 mg sodium, 72 g carbohydrate, 3 g fiber, 5 g protein.

Margarita Pie

1994

When summer's sweltering heat has your family dragging, cool everyone off with this breezy, tantalizing dessert. It's a flaky pastry shell filled with an irresistible combination of vanilla ice cream, lime sherbet, and frozen margarita mix. Tequila, of course, is optional.

1 15-ounce package (2 crusts) folded refrigerated unbaked piecrust
1 teaspoon all-purpose flour
3 cups vanilla ice cream
⅓ cup frozen margarita mix concentrate, thawed

2 tablespoons tequila (optional)
1½ cups lime sherbet
Whipped cream (optional)
Slivered lime peel (optional)
Edible flowers (optional)

1 Let refrigerated piecrust stand at room temperature according to package directions.

2 Trim 1 of the piecrusts to a 9-inch circle. Sprinkle 1 side with the flour. Center the circle, flour side down, in the bottom of a 9-inch pie plate. Using a fluted round cutter, cut remaining piecrust into twenty 2-inch rounds. Brush edge of crust in pie plate with *water*. Arrange and overlap the 2-inch rounds around edge of piecrust to form a rim; press rounds to the edge of piecrust circle to seal. Using a fork, prick the bottom and side of the piecrust.

3 Cover piecrust edge with foil. Bake in a 450° oven for 7 minutes. Remove foil; bake for 5 to 6 minutes more or until golden brown. Cool completely on a wire rack.

4 In a medium mixing bowl stir vanilla ice cream just enough to soften. Stir in margarita mix concentrate. Return to freezer; freeze until nearly firm.

5 If desired, stir tequila into lime sherbet. Return to freezer; freeze until nearly firm.

6 To assemble pie, randomly drop spoonfuls of lime sherbet into ice cream mixture, folding with a spatula just to marble slightly. Do not overmix. If mixture seems soft, return to freezer and freeze until nearly firm. Gently transfer ice cream mixture to the baked piecrust, spreading evenly. Cover; freeze 4 hours or until firm.

7 Before serving, let pie stand at room temperature about 20 minutes to soften slightly. To serve, cut into wedges. If desired, garnish with whipped cream, lime peel slivers, and edible flowers. Makes 8 servings.

Nutrition facts per serving: 417 calories, 21 g total fat (4 g saturated fat), 39 mg cholesterol, 261 mg sodium, 52 g carbohydrate, 0 g fiber, 4 g protein.

Fresh Strawberry & Chocolate Pie

1995

1 6-ounce package (1 cup) semisweet chocolate pieces
1 8-ounce package cream cheese, softened
3 tablespoons honey

1 baked 9-inch piecrust, cooled
4 cups fresh whole strawberries, stems and caps removed
Melted semisweet chocolate (optional)

For generations, strawberries were only a summer treat. Our readers eagerly looked forward to those June and July issues featuring berry-laden dessert extravaganzas. Today our editors can tempt readers with berry recipes anytime because most grocery stores offer strawberries year-round. This chocolate-and-berry delight is a good example; it was published in April 1995.

1 In a small, heavy saucepan heat the 6 ounces chocolate pieces over low heat, stirring constantly, until melted and smooth. Remove from heat; let stand at room temperature to cool.

2 In a medium mixing bowl beat cream cheese with an electric mixer on low speed until softened. Gradually beat in the chocolate and honey. Spread mixture in piecrust.

3 Cover pie; refrigerate 1 to 2 hours. Place berries on pie. If desired, drizzle with additional melted chocolate. Serve immediately. Serves 8.

Nutrition facts per serving: 387 calories, 25 g total fat (8 g saturated fat), 31 mg cholesterol, 154 mg sodium, 40 g carbohydrate, 2 g fiber, 5 g protein.

Vintage Views 1923

A Sweet Ending

In September 1923, a contributing editor and professor of home economics urged serving something sweet at the end of a meal:

"You know a little sweet at the close of a meal makes one feel satisfied. I have [eaten at many places] where they serve plenty of meat, potatoes, bread and other 'fillers' yet I did not feel satisfied. I craved a bit of sweet 'to finish up on.' This may be due to a lack of vegetables and fruit, also, since both contain elements needed in the body. You see, it isn't enough to give our bodies just fuel in the form of starches, sugars and fats. We need the minerals, acids and other regulating elements furnished by fruits and vegetables."

Peach-Praline Cobbler

1994

With a pecan-filled biscuit nestled atop bubbling, cinnamon-spiced fresh peaches, this cobbler earned its bragging rights. Carrie Smart of Rochelle, Illinois, submitted this first-place peach sensation in our August 1994 Prize Tested Recipes contest.

8 **cups sliced, peeled fresh peaches or frozen peaches, thawed**
1 **cup granulated sugar**
1 **cup water**
2 **tablespoons cornstarch**
1 **teaspoon ground cinnamon**
¾ **cup packed brown sugar**

¼ **cup margarine or butter, melted**
1½ **cups chopped pecans**
2 **cups self-rising flour***
2 **teaspoons granulated sugar**
½ **cup shortening**
¾ **cup buttermilk**
Half-and-half or light cream (optional)

1 In a kettle combine the peaches, the 1 cup granulated sugar, the water, cornstarch, and cinnamon. Cook and stir until thickened and bubbly. Transfer to a 3-quart rectangular baking dish.

2 Meanwhile, for filling, stir together the brown sugar and melted margarine or butter. Add pecans; toss to coat. Set aside.

3 For biscuit dough, in a large mixing bowl stir together the self-rising flour and the 2 teaspoons granulated sugar. Using a pastry blender, cut in the shortening until mixture resembles coarse crumbs. Make a well in the center of dry mixture. Add buttermilk all at once. Using a fork, stir until the dough clings together.

4 Turn dough out onto a lightly floured surface. Quickly knead dough by gently folding and pressing for 10 to 12 strokes. Roll to a 12×8-inch rectangle; spread with the filling. Roll up, jelly-roll style, starting from a long side. Cut into twelve 1-inch-thick slices. Place biscuit slices, cut sides down, on top of the hot peach mixture. Bake, uncovered, in a 400° oven for 25 to 30 minutes or until biscuits are golden brown. Serve warm. If desired, serve with half-and-half or light cream. Makes 12 servings.

***Note:** As a substitute for the 2 cups self-rising flour, use 2 cups *all-purpose flour* plus 2 teaspoons *baking powder,* ½ teaspoon *baking soda,* and ½ teaspoon *salt.*

Nutrition facts per serving: 466 calories, 22 g total fat (3 g saturated fat), 1 mg cholesterol, 332 mg sodium, 67 g carbohydrate, 6 g fiber, 5 g protein.

Crunchy Pecan-Pumpkin Custards

1995

3 eggs
1 15-ounce can pumpkin
1 12-ounce can (1½ cups) evaporated milk
¾ cup packed brown sugar
1 teaspoon pumpkin pie spice
1 teaspoon vanilla
¼ teaspoon finely shredded orange peel
1 4-ounce container frozen whipped dessert topping, thawed

¼ cup packed brown sugar
2 tablespoons all-purpose flour
½ teaspoon ground cinnamon
¼ teaspoon ground nutmeg
2 tablespoons butter or margarine
½ cup coarsely chopped pecans
Frozen whipped dessert topping, thawed (optional)

This first-rate dessert, which is like pumpkin pie without the crust, won Carol Gillespie from Chambersburg, Pennsylvania, $100 in 1995.

Elsie, the Borden cow, was a familiar sight in advertisements promoting dairy products during the 1950s.

1 In a medium mixing bowl beat eggs lightly with a rotary beater or wire whisk. Stir in the pumpkin, evaporated milk, the ¾ cup brown sugar, the pumpkin pie spice, vanilla, and orange peel. Fold in the container of whipped topping. Pour pumpkin mixture into twelve 6-ounce custard cups or one 2-quart square baking dish.

2 Bake in a 350° oven about 20 minutes for custard cups, 45 minutes for baking dish, or until side(s) of custard(s) just start to set.

3 Meanwhile, for topping, in a small mixing bowl combine the ¼ cup brown sugar, the flour, cinnamon, and nutmeg. Cut in the butter or margarine until the mixture resembles coarse crumbs. Stir in the pecans. Set aside.

4 Sprinkle custard(s) with the topping. Bake for 10 to 15 minutes more or until a knife inserted near the center(s) comes out clean. Serve warm. If desired, serve with whipped topping. Makes 12 servings.

Nutrition facts per serving: 208 calories, 11 g total fat (5 g saturated fat), 67 mg cholesterol, 74 mg sodium, 25 g carbohydrate, 1 g fiber, 5 g protein.

Pumpkin Cake Roll

1974

November is prime pumpkin time for the magazine. This November 1974 Prize Tested Recipes winner comes from Lucy Feldkamp of Ann Arbor, Michigan. The spicy pumpkin cake is rolled around a satiny cream cheese filling.

3 eggs
1 cup granulated sugar
⅔ cup canned pumpkin
1 teaspoon lemon juice
¾ cup all-purpose flour
2 teaspoons ground cinnamon
1 teaspoon baking powder
1 teaspoon ground ginger
½ teaspoon ground nutmeg

¼ teaspoon salt
1 cup finely chopped walnuts
   Sifted powdered sugar
1 cup sifted powdered sugar
2 3-ounce packages cream cheese, softened
¼ cup margarine or butter, softened
½ teaspoon vanilla

1 Grease and flour a 15×10×1-inch baking pan. Set aside.

2 In a large mixing bowl beat the eggs with an electric mixer on high speed for 5 minutes. Gradually beat in granulated sugar. Stir in pumpkin and lemon juice. In a medium mixing bowl stir together the flour, cinnamon, baking powder, ginger, nutmeg, and salt. Fold into pumpkin mixture. Spread in the prepared pan. Sprinkle with the walnuts.

3 Bake in a 375° oven for 15 minutes or until cake springs back when lightly touched. Immediately loosen edges of cake from pan and turn cake out onto a towel sprinkled with powdered sugar. Starting from a short side, roll up the warm cake and the powdered sugar-coated towel together. Let cake cool.

4 For filling, in a medium mixing bowl combine the 1 cup powdered sugar, the cream cheese, margarine or butter, and vanilla. Beat with an electric mixer on low speed until smooth.

5 Carefully unroll the cooled cake and towel. Spread the filling over the cake, leaving a 1-inch border around the edges. Starting from a short side, roll up the cake and filling. Cover and refrigerate. To serve, sprinkle with additional powdered sugar; cut into slices. Makes 10 servings.

Nutrition facts per serving: 358 calories, 20 g total fat (6 g saturated fat), 83 mg cholesterol, 209 mg sodium, 42 g carbohydrate, 1 g fiber, 6 g protein.

1960

Apple-Walnut Cobbler

One of our readers, Helen J. Tierney, spends part of the year in Connecticut and part in Florida. She enjoys this recipe so much she takes it with her. "In Connecticut, I use chopped walnuts and serve maple-nut ice cream on top," she explains. "In Florida, we have two pecan trees so I use pecans and butter-pecan ice cream. Friends love this dessert and always ask for the recipe. It's easier to make than apple pie!"

5 **cups thinly sliced, peeled cooking apples**
¾ **cup chopped walnuts**
¼ **cup sugar**
½ **teaspoon ground cinnamon**
1 **cup all-purpose flour**
½ **cup sugar**
1 **teaspoon baking powder**

1 **beaten egg**
½ **cup evaporated milk**
⅓ **cup butter or margarine, melted**
Whipped cream or ice cream (optional)
Ground cinnamon (optional)

1 Lightly grease a 2-quart square baking dish. Spread apples in prepared dish. Sprinkle with ½ *cup* of the walnuts. In a small mixing bowl stir together the ¼ cup sugar and the ½ teaspoon cinnamon; sprinkle over apples.

2 In a medium mixing bowl stir together the flour, the ½ cup sugar, and the baking powder. In a small mixing bowl combine the egg, evaporated milk, and the melted butter or margarine; stir into dry mixture until smooth. Pour egg-flour mixture evenly over apples; sprinkle with remaining walnuts.

3 Bake in a 325° oven for 50 to 55 minutes or until a wooden toothpick inserted in the center comes out clean. To serve, cut into squares. Serve warm. If desired, top each serving with whipped cream or ice cream and sprinkle with cinnamon. Makes 9 servings.

Nutrition facts per serving: 304 calories, 15 g total fat (6 g saturated fat), 46 mg cholesterol, 143 mg sodium, 41 g carbohydrate, 2 g fiber, 5 g protein.

Apple Dumplings Deluxe

1929

1 beaten egg
1 8-ounce carton dairy sour cream
2 cups all-purpose flour
2 tablespoons granulated sugar
2 teaspoons baking powder
¼ teaspoon baking soda
¼ teaspoon salt
4 cups very thinly sliced, peeled cooking apples
¼ cup granulated sugar

½ teaspoon ground cinnamon
¼ teaspoon ground nutmeg
1½ cups water
1¼ cups packed brown sugar
¼ cup granulated sugar
2 tablespoons cornstarch
2 tablespoons lemon juice
2 tablespoons margarine or butter
Half-and-half, light cream, or ice cream (optional)

In a January 1929 article, our editors wrote, "Back in the days when Grandmother was a girl and learning to cook in the approved school of her time—Mother's kitchen—sour cream cookery was the thing. All good cooks of that day preferred sour cream because, as they said, it made things more tender." Apple Dumplings Deluxe was one of the featured recipes in that article. It was so special, it appeared again 60 years later in a 1989 issue.

1 Grease a 13×9×2-inch baking pan. Set aside.

2 For dough, in a medium mixing bowl combine the egg and sour cream. In a large mixing bowl stir together the flour, the 2 tablespoons granulated sugar, baking powder, baking soda, and salt; add to sour cream mixture. Mix well.

3 On a well-floured surface, roll out dough to a 12-inch square. Spread apples over dough. In a small mixing bowl combine the ¼ cup granulated sugar, the cinnamon, and nutmeg; sprinkle over the apples. Carefully roll up, jelly-roll style. Cut into twelve 1-inch-thick slices. Place slices, cut sides down, in prepared pan.

4 In a medium mixing bowl stir together the water, brown sugar, the ¼ cup granulated sugar, the cornstarch, and lemon juice; pour over slices in pan. Dot with the margarine or butter.

5 Bake, uncovered, in a 350° oven for 35 to 40 minutes or until golden brown. To serve, spoon warm apple dumplings and the pan juices into individual dessert dishes. If desired, serve with half-and-half, light cream, or ice cream. Makes 12 servings.

Nutrition facts per serving: 264 calories, 7 g total fat (3 g saturated fat), 26 mg cholesterol, 190 mg sodium, 49 g carbohydrate, 1 g fiber, 3 g protein.

Big Apple Dumplings

1950

This was a winner in the October 1950 Cook's Round Table. We pulled the recipe from our files in 1993, when a reader suggested that we run the recipe again because the dumplings were so good. Our taste panelists agreed—they are, without a doubt, mouthwatering. You should use small cooking apples, despite the title of the recipe.

2 cups water
1¼ cups sugar
½ teaspoon ground cinnamon
¼ cup butter or margarine
2 cups all-purpose flour
½ teaspoon salt
⅔ cup shortening
⅓ to ½ cup half-and-half, light cream, or whole milk

2 tablespoons chopped raisins or golden raisins
2 tablespoons chopped walnuts
1 tablespoon honey
2 tablespoons sugar
½ teaspoon ground cinnamon
6 small cooking apples (about 1½ pounds)
1 tablespoon butter or margarine

1 For sauce, in a medium saucepan combine the water, the 1¼ cups sugar, and ½ teaspoon cinnamon. Bring to boiling; reduce heat. Simmer, uncovered, for 5 minutes. Add the ¼ cup butter or margarine. Set aside.

2 Meanwhile, for pastry, combine the flour and salt. Using a pastry blender, cut in shortening until pieces are the size of small peas. Sprinkle *1 tablespoon* of the half-and-half, light cream, or milk over part of the mixture; gently toss with a fork. Push moistened dough to the side of the bowl. Repeat moistening dough, using 1 tablespoon of the cream or milk at a time, until all of the dough is moistened. Form dough into a ball. On a lightly floured surface, roll dough to an 18×12-inch rectangle.* Using a pastry wheel or sharp knife, cut into six 6-inch squares.

3 In a small mixing bowl combine the raisins, walnuts, and honey. In another small bowl stir together the 2 tablespoons sugar and the ½ teaspoon cinnamon. Set aside.

4 Peel and core the apples. Place an apple on each pastry square. Fill centers of apples with raisin mixture. Sprinkle with sugar-cinnamon mixture; dot with the 1 tablespoon butter or margarine. Moisten edges of each pastry square with *water;* fold corners to center over apple. Pinch to seal. Place dumplings in a 2-quart rectangular baking dish. Pour sauce over dumplings. Bake in a 375° oven for 35 minutes or until apples are tender and pastry is golden brown. To serve, spoon sauce over dumplings. Makes 6 servings.

***Note:** If desired, roll pastry slightly larger and use excess pastry to make pastry leaves for garnish. Roll out pastry and cut into leaf shapes. Place on baking sheet. Bake in a 375° oven for about 10 minutes or until golden brown.

Nutrition facts per serving: 722 calories, 36 g total fat (9 g saturated fat), 5 mg cholesterol, 299 mg sodium, 99 g carbohydrate, 3 g fiber, 5 g protein.

Sweet Potato Shortcakes With Berries

1996

Tote this sweet potato version of the old-fashioned classic to your next family outing, and you're sure to get a picnic basketload of compliments. To carry everything to the picnic site, place the shortcake, berries, and whipped cream in separate containers. Pack the berries and whipped cream in a cooler. When you arrive, chill the berries and cream on ice until serving time. (This shortcake is featured on the cover of this book.)

1 16-ounce can sweet potatoes (syrup pack)
½ cup milk
2 tablespoons margarine or butter, melted
2½ cups packaged biscuit mix
2 tablespoons sugar
¼ teaspoon ground cinnamon

1½ to 2 quarts fresh strawberries,* red raspberries, blackberries, and/or blueberries
3 tablespoons sugar
1 to 1½ cups whipping cream
2 tablespoons sugar

1 Grease a large baking sheet. Set aside. Chill a medium mixing bowl and the beaters of an electric mixer.

2 Drain sweet potatoes, reserving 2 tablespoons of the syrup. Mash enough of the sweet potatoes to make ½ cup. (Cover and refrigerate any remaining sweet potatoes and syrup to heat later as a side dish.)

3 In a medium mixing bowl stir together the mashed sweet potatoes, the reserved syrup, the milk, and melted margarine or butter. Sprinkle the biscuit mix, 2 tablespoons sugar, and cinnamon over sweet potato mixture; stir just until dough clings together. (The dough might have some lumps and should be thick.)

4 Drop dough onto the prepared baking sheet in 8 equal portions. Bake in a 425° oven about 12 minutes or until golden brown. Transfer to a wire rack and allow to cool slightly.

5 Meanwhile, in a large mixing bowl combine fresh berries and the 3 tablespoons sugar. Set aside. In the chilled mixing bowl beat the whipping cream and the 2 tablespoons sugar with an electric mixer on medium speed until soft peaks form (tips curl).

6 To serve, split each shortcake in half crosswise; place bottom halves on 8 dessert plates. Top with some of the berries and some of the whipped cream. Place a shortcake top on each serving. Top with the remaining berries and the remaining whipped cream. Makes 8 servings.

*Note: If desired, slice the strawberries.

For a lower-fat version: Use reduced-fat packaged biscuit mix and frozen light whipped dessert topping (thawed).

Nutrition facts per serving: 415 calories, 15 g total fat (8 g saturated fat), 42 mg cholesterol, 704 mg sodium, 65 g carbohydrate, 5 g fiber, 6 g protein.
Lower-fat version: 297 calories, 8 g total fat (3 g saturated fat), 1 mg cholesterol, 496 mg sodium, 52 g carbohydrate, 2 g fiber, 4 g protein.

Amazing Banana-Nut Roll

1 **8-ounce package cream cheese, softened**	½ **teaspoon vanilla**
1 **3-ounce package cream cheese, softened**	⅓ **cup granulated sugar**
½ **cup granulated sugar**	1 **large banana, mashed (about ½ cup)**
1 **egg**	½ **cup finely chopped walnuts**
3 **tablespoons milk**	4 **egg whites**
½ **cup all-purpose flour**	½ **cup granulated sugar**
½ **teaspoon baking powder**	1 **recipe Cream Cheese Frosting**
¼ **teaspoon baking soda**	**Chocolate-flavored syrup (optional)**
4 **egg yolks**	

1 Lightly grease a 15×10×1-inch baking pan. Line bottom with waxed paper; grease paper. Set aside.

2 For filling, in a small mixing bowl combine the cream cheese and the ½ cup granulated sugar. Beat with an electric mixer until smooth. Add whole egg and milk; beat until combined. Spread in prepared pan.

3 For cake, in a medium mixing bowl stir together flour, baking powder, and baking soda. Set aside.

4 In a small mixing bowl beat egg yolks and vanilla with an electric mixer on medium speed about 5 minutes or until thick and lemon colored. Gradually add the ⅓ cup granulated sugar, beating until sugar is dissolved. Stir in the mashed banana and nuts.

5 Wash beaters. In a large mixing bowl beat egg whites on medium speed until soft peaks form. Gradually add the ½ cup granulated sugar, beating on high speed until stiff peaks form. Fold yolk mixture into egg whites. Sprinkle flour mixture over egg mixture; fold in just to combine.

6 Carefully spread batter evenly over filling in pan. Bake cake in a 375° oven for 15 to 20 minutes or until cake springs back when lightly touched. Immediately loosen cake from sides of pan and turn out onto a towel sprinkled with *powdered sugar*. Carefully peel off paper. Starting from a short side, roll up the warm cake using the towel as a guide. (Do not roll towel into cake.) Cool completely. Spread top with Cream Cheese Frosting. If desired, drizzle with chocolate syrup. Serves 10.

Cream Cheese Frosting: In a small mixing bowl combine *half* of a 3-ounce package *cream cheese,* softened, and ½ teaspoon *vanilla;* beat with an electric mixer on medium speed until fluffy. Gradually beat in 1 cup sifted *powdered sugar.* Beat in enough *milk* (1 to 2 tablespoons) to make a frosting of spreading consistency. Makes about ½ cup.

Nutrition facts per serving: 400 calories, 19 g total fat (9 g saturated fat), 146 mg cholesterol, 162 mg sodium, 51 g carbohydrate, 1 g fiber, 8 g protein.

Our food editors are always looking for ways to make recipes easier. In 1993, they came up with this idea that streamlines preparation of a jelly-roll cake. Instead of making, baking, rolling, cooling, unrolling, filling, and rerolling the cake, this practical recipe allows you to bake the cake and filling together and roll everything together just once.

Almond Raspberry Torte

1988

1½ cups all-purpose flour
2¼ teaspoons baking powder
¼ teaspoon salt
¾ cup butter or margarine
1 cup sugar
1½ teaspoons vanilla
3 eggs
¾ cup milk

½ cup seedless red raspberry jam
1 recipe Almond Filling
1¼ cups whipping cream
Sliced almonds, toasted
¼ cup seedless red raspberry jam

We featured this showstopper in our April 1988 issue as the dessert for one of four menus for extra-special occasions. When reassessing the knock-'em-dead torte, our testers decided it was so rich, it could serve 16 people instead of 10 as suggested in the original recipe.

1 Grease and lightly flour two 9×1½-inch round baking pans. Set pans aside.

2 For cake, in a large mixing bowl stir together flour, baking powder, and salt. Set aside. Beat butter or margarine with an electric mixer on medium speed 30 seconds. Add sugar and vanilla; beat until well mixed.

3 Add eggs, *one* at a time, beating well after each addition. Add dry mixture and milk alternately to sugar mixture, beating after each addition (batter may appear curdled). Spread batter into prepared pans.

4 Bake in a 375° oven for 20 to 25 minutes or until wooden toothpicks inserted in the centers come out clean. Cool in pans on wire racks for 10 minutes. Remove cakes from pans. Cool completely on wire racks.

5 Cut cake layers in half horizontally. Stir the ½ cup raspberry jam. To assemble, spread 1 cake layer with one-third of the Almond Filling, then with 2 rounded tablespoons of jam. Repeat layering with the cake layers, Almond Filling, and jam 2 more times. Top with the final cake layer. Cover cake tightly and refrigerate at least 6 hours or overnight.

6 No more than 1 hour before serving, beat whipping cream with an electric mixer on low speed until stiff peaks form (tips stand straight). Spread whipped cream over cake. Press almonds around the base of the cake. Just before serving, stir the ¼ cup raspberry jam. Drizzle jam over cake; if desired, swirl with a knife. Serve immediately. Makes 16 servings.

Almond Filling: In a small mixing bowl crumble one 8-ounce can *almond paste*. Add ⅓ cup softened *butter* or *margarine*; beat with an electric mixer on low speed. Add 2 tablespoons *milk*; beat until smooth.

Nutrition facts per serving: 387 calories, 24 g total fat (13 g saturated fat), 100 mg cholesterol, 239 mg sodium, 39 g carbohydrate, 0 g fiber, 5 g protein.

Chocolate Hazelnut Torte

1988

Enticingly full of nuts and chocolate, this decadent dazzler is perfect for a dessert buffet or as a climax to an elegant dinner party. Warm a serving knife in hot water, then dry it before cutting the torte into wedges. Rewarm the knife as necessary to make cutting easier.

¾ cup butter or margarine
3 ounces unsweetened chocolate
1½ cups packed brown sugar
3 eggs
1 teaspoon vanilla
1 cup all-purpose flour
½ cup coarsely chopped hazelnuts (filberts)

1 ounce white baking bar or vanilla-flavored candy coating, coarsely chopped
½ teaspoon shortening
1 ounce semisweet chocolate or chocolate-flavored candy coating, coarsely chopped
½ teaspoon shortening
Fresh strawberries (optional)

1 Grease and flour bottom of an 8-inch springform pan. Set aside.

2 In a medium saucepan cook and stir butter or margarine and unsweetened chocolate over low heat until melted. Remove from heat; cool slightly. Stir in brown sugar. Add eggs and vanilla. Lightly beat mixture by hand just until combined. (Do not overbeat or torte will rise during baking, then fall and crack.) Stir in flour. Spread mixture in prepared pan. Sprinkle with the hazelnuts.

3 Bake in a 350° oven for 35 to 40 minutes or until a slight imprint remains when torte is lightly touched in the center. Cool in pan on a wire rack for 5 minutes.

4 Loosen side of torte with a knife. Remove side of pan; cool completely on wire rack.

5 Set torte on a wire rack over waxed paper. In a small, heavy saucepan cook and stir the white baking bar or vanilla-flavored candy coating and the ½ teaspoon shortening over low heat until baking bar is melted. Drizzle randomly over torte.

6 In the same saucepan cook and stir the semisweet chocolate or chocolate-flavored candy coating and the ½ teaspoon shortening over low heat until chocolate is melted. Remove from heat; stir until smooth. Drizzle randomly over the torte. Place on a serving plate. Cover loosely and refrigerate at least 4 hours. Bring to room temperature before serving. If desired, serve with strawberries. Makes 12 to 16 servings.

Nutrition facts per serving: 351 calories, 21 g total fat (10 g saturated fat), 84 mg cholesterol, 141 mg sodium, 35 g carbohydrate, 1 g fiber, 4 g protein.

Chocolate Mousse Cake

1986

1½ cups (6 ounces) whole
     hazelnuts (filberts)
3 tablespoons butter or
     margarine, melted
2 8-ounce packages
     semisweet chocolate,
     cut up
1 cup whipping cream

6 eggs
1 teaspoon vanilla
⅓ cup all-purpose flour
¼ cup sugar
1 recipe Chocolate Whipped
     Cream
   Shelled whole hazelnuts
     (filberts)(optional)

During the '80s, Americans were especially passionate about chocolate, as we still are today. Our taste panelists gave this recipe a thumbs up remarking, "It's so creamy and yummy!"

1 Grease a 9-inch springform pan. Set aside.

2 In a blender container or food processor bowl, coarsely grind the 1½ cups hazelnuts to make about 1⅓ cups ground nuts. (If using a blender, blend half the nuts at a time.) Stir together the ground hazelnuts and melted butter or margarine. Press onto bottom and 1½ inches up side of prepared pan.

3 In a medium saucepan cook and stir cut-up chocolate and ½ *cup* of the whipping cream over low heat until chocolate is melted.* Remove from heat.

4 In a large mixing bowl beat eggs and vanilla with an electric mixer on low speed until well mixed. Add flour and sugar; beat on high speed for 10 minutes or until thick and lemon-colored.

5 In a small mixing bowl beat the remaining whipping cream just until soft peaks form (tips curl). Stir about one-fourth of the egg mixture into chocolate mixture. Fold remaining egg mixture into chocolate mixture; fold in whipped cream. Turn into prepared pan.

6 Bake in a 325° oven for 30 to 35 minutes or until puffed on the outer one-third of the top. (The center will be slightly soft.) Cool in pan on wire rack for 20 minutes. Remove side of pan. Cool on wire rack for 3 to 4 hours. Serve at room temperature or refrigerate until completely chilled. Serve with Chocolate Whipped Cream. If desired, garnish with whole hazelnuts. Makes 16 to 20 servings.

Chocolate Whipped Cream: In a small saucepan cook and stir ½ cup *whipping cream* and ½ ounce *semisweet chocolate* over low heat until chocolate is melted. Remove from heat and stir until no chocolate specks remain. Pour into a small mixing bowl; cover and refrigerate until completely chilled. Before serving, beat chilled cream mixture with an electric mixer on low speed until stiff peaks form (tips stand straight).

***Note:** To melt the chocolate in a microwave oven, place cut-up chocolate and cream in a 2-cup glass measure. Cook, uncovered, on high for 2 to 3 minutes or until chocolate is melted. Stir once.

Nutrition facts per serving: 352 calories, 28 g total fat (13 g saturated fat), 116 mg cholesterol, 55 mg sodium, 25 g carbohydrate, 3 g fiber, 7 g protein.

Heavenly Cheesecake

1996

Our readers' continuing interest in healthful foods prompts us to modify traditional dessert favorites, such as cheesecake, to create lower-fat versions. This leaner recipe was so delicious we put it on the cover of our May 1996 magazine. A typical cheesecake with fruit sauce contains 32 grams of fat per serving, but this imaginative version has only 13 grams.

2½ cups Yogurt Cheese
1 cup finely crushed gingersnaps (about 20)
1 cup finely crushed vanilla wafers (about 25)
1 tablespoon all-purpose flour
¼ cup butter or margarine, melted
¾ of an 8-ounce package (6 ounces) reduced-fat cream cheese, softened

1 cup sugar
1½ teaspoons finely shredded orange peel (set aside)
1 tablespoon orange juice
3 eggs or ¾ cup refrigerated or frozen egg product, thawed
1½ teaspoons grated gingerroot
⅓ cup strawberry jelly
2 cups sliced fresh strawberries
1 cup orange segments

1 Prepare the Yogurt Cheese at least 1 day ahead. For crust, in a mixing bowl combine the crushed gingersnaps, crushed vanilla wafers, and flour. Drizzle with the melted butter or margarine. Toss to mix well. Press crumb mixture onto the bottom and 1½ inches up the side of an 8-inch springform pan. Bake in a 350° oven for 5 minutes.

2 For filling, in mixing bowl combine Yogurt Cheese, cream cheese, sugar, and orange juice; beat with an electric mixer on medium speed until smooth. Add eggs or egg product; beat on low speed just until combined. Stir in orange peel and gingerroot. Pour into crust.

3 Bake in a 350° oven about 50 minutes or until the center appears nearly set when shaken. Cool on a wire rack for 15 minutes. Loosen the crust from the side of the pan. Cool for 30 minutes more; remove the side of the pan. Cool completely on a wire rack. Cover and refrigerate for several hours or until completely chilled.

4 For topping, in a small saucepan melt jelly over low heat. Cool slightly. In a bowl stir together strawberries and orange segments. To serve, slice cheesecake. Top each serving with fruit. Drizzle with cooled jelly. Store any remaining cheesecake in refrigerator. Makes 10 servings.

Yogurt Cheese: Spoon 56 ounces *plain nonfat yogurt** into a 100-percent-cotton cheesecloth-lined sieve or colander set over a large bowl. Let yogurt stand in refrigerator about 15 hours or overnight. Discard liquid in bowl. To store, wrap Yogurt Cheese in plastic wrap and store in the refrigerator for up to 4 days. Makes about 2½ cups.

*Note: Be sure to use gelatin-free yogurt. Otherwise, the yogurt won't separate into curds and whey (the curds are the cheese).

Nutrition facts per serving: 404 calories, 13 g total fat (5 g saturated fat), 85 mg cholesterol, 342 mg sodium, 59 g carbohydrate, 1 g fiber, 14 g protein.

Best-Ever Cheesecake

1961

1¾ cups finely crushed graham
  crackers

¼ cup finely chopped walnuts

½ teaspoon ground cinnamon

½ cup butter, melted

3 8-ounce packages cream
  cheese, softened

1 cup sugar

2 tablespoons all-purpose
  flour

1 teaspoon vanilla

2 eggs

1 egg yolk

¼ cup milk

½ teaspoon finely shredded
  lemon peel (optional)

Cheesecake is the quintessential dessert and was especially popular in the '50s and '60s. This version graced the pages of the magazine in April 1961. Myrna Johnston, the food editor at that time, said, "Of all the variations, we love this one best. It's rich, luscious, magnificent!"

1 For the crust, combine crushed graham crackers, walnuts, and cinnamon. Stir in melted butter. If desired, set aside ¼ cup of the crumb mixture for topping. Press the remaining crumb mixture onto the bottom and about 2 inches up side of an 8- or 9-inch springform pan. Set aside.

2 For filling, in a large mixing bowl beat cream cheese, sugar, flour, and vanilla with an electric mixer until combined. Add eggs and egg yolk all at once, beating on low speed just until combined. Stir in milk and, if desired, lemon peel.

3 Pour filling into crust-lined pan. If desired, sprinkle with reserved crumbs. Place on a shallow baking pan in oven. Bake in a 375° oven for 45 to 50 minutes for the 8-inch pan, 35 to 40 minutes for the 9-inch pan, or until the center appears nearly set when shaken.

4 Cool in pan on a wire rack for 15 minutes. Loosen the crust from side of pan and cool 30 minutes more. Remove the side of the pan. Cool completely on wire rack. Cover and refrigerate at least 4 hours before serving. Makes 12 to 16 servings.

Nutrition facts per serving: 429 calories, 32 g total fat (18 g saturated fat), 137 mg cholesterol, 329 mg sodium, 30 g carbohydrate, 1 g fiber, 7 g protein.

Peaches & Cream Tart

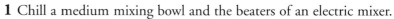

1992

The go-alongs category of our 1992 Barbecue Recipe contest was not lacking in elegance. Rebecca Mae of Carmichael, California, created this prizewinner. The glamorous tart has a coconut macaroon and pecan crust filled with cream cheese, rum, and whipping cream. Fresh peaches and raspberries top it all off.

9 soft coconut macaroon cookies (half of a 13¾-ounce package)
1 cup ground pecans (4 ounces)*
3 tablespoons butter or margarine, melted
½ cup whipping cream
1 8-ounce package cream cheese, softened
⅓ cup sugar
2 teaspoons dark rum or orange juice

1 teaspoon vanilla
¼ teaspoon almond extract
2 to 4 medium peaches, peeled, pitted, and thinly sliced (1½ to 3 cups)
2 tablespoons lemon juice
½ cup fresh raspberries
¼ cup apricot preserves
2 teaspoons honey
Fresh lemon thyme sprigs (optional)

1 Chill a medium mixing bowl and the beaters of an electric mixer.

2 For crust, crumble macaroons (you should have about 2 cups). In a large mixing bowl stir together the macaroon crumbs, pecans, and butter or margarine. Press mixture onto bottom and up side of an 11-inch tart pan with a removable bottom or into a 12-inch pizza pan. Bake in a 350° oven for 15 to 18 minutes for the tart pan, 12 to 15 minutes for the pizza pan, or until golden brown. Cool on a wire rack.

3 For filling, in the chilled bowl beat whipping cream with electric mixer on medium speed until soft peaks form (tips curl). Set aside.

4 In a small mixing bowl beat cream cheese and sugar with an electric mixer on medium speed until fluffy. Add rum or orange juice, vanilla, and almond extract; beat until smooth. Gently fold in whipped cream. Turn mixture into cooled crust; spread evenly. Cover and refrigerate for 2 to 4 hours.

5 Before serving, toss the peach slices with lemon juice. Arrange peaches and raspberries over filling.

6 For glaze, in a small saucepan combine preserves and honey; heat and stir just until melted. Snip any large pieces of fruit in the glaze. If desired, strain glaze. Carefully brush or spoon the glaze over the fruit. If using a tart pan, gently remove side; transfer the tart to a serving platter. If desired, garnish with fresh lemon thyme sprigs. To serve, cut into wedges. Makes 10 to 12 servings.

*Note: To grind the pecans, place nuts, ½ cup at a time, in your blender or food processor. Cover and blend or process until very finely chopped, being careful not to overprocess or the nuts will form a paste.

Nutrition facts per serving: 389 calories, 28 g total fat (11 g saturated fat), 51 mg cholesterol, 115 mg sodium, 33 g carbohydrate, 2 g fiber, 4 g protein.

Ultimate Nut & Chocolate Chip Tart

In 1994, we elected this fudgelike, nut-studded tart to our chocolate hall of fame. Our editors were so impressed with its charms they exclaimed, "With a scoop of rich vanilla ice cream, it's heaven!"

½ of a 15-ounce package (1 crust) folded refrigerated unbaked piecrust
3 eggs
1 cup light-colored corn syrup
½ cup packed brown sugar
⅓ cup butter, melted and cooled

1 teaspoon vanilla
1 cup coarsely chopped salted mixed nuts
½ cup miniature semisweet chocolate pieces
⅓ cup miniature semisweet chocolate pieces
1 tablespoon shortening
Vanilla ice cream (optional)

1 Let refrigerated piecrust stand at room temperature according to package directions.

2 Ease piecrust into an 11-inch tart pan with removable bottom. Trim piecrust even with the rim of the pan. Do not prick piecrust.

3 For filling, in a large mixing bowl beat eggs slightly with a rotary beater or fork. Stir in the corn syrup. Add the brown sugar, butter, and vanilla, stirring until sugar is dissolved. Stir in the nuts and the ½ cup chocolate pieces.

4 Place pastry-lined tart pan on baking sheet on oven rack. Carefully pour filling into pan. Bake in a 350° oven for 40 minutes or until a knife inserted near the center comes out clean. Cool on a wire rack.

5 To serve, cut tart into wedges and transfer to dessert plates. In a small, heavy saucepan cook and stir the ⅓ cup chocolate pieces and the shortening over very low heat until chocolate begins to melt. Immediately remove from heat and stir until smooth. Cool slightly. Transfer chocolate mixture to a clean, small, heavy plastic bag. Snip a very small hole in 1 corner of the bag. Drizzle the melted chocolate in zigzag lines across each tart wedge.

6 If desired, serve tart with vanilla ice cream. Cover and refrigerate any leftover tart for up to 2 days. Makes 8 to 10 servings.

Nutrition facts per serving: 467 calories, 27 g total fat (6 g saturated fat), 86 mg cholesterol, 192 mg sodium, 56 g carbohydrate, 1 g fiber, 6 g protein.

Giant Strawberry Tart

1973

1 recipe Pastry
1 2.9-ounce package custard-
 flavored dessert mix
1¾ cups milk
1 8-ounce package cream
 cheese, cubed
½ teaspoon vanilla
2 cups fresh strawberries,
 halved

1 small peach, peeled, pitted,
 and thinly sliced, or
1 small nectarine, pitted
 and thinly sliced
¼ cup fresh blueberries or
1 small banana, thinly
 sliced
⅓ cup apple jelly
1 teaspoon water

Something about strawberry desserts draws people to pick up our magazine on the newsstand. Consequently, these enticing concoctions often appear on our covers. This strawberry tart appeared on our June 1973 cover. The custard-flavored dessert mix makes the filling super simple. Use fat-free cream cheese to save 8 grams fat and about 60 calories per serving.

1 On a lightly floured surface, roll Pastry to a 14-inch circle; carefully fit into a 12-inch pizza pan. Fold under and flute edge; prick pastry with fork. Bake in a 425° oven about 15 minutes or until golden brown. Cool.

2 In a medium saucepan combine custard mix and milk. Cook and stir over medium heat until mixture comes to a full boil (mixture will be thin). Remove from heat. Stir in cream cheese and vanilla, whisking until smooth with a wire whisk. Cool 10 minutes, stirring once or twice. (Mixture thickens as it cools.) Spread in baked pastry. Cover and refrigerate until firm.

3 Up to 1 hour before serving, arrange halved strawberries around edge, sliced peach or nectarine in a spoke pattern in the middle, and blueberries or banana slices in the center. In a small saucepan combine jelly and the water; heat and stir over medium heat just until melted. Brush over fruit. Refrigerate for up to 1 hour. Makes 10 servings.

Pastry: In a medium bowl stir together 2 cups *all-purpose flour* and ½ teaspoon *salt*. Using a pastry blender, cut in ⅔ cup *shortening* until pieces are the size of small peas. Sprinkle 1 tablespoon *cold water* over part of the mixture; gently toss with fork. Push moistened dough to side of bowl. Repeat with 5 to 6 tablespoons *cold water,* using 1 tablespoon at a time, until all dough is moistened. Form dough into a ball.

Nutrition facts per serving: 382 calories, 23 g total fat (9 g saturated fat), 53 mg cholesterol, 252 mg sodium, 38 g carbohydrate, 1 g fiber, 6 g protein.

Strawberry Crown Trifle

1974

1 **cup sifted cake flour**	3 **pints fresh strawberries**
1 **teaspoon baking powder**	3 **tablespoons granulated**
¼ **teaspoon salt**	**sugar**
½ **cup milk**	⅓ **cup strawberry or orange**
2 **tablespoons butter or**	**liqueur or orange juice**
margarine	1 **recipe Fluffy Filling**
2 **eggs**	**Powdered sugar**
1 **cup granulated sugar**	**Whipped cream**
1 **teaspoon vanilla**	**Fresh mint sprigs**

A time-honored English dessert, trifles usually consist of pieces of cake soaked with brandy, rum, or a liqueur and layered with jam and custard. When we created this 1974 version, we substituted crushed fresh fruit for the jam and a rich vanilla pudding for the custard. Assemble and refrigerate the trifle a day ahead so the pudding, berries, and liqueur have time to flavor the cake.

1 Grease and flour two 8×1½-inch round baking pans. Set aside.

2 In a medium bowl combine the cake flour, baking powder, and salt. In a small saucepan heat the milk and butter or margarine until butter or margarine melts; keep hot. In a large mixing bowl beat whole eggs with electric mixer on high speed for 3 to 4 minutes or until thick and lemon-colored. Gradually add the 1 cup granulated sugar, beating constantly at medium speed for 4 to 5 minutes. Add dry mixture to egg mixture; stir just until combined. Stir in hot milk mixture and vanilla. Turn batter into prepared pans. Bake in a 350° oven for 20 minutes or until wooden toothpicks inserted near the centers of cakes come out clean. Cool on wire racks for 10 minutes. Remove from pans. Cool completely on racks.

3 Set aside a few strawberries for garnish; crush enough remaining berries to make 2 cups. Stir the 3 tablespoons sugar into crushed berries.

4 To assemble, split cake layers in half horizontally to make 4 layers. Fit 1 layer into bottom of a 2-quart soufflé dish (8 inches in diameter); spread 1 cup of the crushed strawberries over the top. Top with second cake layer; sprinkle with half of the liqueur or orange juice. Spread with Fluffy Filling. Place third cake layer on top; spread remaining crushed berries over. Sprinkle cut side of fourth cake layer with remaining liqueur or orange juice; place cake, cut side down, over berries in dish. Cover; refrigerate overnight. Just before serving, sift powdered sugar over trifle. Top with whipped cream, reserved berries, and mint. Makes 12 servings.

Fluffy Filling: In a saucepan combine ⅓ cup *sugar*, 1 tablespoon *cornstarch*, and ⅛ teaspoon *salt*. Stir in 1 cup *milk*. Cook and stir over medium-high heat until bubbly. Slowly stir ½ cup of the hot mixture into 2 beaten *egg yolks*. Return mixture to pan. Cook and stir 2 minutes more. Remove from heat. Stir in 1 tablespoon *butter* or *margarine* and 1 teaspoon *vanilla*. Cover surface with plastic wrap; refrigerate until completely chilled. Just before assembling trifle, in a small bowl beat ½ cup *whipping cream* until soft peaks form; fold into chilled mixture.

Nutrition facts per serving: 342 calories, 16 g total fat (10 g saturated fat), 122 mg cholesterol, 165 mg sodium, 43 g carbohydrate, 2 g fiber, 4 g protein.

Chocolate-Peanut Fondue

1960

During the '60s, millions of Americans got their first glimpse of fondue, a European classic, in Cinerama Holiday, one of the early wide-screen movies. From that time on, fondue was a hit. In addition to the traditional cheese fondue, beef and dessert fondues, such as this chocolate and peanut butter version, also were popular.

1 6-ounce package
   semisweet chocolate
   pieces
½ cup sugar
½ cup milk
½ cup chunky peanut butter

Cubed angel cake or pound cake, assorted fruit dippers (such as banana, apple, or pear slices), and/or marshmallows

1 In a medium saucepan combine the chocolate pieces, sugar, and milk. Cook, stirring constantly, until chocolate is melted. Stir in the peanut butter. Cook and stir until heated through.

2 Pour mixture into a fondue pot; place over fondue burner set on low. Serve with cake cubes, fruit dippers, and/or marshmallows. Makes 8 (¼-cup) servings.

Nutrition facts per ¼ cup sauce and angel cake: 317 calories, 15 g total fat (2 g saturated fat), 1 mg cholesterol, 199 mg sodium, 52 g carbohydrate, 2 g fiber, 7 g protein.

Chocolate Sauce

1994

Want a versatile chocolate sauce that's easy, too? This one is tops. Serve it over ice cream, angel cake, éclairs, or cream puffs. Add just a splash of liqueur, and you've got a sauce that's made for adults only.

4 ounces bittersweet
   chocolate or semisweet
   chocolate, cut up
2 tablespoons margarine or
   butter
¾ cup milk

½ cup sugar
2 tablespoons corn syrup
2 to 4 tablespoons liqueur,
   such as orange, hazelnut,
   or amaretto (optional)

1 In a medium, heavy saucepan cook chocolate and margarine or butter over low heat until melted, stirring frequently. Add milk, sugar, and corn syrup. Bring to a gentle boil over medium heat. Boil gently, stirring frequently, for 8 minutes or until mixture is thickened. Remove from heat. Cool slightly. If desired, stir in liqueur. Serve warm. To store, cover and refrigerate for up to 1 week. Makes 1 cup.

Nutrition facts per 2 tablespoons: 178 calories, 8 g total fat (4 g saturated fat), 2 mg cholesterol, 49 mg sodium, 27 g carbohydrate, 1 g fiber, 2 g protein.

Vintage Views
1930

Prizewinners: Men

A cooking contest for men resulted in some mighty fine dishes, as related here by an editor in the February 1930 issue:

"That the man-person very often chooses the meal is a quite generally accepted fact. … But that the man of the family actually cooks—that has been a moot question. After looking over the hundreds of recipes submitted in the Men's Cooking Contest, conducted by *Better Homes and Gardens,* we have proof positive that he not only can cook but that he excels at it. It may look like a grand gesture when he takes hold of the cooking spoon, but when he turns out a hash—yes, a hash, the most lowly of dishes—to taste as superb as did the San Gabriel Hash, then we shall have to admit that he is good."

Crème Brûlée

1993

Published in our "New American Classics" article in April 1993, crème brûlée was a "must have" recipe. Popular in the '50s, the dessert made a comeback in the '90s and is now a staple in almost every trendy restaurant across the country. This creamy version sports a caramelized sugar topping, which takes a little more effort but is definitely worth it.

2 **cups half-and-half or light cream**
5 **slightly beaten egg yolks**
⅓ **cup sugar**

1 **teaspoon vanilla**
¼ **teaspoon salt**
⅓ **cup sugar**

1 In a small, heavy saucepan heat the half-and-half or light cream over medium-low heat just until bubbly. Remove from heat. Set aside.

2 In a medium mixing bowl combine the egg yolks, ⅓ cup sugar, the vanilla, and salt. Beat with a wire whisk or rotary beater just until combined. Slowly whisk or stir the hot cream into the egg mixture. Place four 4-inch quiche dishes or oval or round tart pans without removable bottoms into a 13×9×2-inch baking pan. Set baking pan on oven rack in a 325° oven. Pour custard mixture evenly into the 4 dishes. Pour *very hot water* into the baking pan around the 4 dishes, about halfway up the sides of the dishes.

3 Bake in 325° oven for 18 to 24 minutes or until a knife inserted near the center of each comes out clean. Remove dishes from water bath; let cool on wire racks. Cover and refrigerate for at least 1 hour or for up to 8 hours.

4 Before serving, remove custards from refrigerator; let stand at room temperature for 20 minutes.

5 Place the ⅓ cup sugar in a heavy 10-inch skillet. Cook over medium-high heat until sugar begins to melt, shaking skillet occasionally to heat sugar evenly. *Do not stir.* Once sugar starts to melt, reduce heat to low and cook about 5 minutes more or until all of the sugar is melted and golden brown, stirring as needed with a wooden spoon.

6 Spoon melted sugar quickly over custards in a lacy pattern or in a solid piece. If melted sugar starts to harden in skillet, return to heat, stirring until it melts. If it starts to form clumps, carefully stir in 1 to 2 teaspoons *water*. Serve immediately. Makes 4 servings.

Amaretto Crème Brûlée: Prepare Crème Brûlée as directed, except substitute 2 tablespoons *amaretto* for all of the vanilla.

Nutrition facts per serving: 364 calories, 20 g total fat (11 g saturated fat), 311 mg cholesterol, 192 mg sodium, 39 g carbohydrate, 0 g fiber, 7 g protein.

Brownie Pudding 1944

1 cup all-purpose flour
¾ cup granulated sugar
2 tablespoons unsweetened
    cocoa powder
2 teaspoons baking powder
¼ teaspoon salt
½ cup milk

2 tablespoons cooking oil
1 teaspoon vanilla
½ cup chopped walnuts
¾ cup packed brown sugar
¼ cup unsweetened cocoa
    powder
1½ cups boiling water

1 Grease an 8×8×2-inch baking pan. Set aside.

2 In a medium mixing bowl stir together the flour, granulated sugar, the 2 tablespoons cocoa powder, the baking powder, and salt. Stir in the milk, oil, and vanilla. Stir in the walnuts.

3 Pour into the prepared pan. In a small mixing bowl stir together the brown sugar and the ¼ cup cocoa powder. Stir in the boiling water; slowly pour over batter. Bake in a 350° oven for 40 minutes. Cool on a wire rack for 45 to 60 minutes. Serve warm. Makes 6 to 8 servings.

Nutrition facts per serving: 368 calories, 12 g total fat (2 g saturated fat), 2 mg cholesterol, 271 mg sodium, 65 g carbohydrate, 3 g fiber, 5 g protein.

A sample of Better Homes and Gardens *wartime pointers to readers: "Not enough eggs, sugar, or butter for a superb Martha or George Washington cake? Skimp on sugar by baking Brownie Pudding. Save eggs, those 20-carat nuggets of nutrition, for main dishes; butter to spread on sandwiches in lunch boxes."*

1976

Almond Cream Crepes

repe in French means "pancake" and is spelled "crêpe." Traditionally, crepes are served on Candelmas, a religious festival held on February 2, and on Shrove Tuesday before Ash Wednesday to celebrate renewal, family, and hope for happiness and good fortune. It is also customary in France to touch the handle of the pan during cooking and make a wish while the crepe is turned. We featured this crepe filled with almonds and cream in our September 1976 issue along with other variations.

⅓ cup granulated sugar
3 tablespoons all-purpose flour
⅔ cup milk
1 egg
1 egg yolk
1 tablespoon butter or margarine
1 teaspoon vanilla
¼ teaspoon almond extract
¼ cup ground toasted almonds
3 egg yolks

¼ teaspoon vanilla
½ cup milk
3 tablespoons butter or margarine, melted
½ cup all-purpose flour
¼ cup granulated sugar
3 egg whites
Cooking oil
Sliced almonds, toasted
Sifted powdered sugar
Mixed fresh berries (optional)

1 For filling, in a small saucepan combine the ⅓ cup granulated sugar and the 3 tablespoons flour. Add the ⅔ cup milk; cook and stir until thickened and bubbly. Cook and stir 1 to 2 minutes more. Beat the whole egg and the 1 egg yolk together slightly. Gradually stir half of the hot mixture into the beaten eggs. Return all of the mixture to the saucepan. Cook and stir over low heat for 2 minutes (do not boil). Remove from heat. Stir in the 1 tablespoon butter or margarine, the 1 teaspoon vanilla, the almond extract, and the ground toasted almonds. Cover and set aside.

2 Meanwhile, for crepes, in a small mixing bowl stir together the 3 egg yolks and the ¼ teaspoon vanilla; stir in the milk and the 3 tablespoons melted butter or margarine. Stir in the ½ cup flour and the ¼ cup granulated sugar until smooth. In a medium mixing bowl beat the egg whites with an electric mixer until stiff peaks form (tips stand straight). Gently fold batter mixture into whites.

3 Brush a 6-inch skillet with cooking oil; heat over medium heat. Spoon a generous tablespoon of batter into the skillet; spread with back of spoon into a 4- to 5-inch circle. Cook over medium heat until underside is brown or about 30 to 45 seconds. Turn and cook just to lightly brown the other side. Invert onto paper towels. Cover; keep warm. Repeat with remaining batter to make 24 crepes.

4 To assemble, spread about 2 teaspoons of the filling onto each crepe; fold in half, then fold in half again to form a triangle. Place crepes in an ungreased 3-quart baking dish. Bake, uncovered, in a 350° oven for 10 minutes or until heated through. Sprinkle with almonds and powdered sugar. If desired, serve with fresh berries. Makes 12 servings.

Nutrition facts per serving: 152 calories, 8 g total fat (2 g saturated fat), 90 mg cholesterol, 78 mg sodium, 17 g carbohydrate, 0 g fiber, 4 g protein.

Weekend Brunch

Turkey-Asparagus Brunch Bake (page 15)

Super-Colossal Cinnamon-Pecan Ring
(page 40)

Fruit Bran Muffins (page 42)

Ginger Marinated Fruit (page 108)

Holiday Feast

Beef Tenderloin with Port Sauce with
puff pastry cutouts (page 212)

Mixed Greens Salad

Glazed vegetables (carrots and Brussels sprouts)

Roasted potatoes or
Sage & Onion Mashed Potatoes (page 260)

Pumpkin Cake Roll (page 286)

A Cold Winter's Night

Yankee Doodle Stew (page 195)

Winter Fruit Bowl (page 107)

Old-Fashioned Popovers (page 110)

Big Apple Dumplings (page 290)

Kids' Night to Choose

Tostada Pizza (page 200)

Zesty Fiesta Corn Salad (page 102)

Fudge 'n' Nut Brownies (page 147)

Spring Celebration

Rack of Lamb
with Rich Brown Sauce (page 227)

Steamed baby carrots

Risotto Primavera (page 258)

Honey-Aniseed Bread (page 115)

Almond Raspberry Torte (page 295)

Party on the Deck

Chicken with Garden Salsa (page 166)

Grilled corn on the cob

No-Chop Potato Salad (page 104)

English Toffee Ice Cream (page 270)

A Simple Summer Supper

Sizzling Vegetable Sandwiches (page 240)

Two-Bean & Rice Salad (page 92)

Assorted melon

Brown Sugar Hazelnut Rounds (page 153)

Globe-Trotter's Open House

Jamaican Shrimp (page 51)

Mexi Meatballs (page 78)

Greek Croustade (page 57)

Zesty Italian Peasant Bread (page 66)

Double Chocolate Chunk Biscotti (page 156)

Toffee Triangles (page 150)

Index

particular, who throughout history have set about hunting the wolf almost to extinction.

For example, the legendary beast of Gévaudan, said to be a giant wolf, reportedly killed about 100 people, over a three-year period, in the Auvergne region of France in the mid-eighteenth century. Such was its ferocity that King Louis XV called out his troops to hunt it down. Even though a large wolf was killed, the attacks continued until two more wolves were slaughtered, both of which were thought to be the beast.

The wolf's association with evil is still fueled today by horror movies, which portray wolf-like creatures transformed by a full moon and driven by a thirst for human blood. So this insatiable interest in the wolf's traditional reputation as a fierce killer continues today. Interestingly, a recent survey, which sought children's attitudes toward the wolf, highlighted that more young people are afraid of the wolf's howl than of the animal itself, which has become familiar to them through modern documentary television programs and natural history books.

In fact, proven attacks by a healthy wild wolf on people are almost non-existent. Wolves that act aggressively toward humans are usually suffering from an illness, such as rabies, and in captivity, attacks are more likely to occur if animals have been poorly handled by their keepers.

Native American legends tell of a sacred pact between wolves and humans to respect each other's families and land. Arguably, the wolf has honored its side of the agreement, but, sadly, we have not, instead we have systematically eradicated the wolf from much of its former habitat.

Today, the dedicated work of conservationists and animal behaviorists has helped us to understand the nature of the wolf and its vital role in the natural world. As ever more wilderness is destroyed due to increased

development and the destruction of natural habitat, nature reserves have allowed the wolf to survive in areas where its very existence was gravely threatened.

This book offers us the privileged opportunity to learn about the secret world of the wolf through the eyes of Shaun Ellis, who was shown the mystical ways of the

SPIRIT OF THE
WOLF

White Protector

According to Native American legend, if a white wolf is seen either in a dream or reality, it has been sent to protect you. The Native Americans respected the wolf's strong family values, among other qualities.

On the brink

Wild wolves live on the brink of starvation for most of their lives, but the adult wolves always return with food for their pups, realizing the importance of the next generation in increasing pack numbers and ensuring hunting success.

wolf by the Nez Perce Native Americans, and who has lived with wolves and studied them for many years.

With stunning photography by Monty Sloan, whose unique viewpoint enables us to glimpse the fascinating world of the wolf from within the pack, this book offers a remarkable insight into the spirit of the wolf.

Natural balance

Top predators, such as the wolf, help to maintain a balanced environment. In wooded areas, deer kill trees by stripping and eating bark, and so by controlling deer numbers, wolves help conserve trees, which are an essential habitat for birds and other wildlife.

SPIRIT OF THE WOLF

Throughout history, wolves have been a constant source of fascination to humans as well as awakening some of our deepest fears. Featured in myths, legends, fables, and folklore, the relationship between humans and wolves is both ancient and complex. From the unsettling children's bedtime story *Little Red Riding Hood* to frightening tales of humans becoming werewolves when the moon is full, we are familiar with the traditional image of the wolf as both a cunning predator and an evil supernatural monster, but is there any truth in these popular myths?

And what of the gentler side of the wolf's nature? Tales of lost children being raised by wolves exist in many cultures, and these ancient stories, together with more recent ones, such as Rudyard Kipling's *The Jungle Book*, suggest that wolves possess superior parental skills. In fact, today the parenting skills of wolves are highly respected by zoologists and animal behaviorists

who consider that, within the entire animal kingdom, only humans and some other primates can equal the care and education they offer to their young.

One of the earliest and best known legends of wolves and human children is the fourth-century story of the Roman twins Romulus and Remus. These sons of Mars and Rhea Silvia, a vestal virgin, were thrown into the River Tiber in a basket by Amulius, who saw them as a threat to his rule of Alba Longa. When they floated ashore, a "she-wolf" heard their cries and suckled them. After being found and brought up by a royal shepherd, the twins later became the founders of Rome.

Wolf mythology is filled with stories about wolves raising orphaned or lost children, and these tales represent a positive attitude toward the wolf and its relationship with human society. Sadly, however, myths also portray the wolf in a negative light, helping to create a climate of fear among the people of Europe, in

Photograph © Paul Herbert

WOLVES IN FOCUS

Though I studied geology at university, wolves soon took over from rocks as a source of inspiration, and I started to focus on these fascinating animals. An interest in photography grew into a career: I have been taking pictures of wolves in color and black and white since 1984 and have accumulated an extensive library of wolf images.

Despite decades of research, both in captivity and in the field; despite success in recovery programs in the upper Midwest and Northern Rockies; despite growing public support for wolves and predators in general; despite the fact that you are far more likely to be killed by a toaster than a wild predator, especially a wolf; this animal remains in peril, or has already become locally extinct in many parts of the world.

So since 1988 to help conserve and promote the wolf, I have been working as a handler, lecturer, researcher, and photographer at Wolf Park in Indiana, USA. Wolf

Park is home to several packs of gray wolves, and part of the proceeds from my photographic sales go to the park to support education initiatives. Working with captive wolves has allowed me to get really close to my subjects, and I've been able to capture intimate behavior that would have been extremely difficult to shoot in the wild. I also design and maintain various websites, most of which are dedicated to wolf conservation.

Field studies, especially those conducted in Yellowstone National Park, have shown the importance of the wolf as a key species in the ecosystem – yet the wolf still remains a maligned, feared, and misunderstood predator. I can only hope that we can now come to accept the wolf for what it is, rather than live in fear for what it is not.

Monty Sloan
PHOTOGRAPHER

KINDRED SPIRITS

I grew up in a farming community where there were few other children, and so I made friends with the wildlife in the surrounding countryside. I felt at home in woodland at night, and I learned to use my senses of smell and hearing to find my way around. I bonded with the badgers and foxes who were fearless and relaxed in my presence. For many years, I was privileged to be able to watch their family groups and study their behavior.

So how did a young man from rural England end up at the foot of the Rocky Mountains in Idaho studying wolves under the guidance of the Nez Perce Native Americans? It was mostly due to hard work, perseverance and a chance encounter with a Native American biologist at a wolf seminar, who I persuaded to take me on as a volunteer. Working with him and fellow students by day, and studying the wolves on my own by night, I slowly earned the respect of the amazing Nez Perce people.

It was here in two to three feet of snow that I realized the best way to learn about wolves was to return to the ways of my childhood and live alongside them. And a few years later, I decided to try to join a wild pack not as a leader but as a low-ranking member, because I understood that only in this position would the wolves be prepared to teach me about their society.

I now work with captive wolves at Wolf Pack Management, Combe Martin, Devon, England and through the in-depth study of their behavior, my colleagues and I are constantly discovering new sides to these fascinating animals. I hope that I can use this knowledge to help protect wolves for future generations to study and admire.

Shaun Ellis
AUTHOR

CONTENTS

Designed, produced and packaged by
Stonecastle Graphics Ltd

Text and captions by Shaun Ellis
Photographs © Monty Sloan
Edited by Maggie Lofts
Designed by Sue Pressley and Paul Turner

Metro Books
122 Fifth Avenue
New York, NY 10011

ISBN: 978-0-7607-8063-3

Printed and bound in China

10 9 8 7 6 5 4 3

The Author

Fascinated by wolves from a very early age, Shaun Ellis dreamed
of living alongside them in the wilderness. Little did he know
that he would one day turn his dream into reality. As a young
man living in the country, Shaun first developed an interest in
foxes and spent many hours observing their behavior. This
eventually spurred him on to leave England and go to North
America to live with and study wolves. He learned to mimic the
wolves' sounds and soon became accepted by the pack. This
privilege enabled him to discover intimate details about their
lives and gain a rare insight into their world.

The Photographer

Monty Sloan finds something deeply inspirational and intriguing
about wolves. Having studied geology at the University of
California, Berkeley, he developed a fascination for wildlife – in
particular wolves and their behavior. Studies of wolf social behavior,
coupled with his hobby as a photographer, quickly turned to a
photographic career – a passion to capture every aspect of wolf
life on film. But wild wolves are elusive, wary, and often difficult
to observe – let alone to photograph – on an intimate and
personal level. Monty found that working with socialized wolves
was the answer. He became a wolf behaviorist and photographer
at Wolf Park, near Battle Ground, Indiana, USA, where nearly
two decades of working with captive wolves have enabled him
to create the world's largest collection of wolf images. His work
has been published in numerous books and magazines
throughout Europe, as well as North and South America.

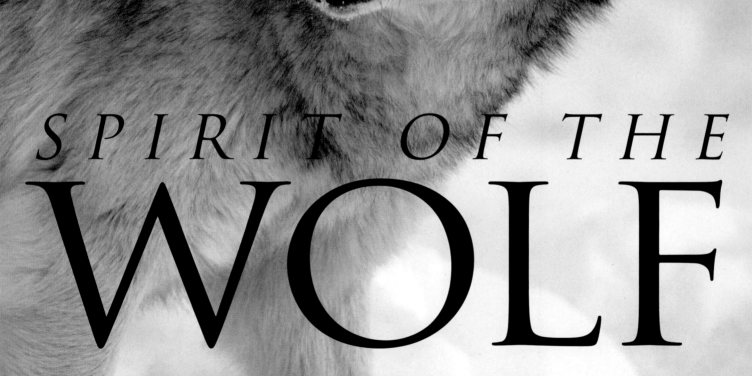

SPIRIT OF THE
WOLF

Written by Shaun Ellis
Photography by Monty Sloan

METRO BOOKS
NEW YORK

The parenting skills of wolves are highly respected by zoologists and animal behaviorists who consider that, within the entire animal kingdom, only humans and some other primates can equal the care and education they offer to their young.

Pup school

Young wolves receiving lessons in life from their nanny. The nanny is selected by the alpha female before the birth of her pups to continue their care and education once they are weaned at four to six weeks of age. This enables the alpha female to devote herself once more to leading her pack.

Dangerous game

There is a constant risk of injury for wolves when hunting large quarry. A kick from a bison or a stab from a deer stag's antlers could be fatal. Adult wolves use the antlers and legs of dead prey during play to teach the young wolves avoidance techniques.

The stuff of myth
Images such as this, with a wolf howling at a full moon, have fueled the human imagination, and horror stories often portray the wolf as a vicious killer with a taste for human blood.

A recent survey, which sought children's attitudes toward the wolf, highlighted that more young people are afraid of the wolf's howl than of the animal itself.

WOLF MYTHOLOGY

From the northern Rockies of North America to the Carpathian Mountains in Europe, wherever there were wolves, human societies have surrounded them with folklore and superstitions, some of which have led to the demise of the wolf in many areas. Other cultures, however, such as Native American ones, have revered wolves and granted them an almost God-like status.

NATIVE AMERICAN CULTURE

One Native American tribe – the Shoshone – believed that coyotes and wolves had created the world and that after death the spirit of a tribal member was taken to the land of the coyote. The wolf guarded the path walked by the dead, and it would first awaken and then wash a human soul in the river. The newly cleaned spirit could then gain entry into the Promised Land.

As human populations increased, wolves began to seek sanctuary in the remote mountainous regions. As a result, Native Americans bestowed even greater mystic importance on the wolf, and they studied the animal in an effort better to understand it and learn from its wisdom. They say that the wolf taught them about co-operation for living together in extended families, and they learned the importance of social structure – they respected their chieftains in the same way that wolves respect the decision-making role of alphas.

Because of its ability to discover new places and find its way around its huge territory, the wolf became known as The Pathfinder. Native hunters often found elk and bison by following the wolves, whose sharp senses of smell and hearing enabled them to detect prey long before their human counterparts. The Native hunters never killed without leaving some meat as a thank you for their wolf helpers. The Native American tribes of the Great Plains believed that they could become great warriors by observing the wolf's hunting

skills. The sign for the Pawnee, one of the most feared tribes on the plains, was the same as the sign for wolf. And the Lakota tribes respected and honored the wolf's loyalty to its mate and family, and before hunting they would smear red dye on their mouths to mimic a feeding wolf.

The Native Americans and the wolf had a pact to support each other, but when Europeans began to colonize North America huge numbers of wolves were killed. Many tribes felt that the pact had been broken, and the Blackfoot and Lakota believed that a gun used to kill a wolf would never shoot straight again.

Native Americans have many stories that tell of shape-shifting: the ability to change from human to a different animal form. According to one old legend, a Native American woman found a wolf pup while out collecting wood for her tribe. The animal was alone, starving and close to death. She carried the wolf back to her camp where she fed him and kept him warm in her tepee. He grew quickly and they became inseparable friends. One morning they went to the river to drink, and in the soft mud the woman saw their tracks from the previous evening; human and wolf footprints turned into two sets of wolf tracks. Confused by what she saw, the woman sought advice from the old chief who told her that as recompense for the tiny life she had saved the wolf had given her the gift of existing in two forms: human and wolf. That evening she sat by the water with her wolf companion and looked at her reflection, and a female wolf looked back at her.

Spiritual cleaner

The wolf's natural love of water inspired some Native American folklore. The wolf was believed to guard the path walked by the dead, where it would wash the human soul in water before the newly cleaned spirit gained entry to the Promised Land.

EUROPEAN CULTURE

The wolf has for centuries captured the imagination of different cultures and features strongly in the complex body of European folklore and mythology. Several of Aesop's fables (c.600 BC) refer to the wolf's cunning; "The Boy Who Cried Wolf" is one of the best known. After the shepherd boy had sounded many false alarms, his cries of "A wolf!" are ignored by the townspeople. To the boy's dismay, his sheep are attacked by wolves and he is left helpless. Similarly, *Little Red Riding Hood*, a children's fairy story which originated in the seventeenth century, reinforces this perception of the wolf as a cunning predator.

Not only are there such stories of wolves dressing up as humans, but there are also ones in which humans turn into wolves. A number of cultures have "were" creatures, often inspired by the most dangerous animal found in the area. There were "were-tigers" in India, "were-leopards" in Africa, and "were-wolves" in medieval Europe. The term "were" is taken from the old English word "wer," meaning "man," thus werewolves or man-wolves were believed to be half-human and half-wolf.

Humans who became werewolves of their own free will were supposed to have made a pact with the devil. Most werewolf transformations took place at night when the moon was full; the werewolf attacked, killed and often ate people and animals, returning to human form at daybreak. On the other hand, people could sometimes inherit the condition. In Greece, for instance, anyone suffering from epilepsy was thought to be a werewolf.

There are various possible explanations for the origin of werewolf myths. A person living in one of the vast European forests 700 to 800 years ago could very easily have been mistaken for a wolf or werewolf. Receding and bleeding gums, sometimes coupled with excessive hair growth, are signs of severe malnutrition, which

would have been common at that time among the poor. Village outcasts trying to scavenge a living might have moved like wolves or mimicked their hunting behavior in an effort to feed themselves. And the wearing of animal skins – often wolfskins because of their outstanding insulating qualities – afforded protection from the cold. Another theory suggests that the poor conditions in which grain was stored at the time might have led to a variety of hallucinogenic

Safe routes

Wolves often use well-worn paths when moving around their territories. With daily scent-marking, these paths become safe areas where attacks from rival packs are unlikely.

reactions. So perhaps something as ordinary as a slice of bread, which might have contained bad rye seed, could have induced a werewolf sighting.

Today we also recognize the existence of a condition known as lycanthropy, which is a form of schizophrenia during which a patient believes that he or she is a wild animal, often a wolf or a werewolf. Sufferers have been observed making growling and snarling noises and chewing on furniture as if it were prey. In other

non-European countries, characteristics of similarly powerful beasts common to the region, such as tigers in India, for example, are displayed by patients.

One of the most famous wolf stories is that of St Francis and the wolf of Gubbio, which can be found in *The Little Flowers of St Francis*, an anonymous fourteenth-century source of St Francis stories. The story tells of how St Francis tamed a large wolf that was terrorizing the good people of Gubbio, a town in

Under cover of darkness

The wolf's nocturnal habits added to its mystery, fueling numerous legends and horror stories. The wolf is, in fact, an intelligent, shy animal that avoids interaction with humans.

Umbria, Italy. While St Francis was staying in the town he was told of a wolf that had become so ravenous that it was not only killing and eating their livestock but also people.

The inhabitants of Gubbio became afraid to go outside the town walls, and so St Francis took pity not only on the people but on the wolf, too, and decided to go out and meet the animal. The townspeople desperately tried to warn St Francis of the danger, but he insisted that God would protect him. One brave friar and several peasants accompanied him outside the town gates, but soon after leaving, the peasants became terrified and refused to go any further. St Francis and the friar walked on, and suddenly the wolf charged at them from the forest, its jaws wide open. St Francis made the sign of the cross at the wolf and it immediately slowed down, and closed its mouth. St Francis then called out

to the wolf: "Come to me Brother Wolf, I wish you no harm," and at once the wolf lowered its head and laid down at the feet of St Francis. He asked why the wolf had been killing the people of Gubbio and their animals. "Brother Wolf", said St Francis, "I would like you to make peace with the townspeople, they will harm you no more and you must no longer harm them, all your past wrongs will be forgiven."

The wolf displayed its agreement by moving its body and nodding its head. In front of the crowd that had gathered, St Francis asked the wolf to make a pledge. He extended his hand and the wolf in turn extended its paw to seal the peace pact. St Francis then invited the wolf to follow him into the town. By the time they reached the square, everyone had gathered to witness the miracle. He then offered the townspeople peace on behalf of the wolf. The townsfolk promised to feed the animal, and St Francis asked the wolf if it could live under these terms. The wolf lowered its head and twisted its body in agreement. This convinced everyone that the wolf was willing to accept the pact. The animal once more placed its paw in St Francis's hand.

From that day the wolf and the townspeople kept their pact. The wolf went from house to house and was given food. When it finally died of old age, the people of Gubbio were sad. The wolf's peaceful ways had been a constant reminder to them of the tolerance and holiness of St Francis, and they had seen it as a living symbol of the providence of God. St Francis had educated them to accept the wolf and, in return, the wolf had accepted them.

Native respect

The Native Americans respected all animals and believed that each one had special qualities and skills that they could learn from: none more so than the bison and the wolf.

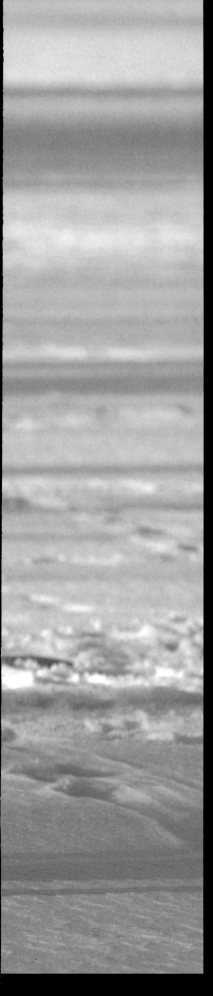

The wolf has for centuries captured the imagination of different cultures and features strongly in the complex body of European folklore and mythology.

Relative differences

European wolves (above) are generally smaller than their North American counterparts (left), and tend to be shorter, darker and more thickly set.

Wherever there were wolves, human

societies have surrounded them with folklore

and superstitions.

Bedtime stories

Children's fairy stories, such as *Little Red Riding Hood,* which originated in Europe in the seventeenth century, reinforced the perception of the wolf as a cunning predator.

THE PACK

Wolves originated in the New World about five million years ago. During the Pleistocene epoch (the last ice age), the dire wolf was the largest known species of wolf ever to exist. But it was a much smaller species that crossed into Siberia from Alaska, and this species eventually developed into the larger gray wolf *Canis lupus* of today. It settled in Eurasia and also migrated back to North America where it populated much of what is now known as Canada and the United States, except for one small region in the south-eastern US, which was home to a smaller wolf known as the red wolf *Canis rufus*.

Thanks to many detailed studies by biologists in the wild, we now know much more about the behavior of gray wolves, including the complex ways they use sound, smell, and posture, which are all specific to a particular rank, to communicate with each other.

The close-knit pack, usually consisting of eight to 12 animals, comprises a pair of high-ranking individuals known as the alpha male and alpha female. These two animals lead the pack but, contrary to previous supposition, are not always the largest wolves. They make all the necessary decisions to protect the pack and its territory, and in return they are usually the only two animals that will breed.

VISUAL COMMUNICATION

The muzzle is one of the most important parts of the wolf's body for communication and to kill prey. The alpha male and female are usually easy to recognize within the family because, among other characteristics, their muzzles are clearly highlighted with bold lines and colors, which act as a clear visual deterrent to members of other packs who will instantly register their status.

It is often said that a direct stare into a wolf's or dog's eyes represents a challenge. But rather than our eyes, it

now seems that it is more likely to be our teeth that convey dominance. Adult wolves teach pups to avert their muzzles when approaching adults in the pack by snapping into the air near the pups' heads to make them turn or lower their heads. Having learned this at an early age, adult wolves lower their heads as a mark of respect to a more dominant pack member.

The head position adopted by each animal depends on its position within the social order. For example, a mid- to high-ranking animal would show respect to a higher family member by moving its muzzle horizontally to either the right or left. If respect is not shown, the dominant animal is entitled to move its own muzzle to either the right or left of the offender's muzzle. This intimidation is usually all that is needed to gain a demonstration of respect, but if more pressure is required, the higher-ranked animal will issue a low, throaty growl, with increasing intensity if necessary, backed up by facial expressions. A snap into the air just to the side of the muzzle will be the final warning before the use of physical force.

The wolf's ear positions also play a vital role in communication. They can be splayed sideways (resembling outstretched wings) to indicate defence, or extended and pointed forward to gain respect by drawing attention to the muzzle.

The hackles are sometimes raised around the neck and shoulders to give the impression of increased size during defensive situations. A dominant animal has a continuous bold line that extends from the neck all the way along the spine to the tip of the tail, the bolder and more continuous the line, the higher the rank of the animal.

One as yet unproven theory among biologists is that the different types of food eaten by the specific ranks within the pack affect their color and markings as well as their scent patterns. An ageing alpha will be demoted when there is a suitable younger candidate in the pack, and the older animal will no longer be able to consume the best parts of the kill. Photographic evidence has recorded a change in the markings and color of demoted individuals sometime after this, suggesting direct links between food, markings and rank.

SCENT-MARKING
The dominant alpha male and female are recognized just as easily by their smell as by their appearance. As the highest-ranking wolves, they will consume the best quality food from each kill: essential organs, such as heart, liver, kidneys, and the best fresh meat, along with possibly the brain, which will give them a stronger smell than any other pack member. Each rank within the pack is allowed to consume a different part of the carcass, ensuring that each emits a different scent.

The strong scent of the alpha pair is essential for defending the pack's territory as rival packs will avoid trespassing into another pack's territory only if the invisible scent barrier is strong and powerful. The alphas will lay scent down in a variety of different patterns – by urinating, defecating and rubbing around trees on the borders of their territory – designed to send different messages either to rival packs or to lone wolves operating within the buffer zones between established families. Raised-leg urination is used only by the alpha wolves as this enables them to spray their strong-smelling urine to a much higher level on trees and bushes, which is essential for marking and defending their territory.

Seasonal changes affect the variety and intensity of scent patterns, continually altering the level of potential threat from neighboring packs. It is the responsibility of the dominant male, as the protector of his family, to maintain and reinforce the scent patterns that define their territory, and it is vital for this purpose that he consumes the best parts from each kill.

Leader of the pack

This alpha wolf can be identified by both its posture and bold coat markings – note the difference in color to the wolf on the left. Alphas are not always the biggest and boldest animals in the pack, but they do have a piercing stare and bold attitude.

A snap into the air just to the side of the muzzle will be the final warning before the use of physical force.

37

VOCAL COMMUNICATION

Growls, yips, yaps, and whines are vocalisations used at close range in combination with body language. The howl is a long-range method of communicating with pack members who are out of sight, or with rival wolves, in which case it is used as a way of avoiding conflict and can be heard several miles away. Each animal has a different sound depending on its pack status. The alpha pair's howl is low in tone, and they can also be identified by the length of the pauses between howls. It may not be the alpha wolves which initiate the howling, but they will quickly assume control of the situation once vocal contact is made with, for example, a neighboring pack, a lone wolf, or a family member that has become lost while hunting. If the alpha wolves consider that the pack needs to prolong its calls, they will offer encouragement to howl by repeating a long, deep howl or if they want to stop the pack, a series of two or three cut-off howls in quick succession.

THE BETAS

Second in rank to the alpha pair are the betas, which are also usually a pair of animals, where numbers permit, which hold disciplinary positions within the family. Betas are easy to recognize because they are often the biggest and boldest animals in the pack; they rely on their strength to establish pack rules passed down by the alpha pair. The beta's role is that of enforcer, deflecting much of the potential danger away from the valuable alphas. Their spine markings, though quite bold, are broken, in contrast to the strong and continuous lines of the alphas.

The betas are vocally quite low in tone: not as low as the alphas but lower than the remaining pack members. They howl for approximately three to four times longer than the alphas, adding strength and continuity to the pack calls.

Top marks

An alpha wolf can also be recognized by its bold facial markings, in particular on the muzzle, ears, and around the eyes, which distinguish it from the other wolves. It will also have a very strong scent.

Alpha line

The alpha's hackles have a bold outline, and a dark line continues down the body, creating the outline of a saddle on its back, and runs right to the base of the tail.

THE LOWER RANKS

Lower in rank than the betas is a group known as the mid-ranking wolves, which are usually led by a pair of more dominant wolves: the female teaches and disciplines subordinate females and the male performs the same role with the male wolves. These animals receive information from the alpha pair via the betas. In large packs of wolves with up to 15 animals, this line of communication is vital in order for the alpha pair to retain control.

The main duty of the mid-ranking wolves is to create the illusion that there are more wolves in the pack than there actually are. This is done in several ways and helps the pack defend its territory. The mid-ranking wolves vary their diet so that their scent-markings never remain the same, thus giving the illusion of a larger number of wolves. And during howling, the mid-ranking wolves use a variety of sounds – yips, yaps, barks, whines, howls, and growls – to make it hard for packs in neighboring territories to identify exactly how many wolves are in the pack. Mid-ranking wolves are naturally suspicious and are always aware of anything new or unfamiliar. The alpha and beta wolves rely on them to alert the pack to any danger.

The pack is completed by the specialists: the hunters, the nannies and the much misunderstood omega wolves. Hunters are often female as they are 20-25 percent smaller than the males and therefore much faster. This gives them the ability to catch the prey or cut off the escape route of the intended quarry. But males

A dominant animal has a continuous bold line that extends from the neck
all the way along the spine to the tip of the tail, the bolder and more
continuous the line, the higher the rank of the animal.

Under exposure

This wolf (opposite) is showing respect by exposing its light underside. It is also showing that it trusts the dominant animal because it has exposed the most vulnerable parts of its body; a single bite to these areas could kill.

Marks of respect

An alpha wolf's bold outlines can be seen from some distance and are used in conjunction with body posture, scent, and sound to gain respect from fellow or rival pack members.

Alpha and beta

The bold markings of the alpha wolf (left) clearly distinguish it from the beta wolf on the right.

Strong second

The beta wolves (opposite) are the biggest and boldest wolves in the pack. They are responsible for enforcing the wishes of the alpha pair and are sent forward to do a recce in times of danger.

are also required for their strength, particularly when hunting large prey such as bison. The female hunter may separate the quarry from the herd and tire it, but she would need the assistance of the larger male hunter to pull the animal down.

Nannies are specialist female or male wolves selected by the alpha female to care for and educate her pups once they are weaned, when she returns to her duties as leader of the pack.

Omega wolves are essential to the survival of the wolf pack. They are responsible for defusing tension within the pack and minimizing injury. From the age of two to three weeks, the omega pup is always at the center of constant bouts of quarreling among its litter-

mates. The omega learns very quickly how to attract attention toward itself by playing games and acting like a "court jester" or clown. Then by using a series of instinctive and learned behaviors, ranging from body postures, facial expressions, and vocal sounds, the omega is able to calm a situation, avoid injury, and restore harmony.

The omega wolf has often been labeled as the "Cinderella wolf" because it was assumed to be low-ranking and mistreated. This could be because when a wolf pack is feeding, the omega has been seen to be chased away, often repeatedly, from the carcass. One possible explanation for this behavior is to allow the high-ranking animals to change position at the carcass without fighting. This ensures that they get the select parts and the right amount of food for their rank. Hungry wolves could seriously injure each other without the distraction provided by the omega. Once the other wolves have fed, the omega is rewarded by being allowed access to some high-quality food that has been saved for it specifically by a beta wolf. So it is probable that, despite appearances, the omega holds a high-ranking specialist position which is valued within the pack.

The omega howl is the most tuneful in the pack, reaching both high and low notes, and by bringing harmony to a bout of howling, it can help to calm the pack when it is on the defensive.

Rival packs will avoid trespassing into another pack's territory

only if the invisible scent barrier is strong and powerful.

Membership application

A lone wolf howls frequently to gain information from surrounding packs. It can tell if a rank is absent from the response and can then decide whether to try to enroll.

Howling from on high

Wolves often prefer to howl from an elevated position in order to project the sound further. They can also be seen standing in a semicircle during howling to project their sound in different directions.

Alpha duet

A breeding alpha pair often indicates their breeding rights by howling. When the alpha female comes into season, there will be visible spots of blood in her urine. By urinating over it, the alpha male is proclaiming his right to mate with her.

Howling lessons

Communication through howling is taught to the young wolves
at an early age, and they are rewarded with food and praise.
Each pup learns the howl relevant to its own rank.

Vocal flare

A wolf away from its pack will often call them using a rallying or locating howl. This wolf doesn't expect to get a reply but is just sending out a vocal beacon so the pack can find him or her again.

Pack jesters

Omega wolves were once wrongly thought to be the lowest ranking in the pack, but they are, in fact, highly respected and allowed to feed on good-quality meat as their reward for defusing tension in volatile situations, such as during feeding.

By using a series of instinctive and learned behaviors, ranging from body postures, facial expressions, and vocal sounds, the omega is able to calm a situation, avoid injury, and restore harmony.

Thanks to many detailed studies by biologists in the wild, we now know much more about the behavior of wolves, including the complex ways they use sound, smell, and posture, which are all specific to a particular rank, to communicate with each other.

Size constraints

A wolf's territory can range from just a few to several hundred miles. This, together with the availability of food, determines the size of the pack.

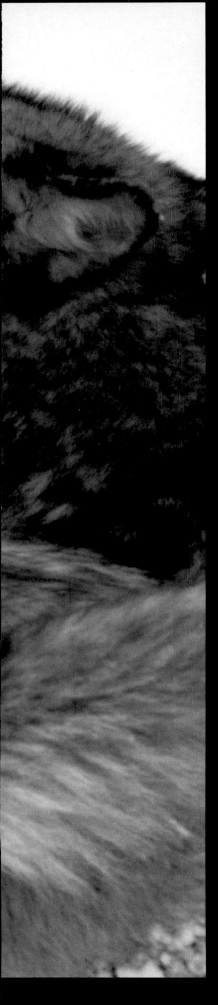

The Magnificent Seven

A wolf pack varies in size from as few as three to twenty animals. Generally, a pack consists of the alpha pair and their young, betas, mid-ranking wolves, and the specialists, such as the omegas.

Wisdom of age

In most wolf packs there are ageing animals that are valued for their knowledge and life experience, like grandparents in human society. These wolves are often selected as nannies and take part in educating and teaching the pups.

The head position adopted by each
animal depends on its position within
the social order.

Variety packs
Pack size depends on the amount of available habitat and how many wolves are needed
to defend and hunt within it. European packs (above) now usually occupy small territories
unlike North American wolves (right), which inhabit vast areas of open plains and forest.

Cleaning contract
It is the right of an alpha to both groom and be groomed by other pack members. Grooming helps the pack to bond and removes dirt and parasites from their fur.

Dual-purpose coat

During winter, the wolf develops a thick fur coat (right) to keep it warm. This is divided into two layers: the top layer of fur, called guard hair, keeps the animal dry in snow and rain, and the layer of soft fur underneath keeps it warm. The thick winter coat is molted in the spring months ready for warmer summer temperatures (above).

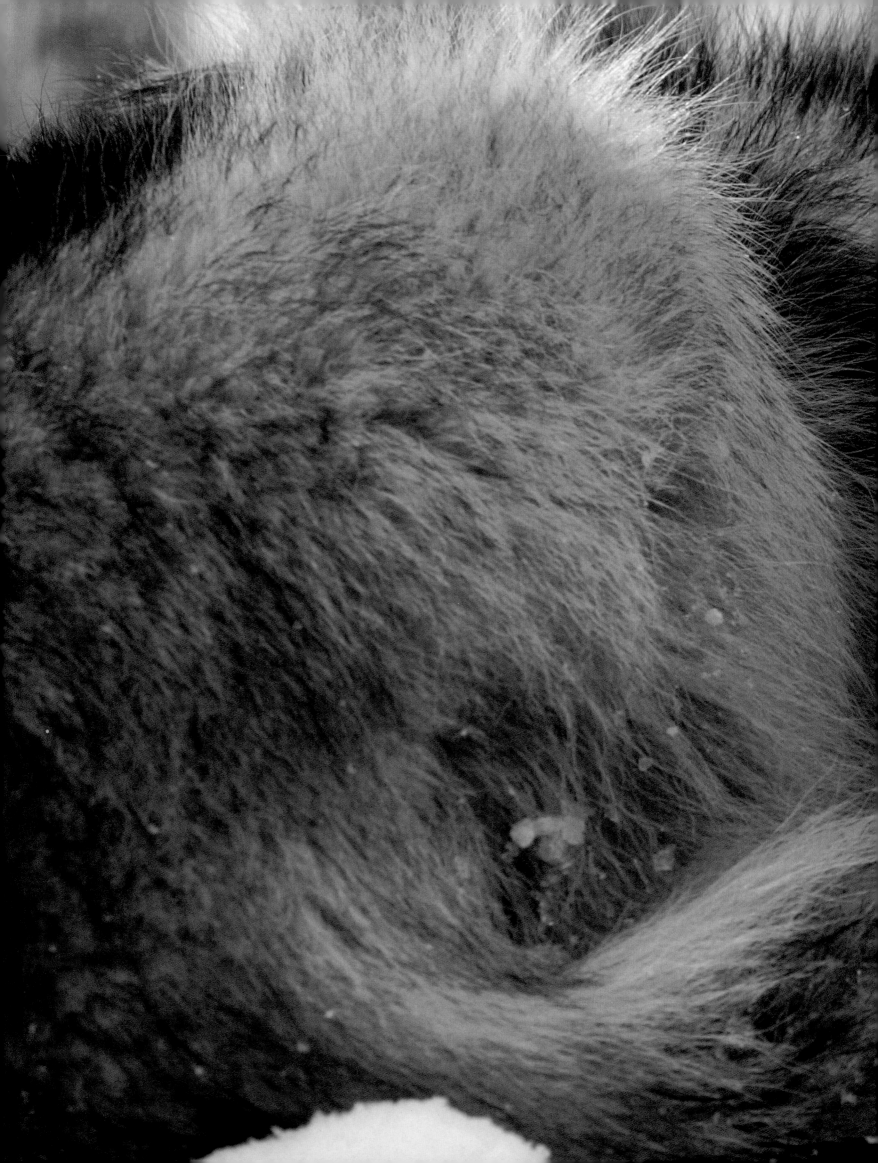

Wolf's clothing
The varied coloration and markings on the wolf's coat allow it to blend into its natural surroundings. Camouflage is vital for hiding from both predator and prey.

No wolf's land

A lone wolf passing through a strange territory will often urinate in water to remain undetected. This wolf has no territory of its own but operates in the buffer zone, a neutral area between existing packs where it is usually safe to travel.

Smelly feet

Wolves can strengthen territorial boundaries by means of scent glands in their feet. A beta wolf will also leave scratch-marks as a visual deterrent along with its scent.

Liquid asset

A wolf pack's territory will usually contain a water source, ranging from lakes to streams.

Wolves need large quantities of water after feeding and during pregnancy.

Natural swimmers

Wolves, with their large feet and long legs, are good swimmers, and they can easily cross lakes and rivers in their territory. Though they catch and eat fish in shallow water, they rarely follow large prey into water.

Fleet of foot

Hunters are specialist animals and tend to be smaller and quicker than other pack members. They therefore tend to be females, but the strength of the males will also be needed to help bring down large prey.

Speed merchants
The maximum speed that a wolf can run is between 30 and 40mph, and this can be maintained for up to an hour if necessary, either to escape danger or during a hunt.

Long-distance runners
Wolves prefer to trot or lope at about 4 to 6mph and
can cover 100 miles in a day in search of food.

Quick thinking

The wolf is very intelligent: its brain is 30 percent larger than the domestic dog's. Captive wolves learn after short periods of observation how to undo simple latches and get to the food rewards behind gates.

Crepuscular canids
The wolf pack is most active at dusk and dawn because it has learned
to operate when humans – its biggest predator – are less active.

Hunting practice

The alpha female instigates a game of tag in which the young wolves will be shown how to catch and bring down their prey by practicing on each other.

When wolves are tracking the movements of quarry, they can follow the scent of the animal's hoofprints, urine and droppings and can also smell any hair, skin particles or parasites in its tracks. They are also able to smell the tooth decay (from chewed vegetation) of an old animal. Indeed, so honed are the wolf's information-gathering skills that it can tell if the quarry is in poor condition, sick, old or injured and how far ahead it is.

Successful hunting requires various techniques, depending on the size of the quarry. Stalking in long grass or ambush are used to catch smaller animals. During an ambush the pack splits into two or more groups, and one will chase the animal toward the remaining pack members, camouflaged in the trees or

bushes. Wolves have been seen to pick up snow in their mouths so that their breath will not be visible to their prey. Once the prey is caught, one bite around the neck and a few shakes will quickly kill the animal.

Another technique is intimidation. Wolves single out their prey and try to get it to run – there is less danger from hooves and horns when the animal moves away from them and cannot turn to defend itself. Wolves have been known to move at a top speed of between 30 and 40 miles per hour, and they can maintain this pace for an hour if they need to. Or, if they are chasing a large, healthy ungulate, such as elk or moose, they can stay the course and deny their quarry food, water, rest and herd security for up to two weeks. The wolves wound their quarry by snapping at it from time to time,

The alpha female will often initiate a practice session

just before the hunt.

and eventually the larger animals will collapse from loss of blood and exhaustion.

TASTE OF SUCCESS

Once the prey has been killed, the pack feeds in an orderly and controlled manner. The alphas do not always feed first but they decide exactly what each wolf is to eat and when. Larger wolves such as the betas need to retain their strength to act as enforcers and will be allowed more food than lower-ranking wolves.

Each wolf is capable of consuming between 5lb and 20lb of meat in one go because it could be several days or even weeks before the pack feeds again. If there is more food than they can eat, wolves have been seen caching the surplus and then marking the spot with urine so that they can locate when food is scarce.

After feeding, the wolf pack relaxes and indulges in play and grooming sessions to ensure that valuable bonds are renewed after the tension and risks of the hunt (wolves make a kill only once in every ten hunts). And then the wolves rest in order to aid digestion. They always remain alert, however, and, if they need to run to escape danger, have been known to regurgitate the contents of their stomachs. Running on a full stomach would not only be uncomfortable and reduce speed, but could cause twisted gut, a potentially fatal condition.

After the hunt and initial feast, the wolf pack often howls to defend its hard-earned meal from other predators. Scavengers such as ravens, eagles, foxes, or coyotes will eventually polish off the leftovers.

By adjusting the position of her tail, the alpha female excretes
an odor which tells the pack which way to turn.

Nose to tail

Here the alpha female uses her lifted tail to release a scent and
to act as a sign for the other wolves to follow her. She will
practice a change of direction when she is some distance ahead
of them.

The deer hunters

The alpha female indicates her intention to hunt deer by using a previously cached leg to teach the pack what to look for, and how to catch it. If the wolves approach her from the front, she will demonstrate potential dangers by turning her head from side to side, and by hitting them with the leg to simulate a kick.

Tracking techniques

Wolves find their prey in three ways: by scent, using their fantastic sense of smell; by following tracks; and by chance encounters.

Winning by a nose

The wolf's sense of smell is so sensitive that they have the ability to smell disease and decay in elderly or injured prey from the tracks they leave in the snow.

118

When wolves are tracking the movements of quarry, they can follow the scent of the animal's hoofprints, urine and droppings and can also smell any hair, skin particles or parasites in its tracks.

Poised for action

This wolf raises himself onto his hind legs as he smells, hears, and finally sees the rest of his pack directing the prey toward him ready for an ambush. This is one of the many techniques used during hunting.

One in ten chance

Wolf packs have a one in ten success rate for catching prey. They compete with both other predators, such as bears and cougars, as well as human hunters.

The alpha female will select the kind of prey most appropriate
to the pack's seasonal needs: in winter, often large animals with a
high fat content, such as bison, elk, and wild boar.

Survival of the fittest

Wolves often test ungulate herds for old, weak, or vulnerable individuals. By hunting these animals, wolves keep deer or bison populations healthy because only the fittest animals will go on to breed.

Risky business

A kick from a large animal, such as a bison, could be fatal. Male
bison often lead and protect their herd and can be very bold
and aggressive. They are not easily intimidated by the wolves.

Deflecting danger
The wolf is most at risk of injury when its prey is charging toward it, and so it circles its prey to try to turn the animal away from him.

Staying the pace

The wolf's slender body and long legs are ideally adapted for the tight twists and turns required when hunting. Moving with a fluid motion, wolves also have stamina over long distances.

Closing in

Having chased this bison for many hours, the wolves will finally pull it down by its nose or rump. Once it has fallen, the wolves close in for the kill.

Once the prey is caught, one bite around the neck and

a few shakes will quickly kill the animal.

Snow blocks

Wolves have been seen holding snow in their mouths when close to their prey. This helps them to avoid detection by lowering the temperature in their mouths so that their breath is not visible.

Food defence

Ears lowered to the sides, head down and baring of teeth indicate that a wolf is defending something. Adult wolves teach the pups to defend their food by stealing it, and then when the pups approach and try to get it back the adults show their teeth and growl. The pups soon learn that they must do the same to keep their food.

Howl of triumph

After a kill has been made, defending territory is just as important as defending the food. The wolves will howl periodically throughout the night to advertise their kill and their intention to defend it.

Cut above the rest

After a kill, the alpha wolves defend their food by baring their teeth and flicking their tongues. These wolves have the right to consume the vital organs such as heart, liver, and kidneys, which will give them the strongest scent.

Sharp warnings

Feeding can appear to be a volatile time, but often the bared teeth and growls are just used to defend a wolf's share of the carcass. The omega wolf is vital in calming such situations and often plays the fool.

Smell of success

This older wolf knows from experience the value in hunting and eating particular prey species to increase his scent. His knowledge is respected and used to teach younger members of the pack. Fish is particularly pungent and may be abundant in some wolf territories.

Hunter-gatherer

Larger wolves, such as the betas, need to retain their strength to act as enforcers and will be allowed more food than lower-ranking wolves.

Tell-tail signs

Tail posture signifies a wolf's position within the pack and where and when it can feed. Each rank of wolf is allowed to eat certain parts of the prey which will give it the correct scent for its place in the hierarchy.

Meatwinner

This wolf (opposite) may be carrying food back to the safety of her own territory before consuming it. Or she may be returning to feed her pups and the nanny she has left to look after them.

Food storage

Burying food for consumption at a later stage. Often this is done close to water or in a riverbank so that the food is refrigerated and kept fresh until needed.

Eating for others
Because the betas rely on their strength and are often
the largest animals in the pack, they have huge appetites.
They are allowed to consume more food than the other
wolves because they protect the pack.

After feeding, the wolf pack relaxes and indulges in play and grooming sessions to ensure that valuable bonds are renewed after the tension and risks of the hunt.

Light relief

Hunting can stretch and test pack relationships. After hunting and feeding, these European wolves enjoy playing together and grooming, which help to establish their bonds with each other again.

Replete

Wolves consume as much meat as they can in one feed – between 5lb and 20lb – because the next meal could be two days or two weeks away. After such a large feed, resting is essential for digestion.

Waking sleep

Wolves have been known to rest for up to 18 hours a day, but they remain constantly alert to their surroundings and can spring into action if predators, prey or rival packs enter their territory.

In the twilight hours

The wolf has adapted its hunting patterns and now prefers to catch its food at dusk and dawn to avoid human conflict.

Night vision

Though poor in comparison to its other senses, the wolf's eyesight is good at night, allowing it to pick up movement in particular.

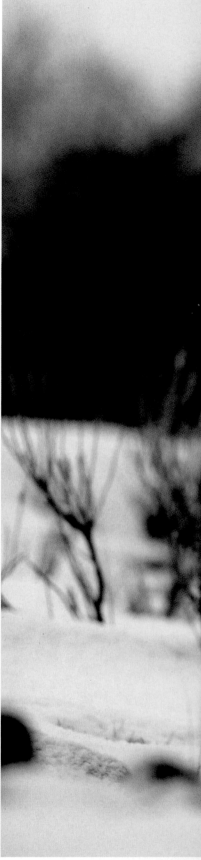

Queuing for the kill

Scavengers, such as foxes, often live close to wolves and, though
rodents and small mammals naturally form the bulk of their diet,
they also feed on the leftovers from a wolf kill.

Canid competitor

Wolves and coyotes often live close to each other. The wolves will chase and kill coyotes because they see them as competition for food. The name coyote comes from an Aztec word *coyotl*, meaning "barking dog" and describes the calls of these smaller canids.

Rich pickings

Scraps of food left by the wolves are cleaned up by birds of prey, such as eagles. They can often be seen and heard circling above a wolf kill and will come down to feed once the wolves have left the carcass.

Big competition

Bears and wolves often live in the same areas and compete for food. The adults rarely fight but will attack and kill each other's young as they are seen as competition for food. Together with humans, bears are responsible for a large percentage of wolf-pup fatalities. An adult bear can easily chase away any guarding nannies and dig out a den of young pups.

BREEDING

Breeding in North America takes place from January to April. Wolves in the southern regions of their territorial range tend to breed earlier than those in the north because food is available earlier. The Ethiopian wolf, for example, which lives only a few degrees north of the equator, breeds anytime from August through to December.

The female wolf reaches sexual maturity at two years old and comes into oestrus only once a year. There are records in some subspecies of females breeding in their first season, but they are usually too young to be able to cope successfully with pups, and the chances of survival are very poor. Females have been known to continue to produce young up to their tenth year, but this is exceptional as wolves rarely live beyond six or seven years in the wild. Although the alpha female is usually the only animal to breed in a pack, subordinate females sometimes produce multiple litters possibly because

significant pack members, such as the alpha female, have been killed, which causes the remaining animals to panic breed to reclaim vacant pack positions or territory.

Scientists are researching whether the type of food the pack eats enables the alpha female to predetermine seven or eight months before her breeding season the number and gender of pups she will have, depending on whether their purpose in life will be to stay with the pack or to move away and establish a new pack in a neighboring territory. Without other wolf packs on the borders of the alpha female's territory, prey is often lost as it escapes into areas where there are no wolves. Wolf packs flush out and drive prey back and forth between territories, so an unoccupied adjacent territory represents potential loss of food.

Adult courtship begins during late winter and early spring, but well before this the alpha female will start to suppress all other potential breeding females by

reminding them of her dominant position in the pack. She does this by constantly wrestling with them and by preventing them from moving in a certain direction by "T-ing," where she blocks their path, thus demonstrating her dominance .

The alpha female also selects nannies who will look after and educate her pups shortly after they have been weaned onto solid food at about four to six weeks, allowing her to get back to her decision-making duties as pack leader. Despite the name, nannies can be of either gender and are selected by the alpha female for their experience and ability to teach pack etiquette to the youngsters. The alpha female employs a complex selection process and initiates play behavior among pack members to determine which wolves are the most balanced and patient and best suited to looking after her pups.

As the female's receptive period approaches, she will increase her suppression of the lower-ranking females to prevent them coming into season at the same time. By growling and snarling and constantly pushing another female around, she can even cause miscarriage.

During mating, the alpha male mounts the female from the rear, and this usually locks them together in a copulatory tie, which happens when a gland in the male's penis swells and the female's vaginal muscles tighten. The tie can last from five to thirty-five minutes; they can even run together for a while if they need to until the tie breaks.

PUPS JOIN THE PACK

The gestation period for wolves is between 60 and 63 days, and birth, from January to April, is usually timed to coincide with the arrival of young prey species to provide the new mother with plentiful food.

For the first four to five weeks of their lives, the wolf pups only have contact with their mother. She suckles them in the den, offering food, security and warmth: the

Peak time
Constant checking of the alpha female's condition is essential near her receptive time. Courtship behavior at this time involves a lot of sniffing and licking.

three vital components they need for survival. These components form the basis of all their future education and are either offered as rewards for good behavior or denied to teach them a lesson.

During the first early weeks in the den, the alpha female will start to introduce the scent of other pack members to the pups. When the mother leaves the den she rubs her face and underside around the other adults and nannies to pick up their scent so that the pups will become familiar with them. She will begin to teach the pups, even at this early stage, what type of respect is required for each rank of wolf. For example, if she has the scent of a dominant member on her muzzle, she will take a young pup's head or neck gently in her mouth and turn the pup over to show the submissive position required in greeting this member of the pack.

The higher-ranking pups quickly discover that the middle teats have better quality milk, and they will begin to show early signs of dominance over their litter-mates by maintaining this position when feeding.

When the pups' hearing and sight are more developed at about four to five weeks, the alpha female brings them above ground for the first time to meet the pack and the nannies who will continue their education and care. When weaning takes place, a similar-ranking adult will regurgitate solid food for a pup, helping it identify the correct food for his or her rank. Once the pups have moved onto solid chunks of meat, the nannies often steal food from the pups to teach them how to defend their food.

The young wolf's education involves vital lessons in communication, social interaction and hunting. Young wolves join in with the hunt at about six to seven months, and lessons taught by older, more experienced members of the wolf family are essential for the youngsters' survival and for the successful future of the pack and of the wolf as a species.

The first six to nine months of the young wolf's life are the most crucial. Many do not survive due to starvation, human persecution or loss to other predators such as bears, cougars, or large birds of prey. Sadly, humans are responsible for a large number of pup deaths either directly through shooting, poisoning and trapping or indirectly through logging and general loss of wolf habitat.

Preparing for pups

Getting ready for the arrival of wolf pups often begins seven to eight months before the alpha female comes into season.

Up close and personal

The alpha male remains close to the alpha female during her season. Her scent will change dramatically when she comes into her short receptive period, and he must be the first male to mate with her to ensure his genes are passed on.

Selection tests
Choosing the right wolves to act as nannies is vitally important. Here an adult wolf is being tested; if selected, it will be responsible for the pups' education from the age of four to five weeks.

Infanticide

Rival packs are fiercely territorial, and in an attack pups are seen as future competitors for territory and are usually killed. But some packs have been known to raise orphaned pups in order to boost their own numbers.

Full-time nanny

During the first few weeks spent below ground both the pups and their mother are watched over by a nanny. These animals are totally dedicated to the safety and training of their future charges and won't leave until dismissed by the alpha female.

216

First outside view
At four to five weeks, the pups venture to the entrance to the den. Their development rate is so fast that in another two weeks they will be exploring up to half a mile away from the den.

The mouth test

The young wolf pup explores its surroundings by tasting

everything and is always on the look out for a potential meal.

The adult wolves will observe and give guidance when required.

Choir practice

The pups listen with interest to the pack howling and will usually attempt to join in with the chorus
at three to four weeks. Perfecting the art of howling is essential for a young wolf pup. Usually it's the
more dominant pups that howl first, but it's not long before all the pups join in the family howls.

Etiquette lessons

The alpha female introduces her pups to the scent of the other pack members while they are still
in their den. She shows them how to respond correctly to the adults depending on their rank.

Early days

For the first four to five weeks of their lives, the pups only have contact with their mother.

Semi-solids

When the young wolf pups are weaned, they receive regurgitated food from the adults after they have fed. This will be replaced by solid meat as the pups' teeth develop.

Once the pups have moved onto solid chunks of meat, the nannies often steal food from the pups to teach them how to defend their food.

What not to eat

These young pups soon establish a feeding routine based on the right food for each rank. They have been taught how to defend their food using body posture and growls.

Hunting howl

Wolves are active and often howl on the night of a full moon. Rather than calling up the devil, it is more likely that the alpha instigates howling because the moonlight increases the pack's chances of a successful hunt.

The first six to nine months of the young wolf's life are the most crucial. Many do not survive due to starvation, human persecution or loss to other predators such as bears, cougars, or large birds of prey.

Test of strength

Three wolf pups practice their skills in a tug of war. The beta pup has the advantage of strength during this game, but the smaller pups are usually quicker and will often run off with the toy if the beta lets go.

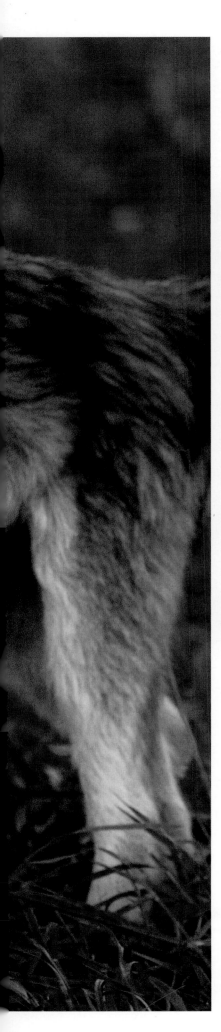

Playing chase

When wolf pups play together, mock hunting is one of their favorite games. Chasing and biting the backs of each other's legs, and running in front of one another are rehearsals for catching prey in the future. Here the nanny is involved in the boisterous play.

Serious play

Constant play-fights help young wolves to learn about pack survival. These sessions teach different hunting techniques, such as the ambush, where some animals hide in the trees and jump out on the other wolves as they approach.

Educational games
Play is used for teaching purposes and to maintain family bonds. Bones or sticks are sometimes picked up and used in chasing games of tag and relay.

CONSERVATION

The gray wolf once had the largest distribution of any mammal, apart from humans, ranging from the Northwest Territories of Canada to Mexico and across much of Eurasia. By the time it was finally protected by the US Endangered Species Act of 1973, it had been wiped out from the lower 48 states except for a few hundred in Minnesota and a few on Isle Royale, Michigan. Similarly, during the nineteenth and twentieth centuries, wolves were exterminated from central and northern European countries.

Governments played a significant part in the decline of the wolf by introducing bounties for dead animals. As early as 600 BC, Greek local government officials paid a bounty of five silver drachmas for each dead male wolf. England introduced wolf bounties in the 1500s, Sweden, in 1647 and Norway, in 1730. The first wolf bounty in North America was issued by the Massachusetts Bay Colony in 1630.

Wolf bounties and legal culls were widespread throughout Europe, Canada and the US. Though culling is an attempt to control wolf numbers, more often than not it has quite the opposite effect, causing what's left of a pack to panic breed.

The gray wolf is now classified as vulnerable by the IUCN (The World Conservation Union) Red List and endangered in the US (lower 48 states) except Minnesota where it is listed as threatened. Despite continued persecution in some countries, such as Russia, the species is now protected by the Endangered Species Act in the US and by the Bern Convention in Europe, which also protects its habitat.

Wolves are now gradually gaining ground in western Europe, with small populations in France, Germany, Norway, Sweden, Finland, Greece, and Italy. There is also now a viable population of about 2,000 Iberian wolves, a gray wolf subspecies, in Spain and Portugal.

period of observation. Electric fencing can be disabled

Worth more alive than dead?

Though a protected species in most European countries, some hunters see no need to stop killing the wolf for sport and will pay large sums of money for the privilege. But with the advent of ecotourism, money can now be generated by people who wish to visit countries to watch wolves, and this has helped to fund conservation work and show local businesses the value of keeping the wolf alive.

Ecotourism is a modern phenomenon which raises funds from tourists who wish to observe or photograph wild wolves in their natural habitat.

Return of the native

The gray wolf (left) became extinct in England in about 1486 and was exterminated in Scotland in 1743. Wolves survived in Ireland until about 1773. The species also vanished from other Western European countries, but now populations can be found in about nine of them.

INDEX